The Edinburgh Comp
Robert Louis Steve

Edinburgh Companions to Scottish Literature

Series Editors: Ian Brown and Thomas Owen Clancy

Titles in the series include:

The Edinburgh Companion to Robert Burns
Edited by Gerard Carruthers
978 0 7486 3648 8 (hardback)
978 0 7486 3649 5 (paperback)

The Edinburgh Companion to Twentieth-Century Scottish Literature
Edited by Ian Brown and Alan Riach
978 0 7486 3693 8 (hardback)
978 0 7486 3694 5 (paperback)

The Edinburgh Companion to Contemporary Scottish Poetry
Edited by Matt McGuire and Colin Nicholson
978 0 7486 3625 9 (hardback)
978 0 7486 3626 6 (paperback)

The Edinburgh Companion to Muriel Spark
Edited by Michael Gardiner and Willy Maley
978 0 7486 3768 3 (hardback)
978 0 7486 3769 0 (paperback)

The Edinburgh Companion to Robert Louis Stevenson
Edited by Penny Fielding
978 0 7486 3554 2 (hardback)
978 0 7486 3555 9 (paperback)

The Edinburgh Companion to Irvine Welsh
Edited by Berthold Schoene
978 0 7486 3917 5 (hardback)
978 0 7486 3918 2 (paperback)

The Edinburgh Companion to James Kelman
Edited by Scott Hames
978 0 7486 3963 2 (hardback)
978 0 7486 3964 9 (paperback)

Forthcoming volumes:

The Edinburgh Companion to Scottish Romanticism
Edited by Murray Pittock
978 0 7486 3845 1 (hardback)
978 0 7486 3846 8 (paperback)

The Edinburgh Companion to Scottish Drama
Edited by Ian Brown
978 0 7486 4108 6 (hardback)
978 0 7486 4107 9 (paperback)

The Edinburgh Companion to James Hogg
Edited by Ian Duncan and Douglas Mack
978 0 7486 4124 6 (hardback)
978 0 7486 4123 9 (paperback)

The Edinburgh Companion to Robert Louis Stevenson

Edited by Penny Fielding

Edinburgh University Press

Edinburgh University Press Ltd
22 George Square, Edinburgh

www.euppublishing.com

Typeset in 10.5 on 12.5pt Goudy
by Servis Filmsetting Ltd, Stockport, Cheshire, and
printed and bound in Great Britain by
CPI Antony Rowe, Chippenham and Eastbourne

A CIP record for this book is available from the British Library

ISBN 978 0 7486 3554 2 (hardback)
ISBN 978 0 7486 3555 9 (paperback)

Contents

Series Editors' Preface

The preface to this series' initial tranche of volumes recognised that some literary canons can conceive of a single 'Great Tradition'. The series editors consider that there is no such simple way of conceiving of Scottish literature's variousness. This arises from a multilingual and multivalent culture. It also arises from a culture that includes authors who move for many different reasons beyond Scotland's physical boundaries, sometimes to return, sometimes not. The late Iain Wright in *The Edinburgh History of Scottish Literature* talked of the Scots as a 'semi-nomadic people'. Robert Louis Stevenson travelled in stages across the world; Muriel Spark settled in Southern Africa, England and then Italy; James Kelman, while remaining close to his roots in Glasgow, has spent important periods in the United States; Irvine Welsh has moved from Leith, in Edinburgh, to a series of domestic bases on both sides of the Atlantic.

All four writers at one time and in one way or another have been underappreciated. Stevenson – most notoriously perhaps – for a time was seen as simply an adventure writer for the young. Yet Stevenson is now recognised not for simplicity, but his wonderful complexity, an international writer whose admirers included Borges and Nabokov. Similarly, the other three have firm international reputations based on innovation, literary experiment and pushing formal boundaries. All have grown out of the rich interrelationship of English and Scots in the literature to which they contribute; they embody its intercultural richness, hybridity and cosmopolitan potential. Some of their subject matter is far-flung: often they are situated not only physically but also in literary terms well beyond Scotland. Yet they are all important contributors to Scottish literature, a fact which problematises in the most positive and creative way any easy notion of what Scottish literature is.

Ian Brown
Thomas Owen Clancy

Brief Biography of Robert Louis Stevenson

Robert Louis Stevenson was born on 13 November 1850 in Edinburgh, the only child of Margaret Balfour and Thomas Stevenson. Following the tradition of his family of lighthouse-builders, he first studied engineering, before switching to law (he qualified, but did not practise). A traveller throughout his life, the young Stevenson took a canoe trip in France, recorded in *An Inland Voyage* (1878) and a walking tour of the Cévennes: *Travels with a Donkey* (1879). By this time Stevenson had met Fanny van de Grift Osbourne, an older, married American woman, and, when she had divorced her husband, he set off in 1879 to join her in California, writing up their exploits as *The Silverado Squatters* (1884). His earliest success came with *Treasure Island* (1883). The Stevensons divided their time between Scotland, England and France, trying various locations for the sake of Louis's continued poor health, and settled in 1885 in Bournemouth. Here Louis developed his friendship with Henry James and wrote *A Child's Garden of Verses*, *Prince Otto* and, with his wife, *The Dynamiter* (all 1885). *Strange Case of Dr Jekyll and Mr Hyde* and *Kidnapped* followed in 1886.

After the death of Thomas Stevenson in 1887, the Stevensons left for America, and from there began their journeys among the Pacific Islands, buying an estate, Vailima, on Samoa. Stevenson's work was now published first in America, and included *The Master of Ballantrae* (1889) and *The Wrecker* (1892). In 1890 the family, including Fanny's son Lloyd Osbourne, decided to live permanently at Vailima. Stevenson became involved with Samoan politics and wrote *A Footnote to History* (1892) in protest at colonial exploitation of the region. The 1890s saw the publication of his great South Seas works: *In the South Seas* (1896), *Island Nights' Entertainment* (1893) and *The Ebb-Tide* (1894). Stevenson died of a cerebral haemorrhage on 3 December 1894, leaving unfinished his last novel, *Weir of Hermiston* (1896).

Introduction

Penny Fielding

Robert Louis Stevenson remains one of the most famous, yet, paradoxically, one of the least well-known writers of the second half of the nineteenth century. Author of two 'classic' works of popular fiction, *Treasure Island* and *Strange Case of Dr Jekyll and Mr Hyde*, Stevenson the writer has become oddly separated from his works. These two texts have become as if disembodied from their author, constantly regenerating themselves in narrative retellings and in theatre and film adaptations, while the author himself lives on in an almost industrial proliferation of biographies and travelogues that promise to trace 'the footsteps of Stevenson'. Meanwhile, a great deal of Stevenson's work remains to be studied, and the connections between what he wrote and the literary, cultural and historical contexts in which he wrote it remain to be explored.

Perhaps Stevenson lived and died at inconvenient times for the literary historian, as his posthumous reputation has had an uncertain relationship with the idea of the literary 'period'. Terms that include 'Victorian', '*fin de siècle*' and 'modernist' have all been used to describe various aspects of his work, without ever succeeding in finally placing him in such a taxonomy of cultural change. One particular difficulty that confronts us today is the decade in which the majority of Stevenson's works were written: the 1880s. Literary and cultural historians are quite used to separating off 'the 1890s' as a separate period, also called the *fin de siècle*, in which new forms of literature were born (although this often means shunting key works like *Dr Jekyll and Mr Hyde*, published in 1886, into 'the 1890s'). Stevenson was in fact writing during years in which publishing practices changed very rapidly, which led to a break-down of the traditional structure of the three-volume novel, and its splintering into new genres and forms. As Ian Duncan's chapter in this volume points out, only a small handful of Stevenson's published work bears much relation to the hitherto dominant tradition of the novel with its modes of realism and architectural unity, and Stevenson threw himself into these newer, shorter and more flexible literary forms to answer the demands of a rapidly-changing reading public. Between the decline of the traditional

1

structure of the 'three decker' novel, and the fashion for the new, self-consciously literary form of the short story, Stevenson wrote stories that did not follow a set idea of how long they should be, who should narrate them and how many narrators a story can have, or whether they should adopt one literary discourse, or several. And, of course, Stevenson did not only write prose fiction but also essays, memoirs of his friends, poems and travel books.

Stevenson's writing career intersects with rapid changes in the cultural idea of what an author was, how literature should be judged, and who was qualified to do the judging. The formation of literary coteries and dining clubs, the cross-over between literature and journalism, and the emergence of the public intellectual all gave rise to the figure of the 'Man of Letters'. Men such as Andrew Lang, W. E. Henley, Edmund Gosse and Leslie Stephen were magazine editors, reviewers, critics, essayists, poets and novelists. They made money from literary culture but they also cultivated the persona of the 'bookman', a figure who also, while exploiting the new professionalism, absorbs the amateur writer and the general bibliophile.[1] Just as the study of literature was becoming professionalised with the advent of the signed, rather than anonymous, literary review and the creation of departments of English Literature in English universities (these had originated much earlier in Scotland), so writers adopted the persona of the cultivated amateur or the 'common reader' who could represent and speak for the reading public in reviews and direct public taste.

Stevenson was a popular author in more ways than one. He was the object of much admiration among the bookmen,[2] to the extent that Andrew Lang reminisced: 'Mr. Stevenson possessed, more than any man I ever met, the power of making other men fall in love with him. I mean that he excited a passionate admiration and affection, so much so that I verily believe some men were jealous of other men's place in his liking.'[3] (This was probably correct: Lang and Henley, for example, both loved Stevenson and heartily disliked each other.) The writer was not the lonely Romantic figure, working in isolation, but one actively engaged in the production of social and cultural values. Participation in the production of late nineteenth-century literature, then, is a social event or performance, and this element of social performativity often extends into the self-consciously stylised rhetoric of the men of letters. Stevenson's style, particularly in his essays, has sometimes attracted adverse comment for its highly self-conscious literary artifice and for the author's apparent relish for archaic syntax and wilful indirection in contrast with the transparent prose of his adventure stories. But Stevenson's style as an essayist marks the way he works through some serious issues about ethics and aesthetics As Alex Thomson argues in his chapter, Stevenson's style was not only the product of an enormous personal industry and a devotion to craftsmanship, which did much to cement his reputation amongst fellow writers, but was also the natural complement to his beliefs about literature's moral function. Literature is indeed a guide for life: not through what it says, but what it is. Stevenson's conception of the centrality of play to literature is not an airy aestheticism, but a conviction that it is not from our schoolbooks but through our childhood games that we learn to obey those impulses which guide right action.

If participation in the literary 1880s was a performance, Stevenson performed himself as a writer and a celebrated, popular author throughout his career, not only in his adoption of different social roles from the Bohemian traveller of his early books to the laird of a Samoan estate, but also in the way he insistently rehearses in his letters to his literary friends the problems of how the writer should live, and how life can be represented in fiction. Living, reading and writing were all, in some way, part of the same experience for Stevenson, as they were for the bookmen, but for Stevenson these were matters of very great seriousness and complexity. In retrospect, the most significant, perhaps the most unexpected, and certainly the strangest, of these literary friendships was the one with Henry James, a relationship that lasted until Stevenson's death and produced one of the key literary exchanges of the 1880s: their discussion in essay-dialogue in *Longman's Magazine* about the condition of the novel and the relations of 'realism' and 'romance'. John Lyon's chapter traces the nuances of this unlikely bond between the great Scottish author of romances, and the American whose intricate inquiries into the 'chamber of consciousness' reinvented nineteenth-century realism in the novel. Lyon delineates this complex relationship as one in which 'realism', the point of dispute in their debate, passes through a series of subtle gradations as both writers contend with the problem of 'the nature of the world and [. . .] how fiction should or should not address it'.

Stevenson's two most frequently-quoted essays – 'A Gossip on Romance' and his 'Humble Remonstrance' to James's *Art of Fiction* – are justly seen as major interventions in literary history, but his discussion of literature was balanced and sometimes agitated by a sense not only of *how* but also *why* one might be an author. Stevenson, especially in the first half of his career, was a productive essayist, writing on a broad variety of topics in widely-circulating magazines such as the *Cornhill*, and these frequently turn to the ethics of being a writer. In 'Some Gentlemen in Fiction' he expresses the idea of the author doing the right thing, but not being able to tell why he does it, an idea characterised by simultaneous confidence and nervousness in the role of the writer: 'We may be sure (although we know not why) that we give our lives, like coral insects, to build up insensibly, in the twilight of the seas of time, the reef of righteousness. And we may be sure (although we see not how) it is a thing worth doing.'[4] At the time, these essays were rather coolly received: George Saintsbury's review of the *Familiar Studies of Men and Books* employs such underwhelming terms as 'pleasant', 'interesting' and 'entirely adequate'.[5] But towards the end of his life and after, his admirers began to feel that it was by his essays that Stevenson would be remembered.[6] This tension is in the essays themselves. On the one hand they are 'familiar', sociable essays written on accessible topics and addressing themselves to the reader in an affable (and to the modern ear sometimes affected) tone. Stevenson sometimes used the term 'gossip' instead of 'essay' as if he were enacting an exchange at a literary club and he often intersperses cultivated argument with anecdotes about himself. Norquay describes this technique: 'The essays create little fictions within themselves, playing with the narrative "I" ; in several instances Stevenson begins by talking about a third-person character until finally "admitting" that this person he knows so well is of course himself.'[7]

Yet the essays are also deeply serious. Stevenson's biographical studies are concerned with ethical character and the exemplary potential of their subjects. In his account of Thoreau, he dwells for some time on Thoreau's statement that 'The cost of a thing [. . .] is *the amount of what I will call life* which is required to be exchanged for it, immediately or in the long run.'[8] Here Stevenson, at the age of 38, is thinking immediately of his own writing career and that he has been engaged in 'bartering for it the whole of his available liberty', but the relations between cost and life occupied him in other contexts.[9] The bookmen had studiously pursued the ideal of 'reading for pleasure' but Stevenson was always worried about the cost of pleasure, and the relation of that cost to ethics. His self-descriptions as a writer toy with the image of the prostitute – 'We should be paid, if we give the pleasure we pretend to give'[10] – yet he also argued against the need to write for the market, claiming instead that writing was, in the title of another essay, 'Child's Play', the spontaneous expression of feelings with no eye on the future.[11] Kevin McLaughlin makes an important point when he shows the link between Stevenson's interest in *adventure*, a form of narrative characterised by chance happenings, and *venture*, or economic speculation.[12] Stevenson uses economic metaphors to describe adventure fiction as a type of speculation on an uncertain future, and recommends, with Thoreau, that no one should 'reckon up possible accidents' in the course of life.[13] But the problem of the cost of things runs throughout his writing: the price Henry Jekyll pays for his experiment in morality (he mistakenly believes the potion will separate out his good and evil sides) is his life; Jim Hawkins pays for his share of the treasure with the nightmares of the 'accursed' island that continue to haunt him as an adult; the parabolic tale 'The Bottle Imp' threatens to set the cost of the satisfaction of desire at eternal damnation.

Stevenson's own fiction and autobiographical travelogues are no less speculative about the act of writing itself than are his essays about fiction and the role of the author. He was a restless writer, and not only in his frequent changes of physical localities across the globe. Caroline McCracken-Flesher's chapter on Stevenson's travel writing shows how in the act of narrating his experiences of new places and people in Britain, France, America and the Pacific, he changes himself as an individual subject. His shifting perspectives, and relations to the available discourses of travel writing, destabilise his own voice as a guide to these places, radically altering the travel genre so that it can no longer provide an external commentary, but becomes, as McCracken-Flesher puts it, an 'inward voyage'. In his fiction, Stevenson is famously diverse. He wrote in different narrative voices, styles and even genres, sometimes within the same work: his unfinished *Weir of Hermiston* moves between a novel of disturbing psychological realism and a compendium of ballad-like tales. Archie Weir can be appalled by the hanging of a criminal condemned by his own father, and listen happily to gruesome tales of murder on the moors committed by his cousins. In *Dr Jekyll and Mr Hyde* the various reporters of the action struggle to make sense of it, continually going over different versions of the same ground to puzzle out the meaning of what they witness. *The Master of Ballantrae* is made up of a variety of competing narrative voices whose information is not always mutually compatible and whose interests in the action are very different. Stevenson – often self-deprecating about his own writing – claimed that he had taught himself to write by aping a string of different authors as varied as Defoe and Baudelaire. Henry James, more approvingly, detected in Stevenson a tendency to start each work with something new and original: 'Each of his books is an independent effort – a window opened on a different view.'[14]

Nevertheless, and despite this obvious diversity, Stevenson has become a by-word for two genres: the boy's adventure of *Treasure Island* and the urban Gothic of *Dr Jekyll and Mr Hyde*. Yet his own attitude to genre is strikingly revisionist. The treasure-hunting theme of his first novel, *Treasure Island* (itself much darker than earlier models such as Ballantyne's *Coral Island*), sits alongside another story that breaks down the classic narrative of adventure. In the novella 'The Merry Men', the treasure-hunting theme becomes murderous as the insane Gordon Darnaway kills the survivor of a wreck to claim the goods from it, and the action is moved uncomfortably closer to the Imperial centre. Far from Jim's vaguely Caribbean island, this treasure-hunting story is set on the west coast of Scotland. (Stevenson wrote 'The Merry Men' and started *Treasure Island* in the same year.) Significantly, Aros in 'The Merry Men' is not a complete island, but separated from the mainland at high tide by 'a little gut of the sea'[15] and the difference between the madness of the living on the land, and the nightmarish quality of the 'charnel ocean'[16] does not mark a complete separation. In *The Master of Ballantrae*, the boyish excitement of the hunt for buried treasure moves away from the island narrative altogether and into the colonising struggles and brutal exploitation of the Seven Years' War in North America. What is buried and dug up in this novel is not treasure but a human body, hideously preserved in a kind of suspended animation. The supposed clear transparency of adventure fiction and the murkiness of late nineteenth-century Gothic are very closely interwoven in much of Stevenson's fiction.

As the chapters by Robert Irvine and Alex Thomson show, the adventure romance, ostensibly simple and exciting fiction for boys, is far from straightforward in Stevenson's hands and his representation and theorisation of childhood in general are exceptionally complex. His children range from the confident and charming playmates of (some of) the *Child's Garden of Verses* to his own accounts of waking screaming from childhood nightmares; from the eager self-sufficiency of *Treasure Island*'s Jim Hawkins, who is quite unperturbed by the death of his father, to the tortured, hypersensitive Archie in *Weir of Hermiston*, whose life is shadowed by the domineering influence of his authoritarian father. Here again, Stevenson is instructive in a revaluation of literary history. Boys' adventure stories had been popular from mid-century, with the emergence of a new figure in British literature: the independent boy cut free from the advice or control of parental figures. R. M. Ballantyne's 1857 novel *The Coral Island* (an influence that Stevenson acknowledged) features three boys who can not only live comfortably on the island on which they are shipwrecked, but also defeat pirates and assist in the conversion of cannibal natives to Christianity. The year 1882, when *Treasure Island* was originally serialised in *Young Folks* magazine, also saw the publication of Richard Jeffrey's novel *Bevis*, chronicling the games of its 10-year-old hero and his friends, and of F. Anstey's equally popular *Vice Versa*, in which a father and son magically change places with the result that the father learns the true value of boyhood freedom and, when the roles revert, resolves not to inflict any further moralising on his son.

In this volume, we see how Stevenson both advances and departs from the model of the freebooting, adventurous boy and the emergence of the new boy hero, cut loose from the demands of moral behaviour, leads us in different directions. Liberated from moral instruction, the child's mind becomes a way of understanding about the nature of growth, and of states of consciousness. Julia Reid's chapter shows us how Stevenson's writing for and about children interacts with evolutionary ideas about psychology which saw children's desires and instincts as natural and instructive rather than in need of control or correction. Evolutionary psychologists, such as Stevenson's friend James Sully, saw children's play as central to understanding the origins of the human species as children retain 'primitive' impulses and behaviours that become obscured in the adult by social and moral compulsion. But at the same time, late-nineteenth-century fears about degeneration and the apparent overdevelopment of civilisation were producing a child whose imaginative capacities shaded into sickliness and unhealthy absorption. As Reid shows, such theories filter into Stevenson's writing in different ways producing both the morbidly introspective child, such as *Weir of Hermiston*'s Archie Weir, and the flourishing Davie Balfour of *Kidnapped*.

Stevenson's most important individual contribution to the theorisation of the child was his repeated argument that we do not – or should not – grow out of our childhood modes of experience, and that the main locus for the continuation of these experiences is the act of reading: 'fiction is to the grown man what play is to the child'.[17] It is tempting to look in Stevenson, as in other late Victorian writers, for ideas that we now associate with Freud, a tendency that Freud, who freely admitted that all his best ideas had already taken shape in the work of creative writers, would probably endorse. It is Stevenson who confronts the Freudian idea that our desires may be darker than we would like to believe, that 'It is not only pleasurable things that we imagine in our daydreams'[18] and Stephen Arata's chapter shows how Stevenson's ideas about dreaming work by what we would later call Freudian forms of imagery and metaphor. But more importantly, Stevenson was attuned to a general turn in the late nineteenth century to the theorisation of an unconscious which operates in our daily lives but below the level of conscious thought and, as Arata demonstrates, it is through the work of fiction that the strange and private meanings of dreams and the unconscious are made public.

Many of Stevenson's darker daydreams have their origins in Scotland. Yet, perhaps because of his peripatetic writing career, Stevenson is not generally typed as an iconic Scottish author, in the way that his predecessors Robert Burns and Walter Scott have been. Stevenson himself admitted to a vexed relationship with his native country, even as it provided an insistent source of material and inspiration for his writing. Writing from his adopted home in Vailima, Samoa, it strikes him that to be truly Scottish is to experience a sense of displacement from Scotland: 'Singular that I should fulfil the Scots destiny throughout, and live a voluntary exile, and have my head filled with the blessed, beastly place all the time!'[19] This sense of dislocation was to result partly in Stevenson's poetic investigation of the nature of home when it is caught up in questions of global time and space, and this is discussed in Penny Fielding's chapter on the neglected topic of his poetry. But Scotland resonates in many ways in Stevenson's fiction. Both Stephen Arata and Julia Reid trace some of Stevenson's darker writing to his early exposure to Calvinism in the graphic and often gruesome stories about Scottish Protestant martyrs told to the young Louis (in fact 'Lewis', as he had not yet changed his name) by his nurse Alison Cunningham (known to the family as 'Cummy'). Reid shows how Stevenson, along with writers on psychology, associates the influence of religion with neurosis, and Arata demonstrates how the Calvinist stress on human fallibility and guilt finds its way into

Stevenson's conception of a dark, violent or even unconscious aspect to Scottish cultural traditions. As Arata argues, Gothic fiction is a particularly potent form for imagining Scotland with its own national tradition split in the nineteenth century between the cultivation of a modern, urban, scientific society, and the invention (sometimes cast as a rediscovery) of a primitive other Scotland, marked by superstition, violence and, in the case of 'The Merry Men', outright madness.

Ian Duncan and Alison Lumsden situate Stevenson within a Scottish literary tradition in which the shadow of Walter Scott, arguably the most widely-read novelist of the nineteenth century, looms large. On the one hand, Stevenson seems to offer a decisive break with Scott, abandoning the idea that the huge historical framework of his novels can demonstrate the course of historical process itself, and replacing the large-scale historical novel with the fractured narrative and multiple points of view of works like *The Master of Ballantrae*. But Lumsden's chapter also shows how Stevenson's position as a Scottish novelist must be read in the context of an abiding interest not only in Scottish history but in historiography itself. Contrary to a common view that sees Scott's novels as a narrative of progress, with Stevenson a commentator on the aridity of Scottish history, Lumsden shows us how both Scott and Stevenson are engaged in acts of memory and commemoration which, as Lumsden says, 'remind the reader of the pain and division which lie behind Scotland's official narrative of historical progress'.

Just as Stevenson's position as a historical novelist has required new attention, so must we take seriously his interest in politics. Throughout this volume, contributors speculate on the various uses of a term that was hugely important for Stevenson, yet curiously difficult to define: 'Romance'. 'Romance' was a loose term sometimes vaguely applied to any stirring adventure writing (Andrew Lang was notoriously guilty of this simplistic use of the term) but to Stevenson it was an important theory of reading. He explodes the idea that 'Romance' is either pure imagination, cut free from the specificities of political engagement, or – as it tends to be represented in modern criticism of the period – as naively right-wing and imperialist. Robert Irvine's chapter on the importance of class in adventure and romance fiction shows how Stevenson plays with the idea of the 'gentleman'. Gentlemen feature prominently in adventure fiction, from Dr Livesey and Squire Trelawney, Jim's ostensible guardians in *Treasure Island*, to the aristocratic figures of the *New Arabian Nights*, and Stevenson maintains some of their glamour while at the same time demystifying the standard Victorian justifications for the gentleman's political privileges. It is the duplicitous pirate Long John Silver, not the Squire or the Doctor, who exercises the greatest political power in *Treasure Island*. Stevenson does not, in any case, see a necessary difference between the abstraction of romance and the specificity of current events. *The*

Dynamiter (written in collaboration with Fanny Stevenson) is in one sense pure romance: picking up on the *Arabian Nights* theme in which multiple stories are told on the same occasion, it is set in a London described as 'the Baghdad of the West' and throws the reader into the pure space of romance action in a city which 'teams and bubbles with adventure'.[20] But this adventure is based on the very recent events of the Irish nationalist bombing campaigns in London in the 1880s. The Stevensons render these events incredible and absurd, splitting them up into fragmentary moments glimpsed in various times and from various angles by the novel's three heroes as if suggesting that the act of terrorism, which seeks to make a political statement by events so shocking they are beyond rational language, is itself absurd.

His most important political intervention, however, was not in British politics, but in what he ironically refers to in the title of an essay as 'A Footnote to History', the fate of the islands of the South Pacific under colonisation. Stevenson's final location was Samoa where he rejected the call of Andrew Lang to return to romance-writing: 'more claymores, less psychology'.[21] The island stories Stevenson wrote in the early 1890s show how far he had come from the bookman culture he left behind him in London. As he undermines the foundations of the nineteenth-century Imperial Romance, in which vigorous and moralistic white heroes regulate the outposts of empire, Stevenson also expresses his disillusion with 'literature' or 'art' in general, as an elevated category.

Stevenson encountered a Pacific already defined in the West in terms of primitivism or an Edenic escape from the complexities of modern life – a place that promised the sexual freedom of Paul Gaugin's paintings. As Roslyn Jolly's chapter shows, what he wrote about there had everything to do with the complexities of modern life. Confronted with an extraordinary diversity of nature and social organisation that was being fragmented by often incompetent and piecemeal colonial interference, Stevenson wrote a series of stories or novellas that sought to map the strangeness and diversity of his new surroundings. 'The Beach of Falesá' describes the attempts of the none-too-bright trader John Wiltshire to understand the island society in which he finds himself, and Stevenson brings to bear on his predicament his own knowledge of the complex trading structures and laws of taboo that he witnessed in Samoa. *The Ebb-Tide* marks, as the title suggests, the low-water mark of the imperial island adventure that had begun so confidently in the works of R. M. Ballantyne. Instead of the three heroic boys of *The Coral Island*, Stevenson offers the washed-up trio of Herrick, Huish and Davis. Where Ballantyne's boyish Ralph, Jack and Peterkin get the better of pirates, the *Ebb-Tide*'s no-longer youthful adventurers steal a boat-load of champagne, only to discover that it is mostly water and an insurance scam. The admirable competence and leadership qualities of the *Coral Island* boys turn into the murder of Huish and abject humbling of Davis by the island's tyrannical overlord Attwater, the embodiment of the pure will and unrepentant violence of the white colonising trader. As Jolly shows us, the old amateur tradition of the adventurer has turned into a model for the violence and duplicity of the 'professional' colonisation of the Pacific.

Stevenson's dark stories of the Pacific from the 1890s are in one sense a shocking break with a tradition that had celebrated colonialism as the site of the twin themes of empire and adventure, but in another sense he was satisfying a new market that was already turning away from such certainties. Joseph Conrad's first novel, *Almayer's Folly* (1895), appeared the year after Stevenson's death, and similarly deals with the failure of trade, the emptiness of the treasure-hunting motif, and the onset of insanity. Stevenson was always a consummate professional, but in ways which ask us to examine what it means to be a 'popular' author at the end of the nineteenth century. Through Stevenson, we see the emergence of many of the concerns that would occupy the twentieth century: psychology, globalisation, the breakdown of racial and social classification. But we also see the last decades of the nineteenth century in all their complexity, as writers such as Stevenson experimented with old traditions of storytelling and new methods of writing, and with the relationship between the author and an increasingly professional literary culture. Stevenson's insistence on writing about 'life' negotiates these encounters with an extraordinary versatility, and this volume addresses the many contexts into which such an exploration led him.

CHAPTER ONE

Stevenson and Fiction

Ian Duncan

Robert Louis Stevenson wrote in a wide variety of literary genres in the course of his brief career. While his essays, travelogues and poems have always had admirers, it is upon his achievements in prose fiction that his reputation rests. Prose fiction overtook poetry to become the dominant form of imaginative literature in nineteenth-century Britain, and we are accustomed to regarding the Victorian period as the heyday of the English novel, encompassing the work of Charles Dickens, W. M. Thackeray, Charlotte and Emily Brontë, Elizabeth Gaskell, George Eliot, Anthony Trollope, Thomas Hardy and Henry James. Modern critical judgments rarely count Stevenson among this august company. F. R. Leavis excluded him from 'the great tradition of the English novel', as a consequence of the more serious exclusion of Walter Scott: 'Out of Scott a bad tradition came [. . .] with Stevenson it took on "literary" sophistication and fine writing.'[1] While the international popularity of *Treasure Island*, *Kidnapped* and *Dr Jekyll and Mr Hyde* remains unshaken, Stevenson's absence from standard surveys and field anthologies appears to confirm his relegation by academic scholars and critics to the status of a minor author.[2]

One way of making sense of this exclusion is to entertain the proposition that Stevenson, however brilliant an author of prose fiction, did not write novels. That is, he did not write 'novels' according to the ways in which the genre came to be defined, and its aesthetic norms established, in the retrospective view of twentieth-century criticism. In *The Great Tradition* (1948) Leavis undertook an official consolidation of those norms, proposing a genealogy and a canon of 'the English novel' in the wake of an Anglo-American modernism that founded itself upon a revolt against Victorian moral and aesthetic values. This reduced the thriving variety of Victorian fiction around a single standard, that of the novel, especially the long, large, multi-plotted, socially and psychologically realist novel that purported to represent the whole of a national society. Its protocols include an effacement of the technical mediations of form and style for a direct mimesis of 'life', in all its dynamic complexity, and the 'high seriousness' that Victorian critic Matthew Arnold held to be the essential moral attitude of great literature: qualities realised in the work of George Eliot above all other novelists. *Middlemarch* (1874) holds its place in critical estimates, more securely now (it seems) than ever, as the summation or perfection of the nineteenth-century novel in English.

In 1924 Leonard Woolf remarked on the 'headlong fall' of Stevenson's once-exalted reputation in the generation since his death.[3] The fall really became headlong with the onset of modernism, and the retrospective normalisation of Victorian fiction around the novel. 'It is no longer possible for a serious critic to place him among the great writers, because in no department of letters – except the boy's book and the short-story – has he written work of first-class importance,' declared Frank Swinnerton in 1914, adding: 'We may question whether Stevenson did not make the novel a toy when George Eliot had finished making it a treatise.'[4] This aesthetic judgment rests upon a biographical diagnosis of arrested development. Stevenson 'was by physical delicacy made intellectually timid and spiritually cautious. He was obliged to take care of himself, to be home at night, to allow himself to be looked after.'[5] In short, he remained a child, skilful in puerile and miniature forms ('the boy's book and the short story') but never mastering the adult complexities of the novel. The developmental scheme undercuts the more interesting suggestion of Swinnerton's comparison between Stevenson and Eliot: that Stevenson's resort to a ludic formalism (making the novel 'a toy') might express a dialectical refusal and critique of the high seriousness of Victorian realism, rather than a failure to grow up to it.

The idea that the novel fully realises the potential of prose fiction for 'greatness' – a term denoting magnitude as well as excellence – rests upon the nineteenth-century claim that the novel is the modern equivalent of epic, which held the highest place in the classical genre system (still authoritative through the eighteenth century). Just as epic was held to be the crowning work in a poet's career (following pastoral and georgic), it occupied a teleological position in the anthropological account of cultural forms developed since the Enlightenment. Epic represented the totality of national historical life for a primitive society; the novel would attempt the same for a modern, commercial age of prose.[6] The example was set at the beginning of the nineteenth century by the historical novels of Sir Walter Scott, which accordingly loomed large over Stevenson's conception of his art, as I shall argue later in this chapter. The view of the novel as the fullest, thus normative, development of fiction still conditions literary historiography and critical hierarchies. It has also conditioned the modern accounts of Stevenson, including Robert Kiely's major critical reassessment in the 1960s. Kiely closes his book *Robert Louis Stevenson and the Fiction of Adventure* (1964) with the verdict: 'The Master of Ballantrae and Weir of Hermiston begin to show the impressive consequences of the transition in Stevenson's fiction from sleight-of-hand to artistry, from adventure as an entertaining counterfeit to adventure as a symbolic chart of the formidable risks in which life involves all men.'[7] At last Stevenson was scaling the mature heights of the novel (here cast in terms of a post-Victorian symbolist aesthetic), just before death cut him off.

The seeds of this modern judgment can be found among a few dissenting critics who challenged what they saw as the overrating of Stevenson's achievement by his admirers in his lifetime, especially in his later years. This criticism comes into focus in the reception of *The Master of Ballantrae*, the first extended work of fiction by Stevenson that could plausibly be claimed as a novel – as opposed to a tale, romance, or 'boy's book'. 'Mr. Stevenson has done it at last,' wrote the reviewer of the *Pall Mall Gazette*: 'he has produced something very like a classic,' thanks to a rendering of psychological complexity ('the combined subtlety and poignancy of its spiritual drama').[8] Other reviewers disagreed: '[It] is nothing short of ridiculous to hear reviewers speak of "great literature" in certain current connections. Fine as Mr Stevenson's work is, he must penetrate more profoundly, and aspire more loftily, and develop more expansively, ere he can assume a position among the larger gods of literature.'[9] After his death, Stevenson's supporters pointed to the unfinished *Weir of Hermiston* as evidence that here, at last, he had achieved that apotheosis. Again his detractors demurred: 'Rich as it is in those perfections of which Stevenson was a supreme master, "Weir of Hermiston" would never have been a great novel, for a great novel he never could have written.'[10]

Indeed Stevenson never wrote a novel, great or otherwise, if we consider the novel as it was defined by nineteenth-century publishing practice. In Stevenson's own ironical summary (in 'A Humble Remonstrance'), 'the fact of the existence of the modern English novel is not to be denied; materially, with its three volumes, leaded type, and gilded lettering, it is easily distinguishable from other forms of literature.'[11] For much of the century publication in three octavo volumes, retailing for the exorbitant price of 31s 6d, was the standard format for new novels. The luxurious 'three-decker' was sustained by the cartel of circulating libraries, whose purchase of the bulk of relatively small print-runs guaranteed publishers' profits. (In 'A Humble Remonstrance' Stevenson refers derisively to 'the modern English novel' as 'the stay and bread-winner of Mr Mudie', magnate of the circulating libraries.)[12] The alternative format was serialisation: either in monthly numbers, each made up of several chapters of a single fictional title, or else in monthly (sometimes weekly) magazines, combined with essays, reviews, short stories and poems by other authors. Extended works of fiction would normally be bound and issued in volumes – as novels – at the close of serialisation.

Most of Stevenson's literary output was written for magazine publication. Only three of his fiction titles – *The Dynamiter*, *Dr Jekyll and Mr Hyde* and

The Wrong Box – were originally issued in book form; of these, the first two were conceived as serials and the third might as well have been.[13] While he contributed work to several periodicals, Stevenson enjoyed a close association with four in particular. His earliest tales appeared in the short-lived weekly *London* (1877–9), edited by W. E. Henley. For the next few years he published much of his work in the *Cornhill Magazine*, the most prestigious literary monthly of the age, edited by Leslie Stephen. After Stephen's resignation from the *Cornhill* in 1882 Stevenson transferred his allegiance to the new *Longman's Magazine*, under the aegis of Andrew Lang. In his last years he became (from the point of view of publishing history) an American author, contributing essays and serial fiction (*The Master of Ballantrae*, *The Wrecker*) to the new *Scribner's Magazine* (founded in 1887). This summary omits Stevenson's most famous works of magazine fiction, *Treasure Island* (1881–2), *The Black Arrow* (1883) and *Kidnapped* (1886), which were serialised in the illustrated juvenile weekly *Young Folks*.

By the 1880s magazines were the ascendant medium for fiction publishing in Great Britain. The independent part-issue format was effectively extinct (following the death in 1870 of Dickens, the only major author who had sustained it with consistent success), and the hegemony of the three-decker was on the wane; in 1894, the year of Stevenson's death, publishers and circulating libraries formally abandoned their commitment to a vehicle that had ceased to be profitable. Stevenson's career, from the mid-1870s to the early 1890s, occupies the first phase of what Philip Waller calls 'both the first and the *only* mass literary age'[14] – the decades of exponential expansion and diversification of the print market before the advent of rival media, film and radio, in the early twentieth century. Various economic and social factors fed this expansion: the increase in national literacy rates following the 1870 and 1872 Education Acts, on top of a general population increase (by 40 per cent from 1840 to 1870 – including a demographic doubling of the professions), and technological developments in publishing (including, from mid-century, the mechanisation of print foundries and the manufacture of paper from wood-pulp). The result was not just a much larger literary market but a more diversified one, with the colonisation of new economic and demographic ranges encouraging a proliferation of new genres and formats. Magazines provided an especially flexible medium for targeting new readers and developing new forms to reach them – such as Stevenson's tales in *Young Folks*, aimed at juvenile readers enfranchised by the 1870 Forster Education Act and the Education (Scotland) Act of 1872.

The death of George Eliot in 1880 (followed by Trollope in 1882) marked the end of an era. The Great Victorian Novel had aspired to represent an entire national society which was also its reading public; Dickens and Eliot could combine popular entertainment with lofty pedagogical and artistic goals in novels that spoke to a putatively unified reading nation. The last quarter of the century saw a splintering of this mid-Victorian literary field, with a chasm opening between the proliferating sub-genres of sensational and escapist entertainment (by H. Rider Haggard, 'Ouida', Marie Corelli, Bram Stoker, Arthur Conan Doyle and others) and stricter codes of novelistic high seriousness (naturalism infused with social purpose in George Moore or George Gissing; a rigorous aestheticism in Henry James). Thanks to Andrew Lang, *Macmillan's Magazine* became an institutional centre for the *fin de siècle* 'romance revival'. Stevenson's career shows a keen attunement to the emergent forms of popular and magazine fiction. More than any other author of the age (until, after his death and to rather different effect, Joseph Conrad), Stevenson confounds the dichotomy that contemporary critics saw reopening between novel and romance – notably, and in contrast to the rough-and-ready craftsmanship of a Haggard or Stoker, by his practice of a high aestheticism at the level of style. We should understand Stevenson's works of fiction, then, in terms of a series of choices and experiments which involved a critical refusal of the Victorian novel and its protocols, rather than a failure to master them, on the one hand; and, on the other, a virtuoso formal refinement of the magazine genres of tale, sensational novella and adventure serial.

While many contemporary readers (including James) admired Stevenson's artistry, some deplored an excessive or obtrusive fashioning of style. Paul Maixner's *Critical Heritage* volume illustrates not just the early vicissitudes of Stevenson's reputation but the high quality of literary reviewing in the last decades of the nineteenth century – such that even (or perhaps especially) the negative criticism aimed at Stevenson's art can bring into relief some of its distinctive formal qualities. The remainder of this chapter will concentrate on two of those qualities: first, the refinement of style, criticised by some as artificial and superficial; second, an alleged lack of organic or architectural unity, the consequence of a radical dispersal of narrative action and setting. The focus will be on three book-length works of late fiction: *The Master of Ballantrae* (1888–9), generally acknowledged as one of Stevenson's finest achievements, the more problematic *The Wrecker* (1891–2), and the unfinished *Weir of Hermiston* (1896), considered by some as his most convincing approach to the aesthetic requirements of the novel. *Weir of Hermiston* modulates from a brilliant pastiche of Scottish Romantic fiction towards a *fin-de-siècle* preoccupation with sexuality as fate; while in *The Master of Ballantrae* and *The Wrecker* we see Stevenson adapting the episodic format of magazine publication for a new, post-novelistic kind of fiction, a planetary narrative which seeks to represent the modern 'world system' in its historical ascendancy – as opposed to the political, moral and aesthetic geographies of region and nation that comprise the traditional domain of the novel.

Stevenson took pains with his style. He characterised himself as playing 'the sedulous ape' to the English and French essayists in his apprentice phase, and displayed a fanatical regard for the acoustic principles of word-choice in an essay of 1885, 'On Some Technical Elements of Style in Literature'. Some of the severest criticism levelled at him came from those who caught him making the effort. Irish novelist George Moore was an especially unforgiving detractor. *The Master of Ballantrae*, Moore complained, '[betrays] the writer who does not think as he writes; but who elaborately translates what he has first written out in very common language into an artificial little tongue which he takes to be gentle'.[15] Several years later (addressing *Weir of Hermiston*) Moore repeats the charge: 'this man's style is but a conjuror's trick – a marvellous trick, but a trick [. . .] To such superficial conception of life Stevenson brought his talent for literary marquetry.'[16] Moore, a disciple of the French naturalist novelist Émile Zola, was the hard-line proponent of a socially purposive realism in Stevenson's generation. His hostility acknowledges the critical thrust of Stevenson's style against novelistic norms – since the realist novel was not supposed to have a 'style', to interpose its artifice between the reader and the life it represents. Stevenson articulated a far subtler conception of style, however, than the technical dandyism with which Moore and other critics charged him. In an appreciation of the romances of Alexandre Dumas, he writes: 'There is no style so untranslatable; light as a whipped trifle, strong as silk; wordy like a village tale; pat like a general's despatch; with every fault, yet never tedious; with no merit, yet inimitably right.'[17] Here Stevenson's prose vibrates with its own echo of the antithetical rhythm of Alexander Pope's *Essay on Criticism* ('Willing to wound, and yet afraid to strike, / Just hint a fault, and hesitate dislike') – an overtone just audible to the attentive reader. In making us aware of it, Stevenson insists that a 'right' style is forged through hard work and discipline, at the same time as he invokes an Augustan standard of cultural authority. (Pope again: 'True ease in writing comes from art, not chance, / As those move easiest who have learn'd to dance.')

Rightness of style consists in a paradoxical renunciation of 'merit': it casts itself as a prose without qualities. And yet, 'wordy like a village tale', it is not a novelist's prose. 'Why complain?' asks the reviewer (cited above) who asserted that *Weir of Hermiston* 'would never have been a great novel': 'Great novelists we have had, but only one man who could give us the Isle of Voices, of all his gems the fairest, rarest, most imperishable.'[18] The reviewer appeals to a work that stands at the opposite end of the formal and historical spectrum of prose fiction from the novel. 'The Isle of Voices' and its companion, 'The Bottle Imp', are exercises in pure fabulation, exquisite simulations of oral traditional narrative – artifices of 'Tusitala', the storyteller, as Stevenson's Samoan neighbours dubbed him. Stevenson himself intended

Island Nights' Entertainments (1893) to be 'a volume of Märchen' (folktales, fairytales),[19] and critics have recognised his late-career renovation of Scottish Romantic techniques of folktale imitation and ballad revival on the anthropological terrain of South-Seas primitivism.[20] With the debatable claim that 'the novelist in Scotland is closer than novelists in other cultures to the storyteller and to the storyteller's relation to his audience', Francis Russell Hart invokes Walter Benjamin's famous essay 'The Storyteller', a meditation on the modern recovery of the traditional kinds of narrative that preceded the rise of the novel, in his discussion of Stevenson.[21] For Benjamin (as for Georg Lukács and other mid-twentieth-century critics) the novel is the paradigmatic literary form of modern culture, written and read by 'the solitary individual' no longer immersed in the common practices of speech, memory and performance that once bound a traditional community.[22] In compensation, the novel seeks to incorporate all the life it is estranged from; an existential necessity drives it to swallow the world – characters, scenery, events, objects, language, information, space and time. Hence the dense, miscellaneous, polyphonic, plot-heavy and rhetorically-rich textual medium of nineteenth-century fiction, from Scott and Balzac to Eliot and Dostoevsky.

Benjamin cites Stevenson together with Edgar Allan Poe and Nikolai Leskov as cases of the modern storyteller, a figure who works historically after and against the novel rather than before it. The storyteller renounces the novel's mimetic and symbolic banquets. 'There is nothing that commends a story to memory more effectively,' writes Benjamin, 'than that chaste compactness which precludes psychological analysis.'[23] Benjamin might be echoing Stevenson's own account of the genesis of *Treasure Island*: 'It was to be a story for boys; no need of psychology or fine writing.'[24] The storyteller lays claim to an artificial simplicity; he defines his art by its refusals. Shortly after completing *Treasure Island*, Stevenson elaborated a theory of fiction in his essay 'A Gossip on Romance':

> Fiction is to the grown man what play is to the child; it is there that he changes the atmosphere and tenor of his life; and when the game so chimes with his fancy that he can join in it with all his heart, when it pleases him with every turn, when he loves to recall it and dwells upon its recollection with entire delight, fiction is called romance.[25]

Stevenson glosses the traditional distinction between novel and romance as one between 'drama', or 'the poetry of conduct', and 'romance[,] the poetry of circumstance'.[26] The first is the domain of ethical agency – of choice, conscience, 'psychology'. As for romance:

> There is a vast deal in life and letters both which is not immoral, but simply a-moral; which either does not regard the human will at all, or deals with it in

obvious and healthy relations; where the interest turns, not upon what a man shall choose to do, but on how he manages to do it; not on the passionate slips and hesitations of the conscience, but on the problems of the body and of the practical intelligence, in clean, open-air adventure, the shock of arms or the diplomacy of life.[27]

Romance becomes a pure praxis of style. What counts is how the game is played, not the conditions under which it was invented, or even what may be at stake. This is not far from George Moore's vision of Stevenson writing out his tales in ordinary language before translating them into a fancy vocabulary – or Lloyd Osbourne's account of his collaboration with Stevenson on *The Wrecker*: 'Well do I remember him saying: "It's glorious to have the ground ploughed, and to sit back in luxury for the real fun of writing – which is rewriting."'[28] Meanwhile the note of wilful boyishness, the insistence on 'obvious and healthy relations' and 'clean, open-air adventure', does suggest a qualitative reduction – a stunting – of what the fiction might be able to include. Such phrases scarcely do justice to the achievement of the 'boy's books' themselves, *Treasure Island* and *Kidnapped*, let alone *The Master of Ballantrae*, *The Wrecker* and *The Ebb-Tide*: in which 'adventure' may yield relations neither obvious nor healthy, and action far from clean. *Catriona*, for that matter, earns its title as the sequel to *Kidnapped* not only by resuming the story of David Balfour but by involving us in a murky atmosphere of 'slips and hesitations of the conscience' which retrospectively overcasts the earlier tale's mood of open-air adventure.

Stevenson realised such a romance aesthetic, without recourse to boyish posturing, in the sets of tales *New Arabian Nights* and *More New Arabian Nights – The Dynamiter*. These scintillating and delightful fictions, which have only recently begun to draw critical attention, constitute the Stevenson out of which came Conan Doyle, Chesterton, Borges and Calvino; they instantiate romance as artifice and play.[29] The figure at their centre, Prince Florizel of Bohemia, performs gentlemanliness as a consummate stylishness. Throughout them, and cognate tales such as *The Wrong Box*, we discern the moves of a great game in a characteristic counterpoint of setting, property and event. Here is the irresistible opening sentence of *The Dynamiter*:

> In the city of encounters, the Bagdad of the West, and, to be more precise, on the broad northern pavement of Leicester Square, two young men of five- or six-and-twenty met after years of separation.[30]

The young men (soon they are three) turn detective, committing themselves to what patterns may emerge from the modern, metropolitan habitus of

'Chance, the blind Madonna of the Pagan'.[31] Theirs is a world of surfaces and appearances which are almost invariably deceptive: empty houses, superfluous mansions, tall tales and masquerades, brown boxes and saratoga trunks that turn out to contain dead bodies or infernal machines. The moves of the game disclose no final, authentic interiority. Somerset's conversion from an idle and inept aestheticism to a knowledge of good and evil at the climax of *The Dynamiter* gives us moral epiphany as burlesque. The world turns out to be one vast, intricately-compartmented wrong box, or rather, an interminable traffic of wrong boxes – and something better than that, an interminable traffic of stories. (There is still a grand piano with a corpse inside it riding around the countryside at the end of *The Wrong Box*.) Stevenson's tales yield an inventory of fatal objects whose wrongness is an effect of their circulation: cadavers, a rajah's diamonds, ticking parcels that fail to explode or explode at the wrong time, a bottle with a devil in it. They also yield, predictably, treasure that turns out not to be treasure, or not where it is supposed to be – indeed, this remains a key motif in Stevenson's fiction right up to *The Master of Ballantrae* (instead of buried gold, a corpse that fails to come back to life), *The Wrecker* (instead of smuggled opium, a tale of massacre), and *The Ebb-Tide* (instead of champagne, water; instead of pearls, damnation). The best that Stevenson's feckless or hapless protagonists can do is to play the game with gusto and hope for luck.

Stevenson's style renders a world made up of surface and circumstance, of change and disguise: a world no longer susceptible (if it ever was) to the meaning-making, totalising apparatus of the Victorian novel. The transparent style is the consummate technique of a narration that finds the world intransigently fragmentary and senseless. Transparency of style is the correlative of the opacity of the world, whereas the semiotically thick and tangled style of the Victorian novelist presumes a porousness between language and the world. In his famous 'Humble Remonstrance' to Henry James, Stevenson repudiated novelistic realism by asserting a Euclidean (rather than Platonic) formalism:

> A proposition of geometry does not compete with life; and a proposition of geometry is a fair and luminous parallel for a work of art. Both are reasonable, both untrue to the crude fact; both inhere in nature, neither represents it. The novel, which is a work of art, exists, not by its resemblances to life, which are forced and material, as a shoe must still consist of leather, but by its immeasurable difference from life, which is designed and significant, and is both the method and the meaning of the work.[32]

There is an odd twist in the anti-mimetic analogy. As life is to art, so is leather to shoe: Stevenson crosses the terms 'resemblance' and 'material consistency', eliding the actual (functional) resemblance of the shoe, to a human foot, as well as the material of which literary art consists, language. Stevenson's technique is in fact mimetic, even as it forges a non-novelistic representation of the world.

In 'A Gossip on Romance' Stevenson criticises the 'slovenly' and 'utterly careless' style perpetrated by Walter Scott. How could a writer with such splendid gifts 'so often fob us off with languid, inarticulate twaddle?' The explanation, he concedes, may be found 'in the very quality of [Scott's] surprising merits'.[33] Stevenson vividly characterises those merits in an early essay (1874), in which he pays tribute to the heroic grandeur of Scott's fiction: 'that canvas on which armies manoeuvre and great hills pile themselves upon each other's shoulders'.[34] Stevenson acknowledges Scott's role as architect of the modern equivalence between novel and epic – the sublime genre that enfolds national historical life in its multifarious entirety. If Scott towered over the landscape of Victorian fiction, his shadow fell the more darkly on Stevenson: first, because Scott instituted the 'classical' form of the modern novel (the establishment of the three-decker format was largely due to the commercial success of the Waverley novels), and second, because he was the great Scottish author of modern times. Stevenson's attitude to him is accordingly vexed. While in his private letters he might acknowledge the epic scale of Scott's achievement, dwarfing the capacity of his own 'weakling generation',[35] Stevenson concludes 'A Gossip on Romance' by belittling him – in terms uncannily close to those his detractors would aim at Stevenson himself: 'He was a great day-dreamer, a seer of fit and beautiful and humorous visions, but hardly a great artist; hardly, in the manful sense, an artist at all. He pleased himself, and so he pleases us [. . .] A great romantic – an idle child.'[36]

In refusing the novel Stevenson sought to circumvent Scott, and find other grounds for his own art, rather than follow in that mighty path. Miniaturisation, and a jeweller's precision of style, offered one way of outdoing Scott's achievement without having to compete with it on its own immense terms. The adventure serial, as Stevenson perfected it in the pages of *Young Folks*, scales down the modern epic form of historical romance for juvenile readers, and *Kidnapped*, in particular, can be read as a Waverley novel in miniature: the epyllion of *Rob Roy*.[37] Stevenson's most intensive engagement with Scott, and with the Scottish tradition of modern fiction, comes in *Weir of Hermiston* – the work hailed by many commentators as promising a novelistic maturity and complexity. In *Weir of Hermiston* Stevenson explicitly invokes epic, setting it in a past that is not just national and local (the Scottish Borders) but literary. Epic has already been claimed by a modern romance aesthetic: Scott's. The narrator relates a bloody episode of murder and revenge:

Some century earlier the last of the minstrels might have fashioned the last of the ballads out of that Homeric fight and chase; but the spirit was dead, or had been reincarnated already in Mr. Sheriff Scott, and the degenerate moorsmen must be content to tell the tale in prose, and to make of the 'Four Black Brothers' a unit after the fashion of the 'Twelve Apostles' or the 'Three Musketeers'.[38]

The Homeric spirit is diluted by post-heroic types of virtue (those twelve apostles). We come too late – later even than Scott's successor Dumas, let alone Scott himself. There can be no more last minstrels.

Weir of Hermiston takes seriously Scott's foundation of the nineteenth-century novel on the passing of an older, traditional, heroic world – the world of epic – and the onset of a modern commercial civilisation. With this acknowledgment, Stevenson explores another aesthetic solution to the challenge of that prior achievement: pastiche. Like *St Ives*, another uncompleted late romance, *Weir of Hermiston* is set 'in that fated year' 1814: fated, for the Scottish author, not just as the year of Napoleon's defeat and exile to Elba, but as the year of Scott's first Scottish historical novel *Waverley*.[39] Scott himself appears in and around the edges of these last tales. The hero of *St Ives* is walking 'among sites which have been rendered illustrious by the pen of Walter Scott' when he falls in with 'a tall, stoutish, elderly gentleman, a little grizzled, and of a rugged but cheerful and engaging countenance'; years later he realises that 'the unknown in the green coat had been the Great Unknown! I had met Scott; I had heard a story from his lips'.[40] *Weir of Hermiston* refers several times to the local poet and improving laird Mr Sheriff Scott. The story abounds in brilliantly stylised evocations of and allusions to Scott, his circle (including the 'Ettrick Shepherd', James Hogg) and his habitat in Edinburgh and the Borders, especially in the first five chapters. The opening pages summon Scott's works as the decisive medium of 'public and domestic history', with references to Claverhouse, 'the chisel of Old Mortality', and the vanished world of faery-lore and riding ballads memorialised in *Minstrelsy of the Scottish Border*. Adam Weir keeps a town house in George Square, like Scott's father, while his wife's family, like Scott's mother's, is named Rutherford. Stevenson based the character of his Lord Justice-Clerk on the Scotts' fearsome neighbour, the 'hanging judge' Lord Braxfield, and the critical tradition has superimposed upon him the biographical profile of Stevenson's own father. The clash between an overbearing lawyer father and a sensitive, artistic son is a recurrent theme in Scots literary biography, with James Boswell, Henry Cockburn, Scott and Stevenson himself (updating the father's profession to engineer) among 'Braxfield's bairns'.[41] By the nineteenth century this had become more than a biographical phenomenon. Scott founded modern Scottish fiction on an analogy between the generational conflict of fathers and sons and the large-scale antagonisms that drive historical change, in *Waverley* and its successors. *Redgauntlet*, Scott's own 'autobiographical' novel, is especially present in *Weir of Hermiston*, with its focus on the vexed relationship between youthful heroes and domineering father-figures, as well as its shift of setting from legal Edinburgh to a primitive, ballad-haunted countryside.[42] Scott, in short, bequeathed to Stevenson the fable of fathers and sons as the psychological plot of Scottish historical romance – and he did so in his own capacity as the formidable father of nineteenth-century Scottish literature.

The evocation of Scott and his world achieves its maximum virtuosity in the trio of essayistic set-pieces that makes up the fifth chapter of *Weir of Hermiston*, 'Winter on the Moors'. Some of Stevenson's early critics complained that he had overdone the Scots dialect, betraying the act of pastiche with this stylistic excess.[43] Certainly the speeches of Adam Weir or Kirstie Elliot are over-egged by comparison with the renditions of Lowland Scots by the great masters of the period in which the tale is set, James Hogg and John Galt as well as Scott himself.[44] Scottishness, as purple passage or pastiche, marks an aesthetic limit. To claim originality Stevenson must turn elsewhere. Where that elsewhere might have lain is hidden by the author's death, although we can find hints in the last few chapters of *Weir of Hermiston*. Chapter 6, in which the narrative begins again with Archie's exile, resounds with allusions to 'the Spirit of the Earth', a 'vast indwelling rhythm of the universe', a 'deeper, aboriginal memory, that was not his, but belonged to the flesh on his bones', and 'the idea of Fate – a pagan Fate, uncontrolled by any Christian deity, obscure, lawless, and august – moving indissuadably in the affairs of Christian men'.[45] If the passages between Archie and Christina are reminiscent of the love chapters of George Meredith's *The Ordeal of Richard Feverel* (1859), the portentous equations between sex and destiny look sideways at Stevenson's great contemporary Thomas Hardy, and in particular at *Tess of the D'Urbervilles* (1891: a novel Stevenson professed not to admire). Stevenson appears to be turning away from the Scottish tradition, available only in pastiche, towards an 'advanced' aesthetic. How successful the turn might have been it is impossible to say.

The earlier long Scottish tale *The Master of Ballantrae* is no less steeped in the great achievements of Scottish Romantic fiction, but to very different effect. The major thematic cluster consisting of the 1745 Jacobite Rising, division in the family, a disputed inheritance, and rivalry between brothers (one dour, one glamorous) recalls several Scott novels, notably *Redgauntlet* but also *Rob Roy*. Stevenson also echoes the anti-Romantic treatments of these themes by Galt and Hogg. Galt alludes to the biblical story of Jacob and Esau, which has a framing role in *The Master of Ballantrae*, in his great chronicle of a blighted inheritance *The Entail*; while Hogg's *The Private Memoirs and*

Confessions of a Justified Sinner provides a model for some of the tale's most striking scenes – the night-time duel (see also Hogg's tale 'Adam Bell') and the final, uncanny exhumation – as well as the diabolical characterisation of one of the brothers.[46] *Confessions of a Justified Sinner* also provides a formal model for *The Master of Ballantrae*, with the authority of its central narrator interspersed with, and compromised by, other sources and voices. The technique points back to a number of other nineteenth-century fictions in which the narration of a family steward or servant is subject to an ironical editorial pressure: Wilkie Collins's *The Moonstone*, Emily Brontë's *Wuthering Heights*, and, the model for all of them, Maria Edgeworth's Irish tale *Castle Rackrent*. (*Castle Rackrent* also gave Stevenson the motif of the reckless heir tossing a coin to decide his fate.) Far from compromising Stevenson's originality in *The Master of Ballantrae*, these sources and precursors make for its firm foundation, so deftly does Stevenson develop them.[47] Meanwhile *The Master of Ballantrae* sustains a withering critique of the nostalgic and idealising constructions of a lost Jacobite Scotland which flourished in Scott's wake. Early critics noted (and some deplored) the morbid intensity of its psychology, in the depiction of the virtuous brother Henry's slow corruption by his obsession with his wicked brother. The bad faith of Romantic Scotland is fixed at the very beginning of the tale: the family divides through a sheerly opportunistic accommodation to the 1745 Rising, and makes a disastrous cult of the martyred Master – who turns out to be not only still alive but a government spy.

The critical anatomy of 'Scotland' in *The Master of Ballantrae* marks its author's repudiation of the Romantic nation, the ideological matrix of the novel after Scott. Stevenson writes a kind of fiction attuned, instead, to the dispersed, disjointed conditions of modern historical life. The narrative tracks, at first, the post-1745 wanderings of the Master across the expanding arena of the British Empire in its late eighteenth-century formation – the Caribbean, North America, India. ('My story was now world-wide enough.')[48] In the last stages of the tale the whole family is transplanted to the wintry deserts of New York, including Mackellar himself – flouting the convention of the narrating steward as indissolubly attached to the estate. The drive of this planetary extension is formal as well as thematic, as the dispersed and miscellaneous texture of the narrative comes into its own. Stevenson declared that *The Master of Ballantrae* 'was to be a story on a large canvas; it was to cover many years, so that I might draw my characters in the growth and the decay of life; and many lands, so that I might display them in changing and incongruous surroundings'.[49] And: 'I saw myself, and rejoiced to be, committed to great spaces and voyages, and a long evolution of time [. . .] I was to carry the reader to and fro in space over a good half of the world, and sustain his interest in time through the extent of a generation.'[50] Critics noted the work's 'various zigzag lights', not always approvingly.[51]

Thus breaking up the unities of time, place and action, Stevenson under-takes a critical development of the formal conditions imposed by magazine serialisation for a new mode of novel-length fiction. The lightly-connected series of tales in *New Arabian Nights* and *The Dynamiter* had pointed the way forward. *The Dynamiter*, in particular, ranging across time, geography and even different genres (not to mention authors), anticipates Stevenson's most radical fictional experiment, *The Wrecker*, in which the formal dispersal of the narrative tracks a planetary movement of capital rather than of persons – or rather, circulations and fluctuations of capital to which the 'singular zigzags' of the tale's human subjects are accessory.[52]

The Wrecker articulates a series of extreme and arbitrary reversals of fortune as it shifts from the Marquesas (site of a tale-telling frame that is never resumed), through the imaginary midwestern state of Muskegon (where the hero's education consists of gambling on a mimic stock-exchange), 'Old Europe' in the now tarnished shapes of Edinburgh and Paris, a luminously evoked San Francisco, the desolation of Midway Island, Dorset, Barbizon and New South Wales. The narrative texture is notably episodic and discon-tinuous, with sudden gleams of light cast on characters, scenes and events that as often as not turn out to be incidental or irrelevant. A spectacular instance occurs in the second chapter, 'Roussillon Wine'. Late one night, the protagonist, Loudon Dodd, returns to his hotel drunk after a dinner party. He finds himself unable to navigate the interior of the building, which has mysteriously acquired new heights and depths:

The house was quite dark; but as there were only the three doors on each landing, it was impossible to wander, and I had nothing to do but descend the stairs until I saw the glimmer of the porter's night light. I counted four flights: no porter. It was possible, of course, that I had reckoned incorrectly; so I went down another and another, and another, still counting as I went, until I had reached the preposterous figure of nine flights. It was now quite clear that I had somehow passed the porter's lodge without remarking it; indeed, I was, at the lowest figure, five pairs of stairs below the street, and plunged in the very bowels of the earth. That my hotel should thus be founded upon catacombs was a dis-covery of considerable interest; and if I had not been in a frame of mind entirely businesslike, I might have continued to explore all night this subterranean empire. But I was bound I must be up betimes on the next morning, and for that end it was imperative that I should find the porter. I faced about accordingly, and counting with painful care, remounted towards the level of the street. Five, six, and seven flights I climbed, and still there was no porter. I began to be weary of the job, and reflecting that I was now close to my own room, decided I should go to bed. Eight, nine, ten, eleven, twelve, thirteen flights I mounted; and my open door seemed to be as wholly lost to me as the porter and his floating dip. I remembered that the house stood but six stories at its highest point, from which it appeared (on the most moderate computation) I was now three stories higher than the roof.[53]

Eventually Dodd walks into one of the rooms and surprises a half-dressed young lady in the act of going to bed. Unperturbed by the intrusion, she guides him to his room and leaves him to sleep it off. The next day, Loudon catches sight of 'the heroine of my adventure' in the Luxembourg Gardens. He hastens to apologise, but runs instead into another character, Jim Pinkerton, who will turn out to be consequential in his story. 'As for the young lady with whom my mind was at the moment chiefly occupied,' Dodd closes the chapter, 'I was never to hear more of her from that day forward: an excellent example of the Blind Man's Buff we call life.'[54]

The perhaps unnecessary editorial comment draws attention to the essentially arbitrary structure of the plot of The Wrecker. Meanwhile the night-time hotel, the site for Dodd's adventure, provides an emblem of Stevenson's narrative method, rather like the allegorically dense enclosures that periodically interrupt the chivalric quest in Edmund Spenser's The Faerie Queene. Dodd's toiling up and down interminable, hallucinatory flights of stairs enacts a satiric rejection, on Stevenson's part, of the sublime effects of elevation, profundity, obscurity and (in sum) interiority – effects claimed, for example, in the drastically different symbolist aesthetic of Conrad, with whom Stevenson is frequently compared. Instead of Conrad's vertical or metaphoric art, which seeks significance in depth, darkness, interiority and difficulty, Stevenson commands a horizontal and metonymic art of surface, extension, sequence, juxtaposition, friction and flow. This becomes starkly clear in the treasure-hunt towards which (it seems) the tale has been leading. Dodd and his men ransack the inside of a wrecked ship for smuggled opium. As they begin to tear the vessel apart in their increasingly frenzied search, the question of what constitutes an *inside* (a concavity that will yield a precious core) becomes critical. The treasure, the secret upon which huge sums of money have been staked, turns out to be something and somewhere else entirely: a story, its content a pointless, random outburst of catastrophic violence.

In a letter to Colvin, Stevenson characterised The Wrecker as a representation of the modern world system: 'a long tough yarn with some pictures of the manners of to-day in the greater world'.[55] In an unusual move, he supplied the tale with an epilogue, where he claimed to have adopted 'the method of Charles Dickens in his later work'. As in Dickens's vast serial novels of the world-city (London), from Bleak House (1853) to Our Mutual Friend (1865), Stevenson sought to invest 'that very modern form of the police novel or mystery story' with the 'tone of the age, its movement, the mingling of races and classes in the dollar hunt, the fiery and not quite romantic struggle for existence with its changing trades and scenery'.[56] Unlike Dickens's masterpieces, Stevenson's 'yarn' offers no promise (or threat) of a revealed symbolic totality. *The Wrecker* is more reminiscent, perhaps, of Dickens's earlier *Martin Chuzzlewit* (with its satiric American episodes) or other nineteenth-century fictions of the confidence trickster, by Herman Melville or Mark Twain, not least in its deceptive lightness. Stevenson described *The Wrecker* as

> a tale of a caste so modern; – full of details of our barbaric manners and unstable morals; – full of the need and the lust of money, so that there is scarce a page in which the dollars do not jingle; – full of the unrest and movement of our century, so that the reader is hurried from place to place and sea to sea, and the book is less a romance than a panorama; – in the end, as blood-bespattered as an epic[.][57]

As blood-bespattered as an epic; but it no longer claims the epic ambition of organic totalisation that the novel had assumed in Scott's wake. Stevenson's work of fiction, less a romance than a panorama, commits itself to the serial extensions and dislocations of a new kind of space constituted by the planetary zigzags of capital – and holds out no assurance that its parts will add up to make a whole.

CHAPTER TWO

Romance and Social Class

Robert P. Irvine

The adventure story, like any fiction written and read within the conventions of a popular genre, does not present itself as a way of knowing a complex social world represented within its pages. It promises the pleasures of genre itself, of narrative expectations aroused, frustrated and fulfilled, rather than the effect of encountering the reality of a specific society in all its historical complexity. In Stevenson's early essays such as 'A Gossip on Romance' (1882), this manifest discontinuity with the everyday social world is the defining feature of 'romance', a term Stevenson uses interchangeably with 'adventure'. But critics have long recognised that, far from floating free of the categories that structure social existence at a particular historical epoch, romance narrative has been a powerful way of reproducing and reinforcing them; powerful precisely because of its apparent autonomy from the politics of everyday life, because it seems to be 'just a story'. In the case of the late-nineteenth-century romance of adventure, critical attention has mostly been paid to its mediation of categories of race and gender, which were under particular kinds of stress in this period.[1] But in Britain, the last decades of the nineteenth century also saw the monopoly in political power of property-owning men broken up for the first time, by the extension of the parliamentary vote to sections of the male working class in the Reform Acts of 1867–8 and 1884. The exclusivity of the franchise had served to confirm the difference of 'gentlemen', whether born into wealth or enriched by commerce, from their labouring brethren. Its loss required conservatives to revisit a longstanding uncertainty about what constituted a 'gentleman' apart from his political agency, to justify the survival of a social difference where there was no longer a constitutional one. Late-nineteenth-century adventure stories often use their remote or exotic settings to confirm the naturalness of social hierarchy, precisely because that naturalness was far from obvious at home. Stevenson's version of the adventure romance addresses the same question, but refuses to offer any clear-cut confirmation of the natural superiority of the gentleman.

We can begin with Stevenson's claim in 'A Gossip on Romance' that this type of fiction displays the hero's physical resourcefulness, rather than the inner workings of his consciousness, because '[t]here is a vast deal in life and letters both which is not immoral, but simply a-moral; [. . .] where the interest turns, not on the passionate slips and hesitations of the conscience, but on the problems of the body and of the practical intelligence, in clean, open-air adventure, the shock of arms or the diplomacy of life'.[2] 'A Gossip on Romance' was written in February 1882, just after the last episode of *Treasure Island* had appeared in the magazine *Young Folks*, and here it describes in theory what the preceding fiction had carried out in practice. On the island, Jim Hawkins acts with some practical forethought, but without moral heart-searching, when he repeatedly absents himself from the forces of law and order (Captain Smollett, Doctor Livesey, Squire Trelawney) to act on his own. Resolving to leave the stockade when it is under siege by the mutineers, for example, he knows that he would 'not be allowed to leave the enclosure' if he requested it, and must therefore 'slip out when nobody was watching; and that was so bad a way of doing it as made the thing wrong in itself. But I was only a boy, and I had made my mind up.'[3] Similarly, Jim carefully explains how he got onto the island, and took control of the ship, but only fleetingly mentions the thought-processes that preceded or accompanied his actions. Describing his shooting of Israel Hands, Jim 'scarce can say it was by my own volition, and I am sure it was without a conscious aim' (p. 142).

That the hero who embodies this genre-defining capacity for spontaneous action is a boy, rather than a mature man, also returns us to Stevenson's essays. There Stevenson often links the appeal of romance to the world of make-believe and day-dream inhabited by the child: 'Fiction is to the grown man what play is to the child; it is there that he changes the atmosphere and tenor of his life; and when the game so chimes with his fancy that he can join in it with all his heart, [. . .] fiction is called romance.'[4] But there is more to *Treasure Island* than Jim's actions, and the reader's vicarious participation in those actions. There is also the world of the adults whom Jim accompanies on the voyage, and this is a world split by class division, between the gentlemen leading the expedition, and the men who, initially at least, follow. The text certainly discourages the reader from thinking of the adults in this way: it represents most of the action from Jim's point of view, and Jim, as a child, understands the conflict in simple terms of right and wrong, unmediated by social categories such as class. But the text also wastes no time in staging a scene in which the social power of the gentleman over the lower classes is unambiguously displayed. Chapter 1 ends with a confrontation between Black Dog and Dr Livesey in the parlour of the Admiral Benbow. When the old pirate demands silence, Livesey replies with a cool 'Were you addressing me, sir?' Then the pirate pulls a knife:

The doctor never so much as moved. He spoke to him, as before, over his shoulder, and in the same tone of voice; rather high, so that all the room might hear, but perfectly calm and steady: –

'If you do not put that knife this instant in your pocket, I promise, upon my honour, you shall hang at the next assizes.'

Then followed a battle of looks between them; but the captain soon knuckled under, put up his weapon, and resumed his seat, grumbling like a beaten dog. (p. 6)

The upright doctor refuses to recognise his antagonist as a social equal, not even to the extent of turning to face him as a physical threat. And this in itself forces the drunken sailor to back down, accepting his own subordination to the gentleman. Social hierarchy is enforced by nothing more than the gentleman's quiet but absolute assurance of his superiority. Livesey's power over others may be the result of particular legal-political institutions (he reminds Black Dog that he is a magistrate as well as a doctor), but in this scene such power is so perfectly embodied in him as an individual that it seems like a natural expression of his personality.

Treasure Island's setting in the mid-eighteenth century allows Stevenson to imagine a Britain in which the authority of the gentleman has not been jeopardised as it had been in Stevenson's own time, by, for example, the extension of the franchise, and the rise of autonomous working-class organisations such as trades unions. The gentleman's authority is secure on the mainland; it will indeed be overthrown by the pirates' rebellion in the course of the adventure on the island, but then restored, largely by Jim's agency. So the story, reassuringly for a late-nineteenth-century middle-class readership, acts out the survival of traditional social hierarchy in the face of a working-class revolt.[5] At the same time, however, the leader of the revolt is represented in a way that undermines that hierarchy's naturalisation in the personal authority of the gentleman. For Long John Silver is able to feign the subordination that Black Dog instinctively feels. He is also able to adopt the manners of the men set over him, and this gives him something of their authority, too, as Ben Gunn confirms when he tells Jim that Captain Flint 'were afraid of none, not he; on'y Silver – Silver was that genteel' (p. 98). Silver aims, moreover, to take this acquisition of gentility to its logical conclusion by acquiring not only the wealth, but the political power of the gentleman, looking forward to the time '[w]hen I'm in Parlyment, and riding in my coach' (p. 61). In Silver, gentlemanliness appears, not as an inherent personal authority such as Dr Livesey's, but as a form of behaviour which can be assumed in order to disguise the true personality. The story of *Treasure Island* works to preserve the social hierarchy that the gentlemen represent, but the 'naturalness' of the gentleman's authority is simultaneously undermined by the ease with which Silver threatens to appropriate it.

The category 'gentleman' was a problematic one, not just for Stevenson, but in nineteenth-century discourse generally, on precisely the grounds that separate Dr Livesey from Long John Silver. On the one hand it named a set of manners that could be acquired by the newly wealthy male (such as Silver hopes to be) as a way of gaining acceptance within a socially and politically empowered élite. On the other hand it was often mystified as a status that could not be consciously acquired, but only experienced as an instinctive knowledge of what was right and what was not, inherited by the gentleman from his ancestors along with (or perhaps instead of) material wealth. Its ambiguity made the concept 'gentleman' useful when the aim was to blur the distinction between old and new wealth; but when gentlemen, however defined, found their authority challenged by those with no wealth at all, this ambiguity was bound to be the cause of some anxiety. Where does Jim Hawkins, and the celebration of spontaneous action that he represents, fit into *Treasure Island*'s portrayal of social authority, once we understand it in these terms? We have identified Jim's mode of action with Stevenson's idea of romance as a genre, so this is also a question about the social politics of the boy's adventure story as Stevenson reinvents it at this early stage of his career.

We can answer it by comparing Jim to the hero of an earlier tale of maritime adventure set in the historical past, Charles Kingsley's *Westward Ho!* (1855). The hero of this story, Amyas Leigh, is, like Jim, a brave, impulsive lad from the West of England. He is much older and more experienced than Jim: by the novel's second chapter he is 21 and has sailed around the world with Francis Drake. But he is described in ways that prefigure both Jim's role in *Treasure Island* and Stevenson's discussion of romance as a genre in his essays. Chapter 3 contrasts Amyas with his cousin Eustace, who has trained as a Jesuit on the continent, and Kingsley sums up the difference between them thus:

> I cannot tire myself or you (especially in this book) with any wire-drawn soul-dissections. I have tried to hint to you two opposite sorts of men. The one trying to be good with all his might and main, according to certain approved methods and rules, which he has got by heart; [. . .] The other, not even knowing whether he is good or not, but just doing the right thing without thinking about it, as simply as a little child, because the Spirit of God is with him. If you cannot see the great gulf fixed between the two, I trust that you will discover it some day.[6]

In one obvious way *Westward Ho!* is a very different type of boy's story from *Treasure Island* in its explicit religious and moral didacticism. Such didacticism is routine in boy's adventure fiction before Stevenson: for all that *The Coral Island* (1857) by R. M. Ballantyne is an important precursor text for *Treasure Island* (Stevenson hymns 'Ballantyne the brave' in its opening verses), it is shaped around a Christian message as explicit as Kingsley's. Yet Kingsley's rejection here of 'wire-drawn soul-dissections', the valorisation of action over thought and the deployment of the unreflective 'little child' as a touchstone, are all moves that will be repeated in Stevenson's critical writing as discussed above, and all find expression in the hero of *Treasure Island*. The important difference between Amyas and Jim from our point of view is that Amyas is a gentleman, in the very unambiguous sense pertaining in the England of Elizabeth Tudor: he is a male member of a family that owns land, and has the social and political power that went with owning land at that period. Although Kingsley does not spell out the connection, Amyas's unconscious ability to distinguish right from wrong is clearly an aspect of his role in the story as the perfect example of a gentleman in this sense. His vigorous physicality and moral instinct thus mystify the gentleman's social authority by locating its origin somewhere other than in political and economic institutions: namely, in the impulses of his body and, ultimately, the God who created them.[7]

In this relation, the role of Jim in the politics of *Treasure Island* becomes clear. Jim embodies the attributes attached by writers such as Kingsley to the ideal gentleman, without himself being a gentleman. Those attributes are in the service of the gentlemanly hierarchy, certainly, for Jim enables the defeat of the pirates; but the class ideal that he embodies has been detached from the class in which it originated, thus suspending the question of whether the qualities that define the gentleman are inherited or acquired.[8] *Treasure Island* asks to be read as pure adventure, floating free of any engagement with contemporary social categories; in fact this very demand, as expressed in the figure of the boy hero, is generated by the ambiguity within one of those categories, the idea of the gentleman. Stevenson's story vindicates the naturalness of social hierarchy through the spontaneous allegiance to it of the 'natural' being which is the untutored child, and not through the special qualities of the particular gentlemen whom the child actually serves; by the opportunity it offers the boy-hero to serve heroically under them, rather than the chance it presents the gentlemen heroically to lead.

Treasure Island's combination of a conservative commitment to the principle of social hierarchy with scepticism about the gentlemen actually occupying its upper storeys is characteristic of Stevenson's fiction in general. *Strange Case of Dr Jekyll and Mr Hyde* (1886), for example, has received some revealing critical attention in this regard. Stephen Arata has pointed out the extent to which Hyde, rather than simply representing the opposite of the gentleman, undergoes an education that makes him more and more like the gentlemen from whose point of view the story is told.[9] But the effect, as Robbie Goh has argued, is not to discredit gentlemanliness as such by embodying its 'decadence' or 'hypocrisy' in the figure of Hyde. Rather, it is to postulate 'an "abstract" gentility whose basis is no known or recognisable social grouping or category', but is instead expressed in the interpretative strategies adopted by Utterson and Lanyon, strategies that the reader is invited to share.[10] Rather than rehearse the complex arguments of Arata and Goh, however, it is more useful for our present purposes to look at a pair of texts from the start of Stevenson's career in fiction, in which the implication of romance narrative form in the politics of social class is more clearly visible, and which prefigure *Dr Jekyll and Mr Hyde*'s concern with the transformation of the gentleman in the nocturnal metropolis.

These are the story-cycles 'The Suicide Club' and 'The Rajah's Diamond', which first appeared in *London* magazine in 1878; they are usually referred to as *New Arabian Nights*, the title under which they were published, with some other stories, in book-form in 1882, and a title which advertises their revival of romance tradition. Each consists of a series of tales within a frame narrative. Linking them is the figure of Prince Florizel of Bohemia, a charismatic foreigner seeking adventures in the criminal underbellies of Paris and London with his sidekick, Colonel Geraldine. In 'The Suicide Club', Florizel joins a secret society which facilitates the deaths of its members, young gentlemen who have failed in life in various ways; it does this, Florizel discovers, by arranging for them to murder each other. Florizel sets about destroying the club by having its president killed in a duel, first at the hands of Geraldine's brother, then, when the president has the latter murdered, at Florizel's own. The second story, 'The Rajah's Diamond', follows the titular jewel from its loss by a hapless servant, through its luring a young curate into criminal connections, to its eventual recovery by Florizel, who throws it into the Seine so it cannot cause any more trouble.

What concerns us here are less the details of the particular stories than the narrative pattern that they repeat, and the politics that this repetition encodes. Only the first story in *New Arabian Nights* is told from Florizel's point of view. The others follow the experiences of a series of young gentlemen who get caught up in the intrigue quite inadvertently. The protagonist of each tale begins in complete ignorance of what has gone before, and the underworld plot in which he is about to become enmeshed. Then as soon as the nature of that plot is fully revealed to him, his tale is broken off short, and his fate described in a few lines from the editor, so that the same plot can be discovered all over again by a new protagonist in a new story. This chapter began by suggesting that 'adventure' or 'romance' was constituted as a genre by its manifest discontinuity with the everyday life of contemporary society. In *New Arabian Nights*, that discontinuity is experienced by each protagonist in turn, as he enters a world of adventure and, in Stevenson's words, 'changes the atmosphere and tenor of his life'.[11]

The complex narrative structure of *New Arabian Nights* is not, however, only a playful exercise in generic self-consciousness. It is also a means of dramatising a social ethic similar to the one we found in *Treasure Island*. The recurring introduction of new protagonists, each discovering the plot for the first time, allows each to encounter Florizel for the first time as well; and in every case he immediately impresses the protagonist with his quiet author-ity. The young curate of 'The Rajah's Diamond' approaches him at his club because 'there was something in his air which seemed to invite confidence and to expect submission';[12] another protagonist, finding the diamond in his pocket, instantly hears Florizel's voice in his ear, 'a quiet voice, which yet had the ring of command' (p. 143). This effect is experienced by observers who often do not know his royal status, and in contexts where his power as a monarch has no bearing. The origin of his authority seems to lie simply in himself, just as Livesey's authority as a gentleman and a magistrate was assimilated to his personality in *Treasure Island*. The encounters between prince and protagonist in the *New Arabian Nights* should be thought of as equivalent to what happens in the parlour of the Admiral Benbow: scenes of subordination in which the social underling recognises the inherent author-ity of a social superior over him. In the *New Arabian Nights* this recognition is usually relieved rather than resentful, but the naturalisation of authority that it effects is essentially the same.

However, these stories refuse to confirm that Florizel is quite as special as he is perceived to be by the gentlemen whom he assists. As Lisa Honaker points out, Florizel's decisiveness is revealed to be limited near the beginning, and near the end, of *New Arabian Nights*: on being dealt the death-card in the Suicide Club, and on being caught in possession of the diamond in Paris, he hesitates, doubts himself and is uncertain of the right course of action.[13] This is not the instinctive knowledge of right and wrong enjoyed by that ideal gentleman Amyas Leigh in *Westward Ho!* And we can note that Florizel appears limited at these points because here, and not elsewhere, we are given access to his consciousness through free indirect discourse. Only from the perspective of others does he impress with his effortless authority over lesser men. Florizel's authority is not, in fact, an expression of anything inherent in him, but the effect of others' need to find in him an organising authority of this kind. In this way *New Arabian Nights* posits, not an instinct for command on the part of the governors, but an instinct for subordination on the part of the governed.

Recent critics have tended to reappraise Stevenson's formal experiments as prefiguring the modernist novel of the early twentieth century.[14] But the form of *New Arabian Nights* is shaped by a distinctly Victorian social poli-tics, and particularly that of the mid-nineteenth century's most influential social commentator, Thomas Carlyle. Carlyle's work in the 1840s casti-gated Britain's hereditary ruling class, the land-owning aristocracy, and the recently-enfranchised middle class of the new industrial towns and cities, for their failure to provide disinterested leadership to a population suffering terrible living and working conditions. But Carlyle's answer to this situation was not the empowerment of working people. Instead, he called for a new type of ruler, one in tune with the secret aims of history; because, for Carlyle, the mass of people (middle-class and working-class alike) will always find their greatest happiness in following those few who embody the transcendent purposes of historical change. The problem, Carlyle wrote in 1841, lies in recognising who these privileged individuals are:

> There is no act more moral between men than that of rule and obedience [. . .]
>   I say, Find me the true *Könning*, King, or Able-man, and he *has* a divine right over me. That we knew in some tolerable measure how to find him, and that all men were ready to acknowledge his divine right when found: this is precisely the healing which a sick world is everywhere, in these ages, seeking after![15]

In their encounters with Florizel the protagonists of *New Arabian Nights* acknowledge a leader figure, seemingly set apart from the mass of men, and 'loyally surrender themselves, and find their welfare in doing so'.[16] But, as we have seen, Stevenson withholds from Florizel the quasi-divinity that would explain the benefit they gain from this on Carlyle's account. Instead, Stevenson's emphasis is on what Carlyle calls 'our faculty, our necessity, to reverence Heroes when sent'.[17] What the young gentlemen primarily gain from meeting Florizel is an occasion to exercise this faculty, rather than any moral or practical guidance he is able to offer. Florizel's appeal to such characters makes sense if we understand them to be living with the uncertainty, discussed above, as to precisely what qualifies them as 'gentlemen' in the first place. By engaging in what Carlyle calls 'hero-worship', the protagonists confirm to themselves the reality of social hierarchy as a fact of nature, and thereby their own privileged status within it, evading the fraught questions of heredity and education otherwise required to justify their privilege. The salvation that Florizel represents for these young gentlemen is the reassurance that they are, as gentlemen, worth saving; where others, implicitly, are not. Stevenson strips the Carlylean charismatic leader of his unique relation to history, and justifies him purely in terms of the hierarchical effects that he produces in his society. And without his quasi-divine status, the hero-king stands revealed as an idea that tends to consolidate, rather than challenge, the authority of established gentlemen, even while he appears glamorously outside the world of mundane routine that this class inhabits.

We have seen that *New Arabian Nights* and *Treasure Island* alike understand social hierarchy as a moral good even while tending to demystify the authority of those in its higher ranks. There is one trait, however, which Florizel shares with Jim, rather than with the adult gentlemen of *Treasure Island*, and that is his special relationship to violence. Jim's instinctive violence is explained by his immaturity; similarly, Florizel's insistence on killing the president in a duel is only explicable by reference to his high birth. For duelling, ritualised single combat in defence of a point of personal or family honour, was understood as a specifically aristocratic practice, indeed as 'the linchpin holding together the highly selective principles of aristocratic gentlemanliness'.[18] By the mid-nineteenth century it was also understood as absurdly anachronistic, even by conservatives. Yet Florizel's killing of the president is offered as a satisfactory ending towards which the narrative, set in contemporary times, can move. This use of a duel to provide closure is all the more striking given Stevenson's portrayal of duels in eighteenth-century settings, where, although not anachronistic, they either fail to get started, or end indecisively: Alan Breck cannot bring himself to accept David Balfour's challenge in *Kidnapped* (1886), and in *The Master of Ballantrae* (1889), Henry Durie thinks he has killed his brother, only to find that the 'body' has vanished on his return to the duelling-ground. Certainly, judged by the usual rules of the aristocratic duel, the fights that Florizel arranges in 'The Suicide Club' are very dubious affairs, as Honaker notes.[19] Yet compared to its revelation of Florizel's limitations in other respects, *New Arabian Nights* seems untroubled by his quick resort to violence. It seems to be the one aspect of Florizel's high status that genuinely belongs to him, not a projection onto him by socially-insecure gentlemen in search of a leader.

The possibility that social order is ultimately based on the threat of violence is one to which Stevenson persistently returns: if anything, it tends to become more explicit as his career progresses. *Prince Otto* (1885), a historical romance set in a tiny German state at the time of the nationalist revolutions of 1848, is a case in point. Otto, Grünewald's monarch, begins the story unaware of the plot to overthrow him, long in preparation and headed by his wife Seraphina and his prime minister. He is the opposite of Florizel: ignorant and powerless where Florizel usually appears both omniscient and omnipotent. Book I of *Prince Otto*, 'In which the Prince plays Haroun-al-Rashid' (as Chapter 2 has it), is an exploration of this contrast. Both princes doubt themselves, but where the disguised Florizel's authority is confirmed by others' reactions, Otto's subjects consistently condemn him as an ineffectual and decadent prince. However angry these judgments make him, it is striking that Otto never simply assures himself that they are false, as if he had no privileged knowledge of himself to compare them with. As Florizel's social authority was an effect created by others in their perception of him, so Otto seems only to know himself through the expressed opinions of others.

It is therefore significant that the one action taken by Otto which has a positive effect on the outcome of his story is his attempt to fight a duel. This provides the climax to the first section of the book, before Otto's reassertion of his authority in the state and the counter-plots that this puts in motion, and is occasioned by his encounter with the English traveller and satirist, Sir John Crabtree. Sir John, an 'old radical' as well as an old courtier, has been arrested in possession of a manuscript 'Memoirs of a Visit to the Various Courts of Europe' which culminates in a coruscating portrait of Grünewald.[20] Among other calumnies, Otto is described as 'the nearly perfect fruit of a decadent age' (pp. 52–3) and Seraphina as the abject slave of her passion for his prime minister. Otto, once informed of his arrest, signs Sir John's passport for Vienna, and then, waiving his superior station as a prince ('I would be regarded simply as a gentleman', p. 62) challenges Sir John to a duel in defence of the honour of his wife. Sir John, of course, laughs this off: Otto cannot simply make his status as sovereign disappear in this way, and it is part of the aristocratic code that a duel cannot be fought with a reigning monarch. However, Sir John is greatly impressed by Otto's willingness to fight:

'This is a day that I shall still recall with gratitude, for I have found a sovereign with manly virtues; and for once – old courtier and old radical as I am – it is from the heart and quite sincerely that I can request the honour of kissing your Highness's hand?'

'Nay, sir,' said Otto, 'to my heart!'

And the Englishman, taken at unawares, was clasped for a moment in the Prince's arms. (p. 63)

This is the only scene in *Prince Otto* in which the protagonist's aristocratic virtues are recognised by a stranger, as Florizel's always were. Moreover, the motivation of the scene has been reversed, for it is now the monarch who craves the recognition of the English gentleman, and not the other way round. In any case, Sir John's approval of Otto's 'manly virtue' makes no difference to his fate as a monarch: a series of accidents precipitate the revolution, Otto is deposed, and a republic declared in Grünewald. Sir John's opinion does make a difference to his fate as a husband, however. It is the fact of Otto's challenge, as recounted by Sir John (p. 165), that prompts a change of feeling in Seraphina towards him, and thus makes possible the reconciliation with which their story ends. Looking back on his declaration of love before their division became an open party-political one, she discovers (extrapolating somewhat from Sir John's description) that Otto 'had come to her, still thrilling under recent insult, and not yet breathed from fighting her cause; and how that knowledge changed the value of his words!' (p. 168). Just as in a novel by Charles Dickens or George Eliot, a happy married life seems to be the only felicity that can be rescued from the evident failure of other traditional social forms. Yet where violence appears in the realist novel, it is as a threat to that felicity: a ghost from a banished aristocratic past, or a menace from the alienated workers below. In *Prince Otto*, in contrast, the threat of aristocratic violence, the 'manly virtue' that it demonstrates, is a condition of securing domestic happiness in the first place.

All the themes I have been tracing find their most explicit expression in 'The Ebb-Tide', written by Stevenson in collaboration with his step-son Lloyd Osbourne and published in the year of his death (1894). This is a return to the island romance of piracy and treasure, but set in an entirely contemporary South Pacific, and more obviously concerned with the contemporary politics of social hierarchy in the imperial centre. We should not be surprised that British class relations are the central concern of a story set in such an exotic location. Recently, the historian David Cannadine has argued that class was always crucial to the British experience of empire. 'The British exported and projected vernacular sociological visions from the metropolis to the periphery, and they imported and analogized them from the empire back to Britain, thereby constructing comforting and familiar resemblances and equivalencies and affinities.'[21] In just this way, 'The Ebb-Tide' uses the imperial periphery as a stage on which to dramatise the domestic sociological vision implicit in Stevenson's earlier work.

The first part of this story centres on three white drifters who have fled from various failures in life until they have ended up in the French colony of Tahiti. One, Robert Herrick, can claim to be a gentleman by upbringing; the son of a successful London merchant, sent to 'a good school' and then Oxford University, he is nevertheless 'deficient in consistency and intellectual manhood,'[22] and has failed in every job that gave him a place through simple incompetence. His companions are an alcoholic American sea-captain, Davis, who lost a ship and its passengers while drunk in command; and Huish, 'a vulgar and bad-hearted cockney clerk' (p. 127). A rare chance of activity and remuneration comes their way when Davis is offered the command of a ship, the *Fallarone*, apparently full of California champagne, whose white officers died of smallpox before she could make it to her destination, Sydney. The three whites decide to steal the ship, sail her to Peru, and there sell both ship and cargo. But the plan goes wrong when provisions run short and most of the 'champagne' turns out to be water: the ship set sail as part of an insurance scam, and was never intended to reach Sydney in the first place. The second part of the story narrates their experiences on the island at which they are forced to stop, ruled by an Englishman, Attwater. Attwater is a clergyman, but also a businessman: the island lagoon is rich in pearls, and Attwater has been overseeing their exploitation with indentured native labour, driven at the point of a Winchester rifle: 'I gave these beggars what they wanted: a judge in Israel, the bearer of the sword and scourge' he tells Herrick later (p. 204).

In their backgrounds Herrick, Davis and Huish can be seen as a cross-section of male Anglo-Saxon society, but in Tahiti their poverty, material and spiritual, puts them on a level; and on the ship not even Davis's expertise establishes any hierarchy among them. At their first meeting, the instant effect of Attwater's presence on the ship is to distinguish the gentleman, Herrick, from the other two. Huish tells Attwater that, while Davis may be captain on deck, 'Below, we're all equal':

> '[. . .] and what I say is, let's go into the 'ouse and have a lush, and talk it over among pals. We've got some prime fizz,' he said, and winked.
>
> The presence of the gentleman lighted up like a candle the vulgarity of the clerk; and Herrick instinctively, as one shields himself from pain, made haste to interrupt.
>
> 'My name is Hay,' said he, 'since introductions are going. We shall be very glad if you will step inside.'
>
> Attwater leaned to him swiftly. 'University man?' said he.
>
> 'Yes, Merton,' said Herrick, and the next moment blushed scarlet at his indiscretion.
>
> 'I am of the other lot,' said Attwater: 'Trinity Hall, Cambridge, I called my schooner after the old shop. Well! this is a queer place and company for us to meet in, Mr Hay [. . .]' (p. 193)

On a stolen ship in a tropical lagoon in the South Pacific, two English gentlemen recognise each other as members of the same class, and find confirmation in the reciprocal naming of an Oxford college and a Cambridge one. The threat of violence is muted in this first encounter, but the gentlemen's recognition of each other is 'swift' and physical (Attwater's leaning to Herrick, Herrick's blush); Herrick's knowledge of the right thing to do is 'instinctive' just as it was for Jim Hawkins and, before him, Kingsley's Amyas Leigh. The missionary already knows that the men of the *Farralone* are, all three, pirates, but in his eyes Herrick's status as a gentleman transcends any involvement in crime, and Attwater's presence on the ship immediately re-establishes the class hierarchy of the imperial centre among the degraded exiles.

Herrick comes to see in Attwater, not a minister of the divine, but a type of divinity: '"he looks at us and laughs like God!"' he warns Davis (p. 222). But to Davis, the son of a republic, he appears as simply '"the real, first-rate, copper-bottomed aristocrat. [. . .] No, that couldn't be nothing but genuine; a man got to be born to that"' (p. 197). When Davis and Huish plot to murder Attwater, Herrick attempts suicide, but fails even at this. He finds himself at Attwater's feet with the question, '"Can you do anything with me?"' He continues, '"you are cold, cruel, hateful [. . .] But you are an honest man, an honest gentleman. I put myself, helpless, in your hands"' (p. 230). Thus, at the end of Stevenson's career, we find a drama of subordination remarkably similar to those acted out at the beginning, in *New Arabian Nights*. The morally-compromised middle-class gentleman recognises the higher authority inherent in the natural aristocrat. Further, two aspects of this scenario left implicit in *New Arabian Nights* are made quite explicit in 'The Ebb-Tide'. One is that the effect of the middle-class gentleman's encounter with the aristocrat is confirmation of their mutual difference from the mass of men below them, a class represented here by Davis and Huish, but effectively invisible in *New Arabian Nights*. The other is the role in the aristocrat's charisma of his capacity for violence. Attwater is a virtuoso with the Winchester, and the culmination of the action on the island is an act of violence as ritualised as any duel: the inflicting on Davis of a death-ordeal, as Attwater shoots close to the captain's head three times, then withholds the expected, fatal, bullet. The effect is the Christian rebirth of Davis, who becomes, in Herrick's words, '"Attwater's spoiled darling and pet penitent"' (p. 252). Herrick remains an unbeliever, however; and in the story's closing scene, disillusion with Attwater seems to be setting in. The lower classes dead, or tamed by evangelical religion, the middle-class gentleman no longer depends on aristocratic recognition as he did while he was enduring assimilation to their ranks. Just as *New Arabian Nights* refuses to confirm the reality of Florizel's power beyond the gaze of those who need him, so 'The Ebb-Tide' withholds any suggestion that his encounter with Attwater has produced a lasting moral or spiritual change in Herrick. 'The Ebb-Tide' uses its colonial space to fantasise an authoritarian solution to the erosion of the social power of the British gentleman, but gives no indication that this solution can be exported back to the metropolis. In doing so, it does not demystify or critique the romance of adventure as Stevenson had earlier practised it, so much as spell out the social logic inherent in that practice from the start.

Treasure Island apart, this chapter has taken its examples from what has been until recently Stevenson's least-valued work; yet these texts, easy to put to one side as experiments (*New Arabian Nights*), aesthetic failures (*Prince Otto*), or compromised by collaboration ('The Ebb-Tide'), reveal particularly clearly a social politics also subtly operating in canonical work such as *Dr Jekyll and Mr Hyde* or *The Master of Ballantrae*. The distinctive version of class relations that we find in Stevenson's romance of adventure might best be named an 'anti-liberal' one. Liberal political thought, in its broadest sense, imagines society to be composed of autonomous individuals, who come together to agree, freely and peacefully, the rules by which they live together. On this view, successful social forms emerge from common interests identified through debate; they are not imposed by violence. Liberal thinking dominates the politics of nineteenth-century Britain, but Stevenson's protagonists are just not autonomous in this way: their identity as individuals is only stable within pre-existing hierarchies of power. Consolation comes not from compromise with those hierarchies, but from their confirmation, by violent means if necessary. Yet despite this anti-liberal stance, Stevenson refuses to confirm any metaphysical justification for social hierarchy, either divine (as in Kingsley) or historical (as in Carlyle); its justification is no more than the closure it offers a set of gentlemanly protagonists who are, by and large, a pretty mediocre bunch. Anti-liberal though he may be, Stevenson offers no reassurance to those conservatives seeking a more solid grounding than this for the defence of the traditional class distinctions of British society.

CHAPTER THREE

Childhood and Psychology

Julia Reid

For admirers as well as detractors, Stevenson was a boy who never grew up. Edmund Gosse celebrated his 'childlike mirth', his stepson Lloyd Osbourne lauded his 'abiding spirit of the child', and others have even speculated that J. M. Barrie's play *Peter Pan* (1904) was partly inspired by Stevenson.[1] This idea of his perpetual boyhood was a key-note of the critical turn against Stevenson soon after his death, when he became remembered chiefly as a children's author. Drawing on the evolutionary notion of arrested development, the critic John Jay Chapman wrote that '[w]hether or not there was some obscure connection between his bodily troubles and the arrest of his intellectual development, it is certain that Stevenson remained a boy till the day of his death'.[2] While the critical climate is now much more favourable to Stevenson, the idea of his childlike quality has persisted: for Morag Styles, in *A Child's Garden of Verses* 'Stevenson captured, as faithfully as it is possible for an adult to do, what it feels like to be a child', and for Ann Colley the same volume enabled him to 'walk back into the space of his early years'.[3]

Yet this idea that Stevenson was able to capture some timeless essence of childishness is at odds with his self-conscious participation in the contemporary debate about the nature of childhood. This chapter will show that Stevenson engaged in a sophisticated manner with evolutionist understandings of childhood, the imagination and the unconscious. The chapter will start by examining Victorian understandings of children's psychology and corresponding forms of children's literature. It will then survey Stevenson's engagement with ideas about the childhood imagination across a wide range of his writing, including his fiction for adults and for children, memoirs, letters, essays and poetry.

Stevenson was the inheritor of the nineteenth century's diverse and contested construction of childhood, in which Puritan moralism was confronted by conceptions of the natural child originating in the Enlightenment and Romantic periods and, later, by evolutionary science. By the early-Victorian period, the old Puritan and Evangelical notion of the child's original sin was much eroded, although it endured in particular contexts and locations (notably in strictly Calvinist households in Scotland). It was challenged by a concept of the child as part of the natural order which derived from the Enlightenment: John Locke and Jean-Jacques Rousseau had both fostered a belief that the child's behaviour was natural for its particular stage of development.[4] This sense of the child as more than merely a miniature adult informed the Romantic idealisation of childhood innocence and, later, evolutionary scientists' vision of childhood as a re-enactment of primitive life. Romantic works such as William Blake's *Songs of Innocence* (1789) and William Wordsworth's 'Ode: Intimations of Immortality from Recollections of Early Childhood' (1807) evoked the child's access to an imaginative insight denied to adults: mourning the loss of childhood, the speaker in Wordsworth's poem asks 'Whither is fled the visionary gleam? / Where is it now, the glory and the dream?'[5] From the mid-nineteenth century, evolutionary scientists including Charles Darwin offered a scientific basis to the Enlightenment belief that humans were part of the natural world.

According to the popular evolutionary doctrine of recapitulation, the individual repeated the development of the species. Thus the child, like the animal or 'savage', represented an early stage of evolutionary development. Darwin described his own child in these terms, portraying his rage as 'an instinctive sign of anger, like the snapping of the jaws by a young crocodile just out of the egg', and suggesting that his fear of large animals reflected 'the inherited effects of real dangers and abject superstitions during ancient savage times'.[6] The new science of child psychology developed from these evolutionist antecedents. Recapitulation was central to the work of nearly all early child psychologists, including Wilhelm Preyer, G. Stanley Hall, G. J. Romanes and Stevenson's friend, James Sully.[7] In 1895, Sully compared the interest underlying the 'careful study of infancy' to the 'curiosity which prompts the geologist to get back to the first stages in the building up of the planet'. The 'first years of a child', he continued, have an 'antiquarian interest', as they illuminate 'the probable condition of primitive man'.[8]

Sully's words echo Stevenson's essay on his childhood literary tastes, '"Rosa Quo Locorum"' (written in 1893 but not published until 1896). Here, Stevenson asserted that '[f]rom the mind of childhood there is more history and more philosophy to be fished up than from all the printed volumes in a library'.[9] Indeed, Sully repeatedly cited Stevenson's observations about childhood 'make-believe', associating him with Rousseau, Johann Heinrich Pestalozzi, George Sand, and other '[c]areful observers of children and conservers of their own childish experiences'.[10] Stevenson's thoughts were influential, as we shall see, and this was perhaps because evolutionist ideas about play and the imagination stood at the heart of the new child psychology. Herbert Spencer, an early and enduring influence not only on the new science but on Stevenson himself, had drawn on his memories of Friedrich

Schiller's work to figure the 'play-impulse' as an embryonic form of the 'æsthetic sentiments'.[11] The burgeoning scientific interest in the child's nascent artistic appreciation which Stevenson predicted in '"Rosa"' ('[a] matter of curiosity to-day, it will become the ground of science to-morrow') was well under way by the turn of the century.[12]

As suggested by the indulgent approach to childhood play and fantasy (no longer associated with deceit), evolutionary child psychology apparently took the moral sting out of the study of children's development. The evolution of imagination – and of will and instinct – was now interpreted as a natural process, unconnected with morality: Sully reminded his readers that the 'infant [. . .] is not as yet a moral being; and there is a certain impertinence in trying to force it under our categories of good and bad, pure and corrupt'.[13] Yet, on another level, the representation of children as 'primitive' retained a strong – if ambiguous – moral resonance, constructing them either as untamed animals or as dwellers in an innocent Golden Age.

The conflicting contemporary understandings of childhood – Puritan, Enlightenment, Romantic and evolutionary – clearly shaped the developing tradition of children's literature and fuelled debate about what children should read. By mid-century, in most quarters, the Evangelical diet of didactic literature had largely been superseded by lighter fare, and disapproval of fairy tales and nursery rhymes had given way to an active encouragement of imagination and fantasy.[14] In 1865, Charles Lutwidge Dodgson, writing as Lewis Carroll, was even able to parody the Puritan Isaac Watts's *Divine Songs Attempted in Easy Language for the Use of Children* (1715), in *Alice's Adventures in Wonderland*, while others including Charles Kingsley and Edward Lear offered fantastic literature to a newly valued child readership.[15] Increasingly, and especially after the 1870 Forster Education Act, and the Education (Scotland) Act of 1872, publishers took seriously the market for children's literature.[16] Imperial adventure fiction enjoyed a surge in popularity: violent action replaced Christian ethics as the centre of narrative attention, and was defended as appealing to the child's primitive heritage. The *fin de siècle* also saw a renewed sentimentalisation of childhood in books such as Frances Hodgson Burnett's *Little Lord Fauntleroy* (1886), which appealed to adults' nostalgia for their own lost childhoods as much as to children's presumed innocence.

Stevenson's writing for and about children engaged with all of these divergent impulses within children's literature: the didactic, fantastic, violent and sentimental. Underpinning the apparent diversity of his output, however, is a central preoccupation with the value of the childhood imagination, which he represented ambivalently, as either invigoratingly primitive or dangerously morbid.

The childhood imagination, for Stevenson, was a survival from 'savage'

times. Subscribing to the recapitulationist view in which children represented an early stage of evolutionary development, he aligned the childhood
imagination with romance, oral narratives, dreams and popular literature. In
'Popular Authors' (1888), he linked children and 'readers of the penny-press',
and compared popular fiction to ancient, spoken narratives, claiming that
cheap novels are 'unhatched eggs of Arab tales; made for word-of-mouth reci-
tation'.[17] This evolutionist approach to the childhood imagination centrally
informs Stevenson's essays and poetry including 'Notes on the Movements of
Young Children' (1874), 'Child's Play' (1878), and A Child's Garden of Verses
(1885). However, where most evolutionists adhered to a progressive narrative of gradual imaginative refinement, Stevenson celebrated the endurance
of states of primitive consciousness, and even suggested that they might reju-
venate an overcivilised modern world. Ironically, he drew on the resolutely
forward-looking evolutionism to offer a revitalised Romantic conception of
childhood as a visionary Arcady.

As a young man in the early 1870s, Stevenson was fascinated by the childhood imagination, drafting autobiographical reminiscences which he would
use twenty years later in '"Rosa Quo Locorum"'.[18] Evidently interested in
contemporary debate about child psychology, he also wrote an article that
attempted the empirical study of childhood play, 'Notes on the Movements
of Young Children' (1874). Here, Stevenson hailed the sight of children
dancing as 'a reminiscence of primitive festivals and the Golden Age'.[19]
Although he evoked a transition from children's 'natural' and 'spontaneous' movements to adults' 'restraint of regulated dance', a further, racial-
ised contrast between 'conscientious' British dancing and a more natural
Mediterranean style suggested that some adults at least might retain their
'primitive' spontaneity.[20]

His later essay, 'Child's Play' (1878), marked a more sophisticated and
influential intervention in debate about childhood: it envisaged childhood
make-believe as a primitive archetype of adult creativity but also suggested
it could reinvigorate a prosaic modernity. By this time, Stevenson had met
James Sully, who later described how their 'synchroniz[ed] [. . .] contribu-
tions to the Cornhill [Magazine]' made them 'brotherly companion[s]'.[21] In
1876, in a Cornhill essay, Sully had described how a 'primitive' animism
united the 'uninformed mind of the savage, and the naïve intelligence of the
child': 'Everybody who has watched young children closely,' he explained,
'knows that they have the habit of regarding the most insignificant objects
[. . .] as possessed of life.'[22] Stevenson's 'Child's Play', also published in the
Cornhill, illustrated this childhood animism, recalling how he and his cousin
imagined a sugar-topped porridge bowl as 'a country continually buried under
snow' and a milk-filled bowl as 'a country suffering gradual inundation'.[23]
Childhood emerges as a primitive time: describing how children see their

parents as 'bearded or petticoated giants' or 'deities' who 'move upon a cloudy Olympus', Stevenson exclaims, '[s]urely they dwell in a mythological epoch, and are not the contemporaries of their parents'.[24] Sully's *Studies of Childhood* (1895) registers the influence of Stevenson's essay. Examining childhood play for 'early traces of children's artistic tendencies', Sully declares that children's games such as 'the making of a river out of the gravy in the plate' demonstrate a developing artistic impulse. 'Such table-pastimes are known to all observers of children,' he writes, 'and have been prettily touched on by R. L. Stevenson.' Indeed, Stevenson's description of his solitary childhood games leads Sully to claim that the doctrine of 'art for art's sake' demonstrates art's affinity with 'child's play'.[25] Sully's words interestingly echo Stevenson's assertion that '"[a]rt for art" is [children's] motto'.[26]

Yet while Sully, like most evolutionists, represented the childhood imagination as enduring only in the 'poetic mind', Stevenson celebrated the survival of this primitive heritage, in the shape of the adult romance.[27] 'It is when we make castles in the air and personate the leading character in our own romances,' he writes, 'that we return to the spirit of our first years.'[28] This account of the link between childhood make-believe and adult dreams resonates with later Freudian notions of the unconscious, intriguingly anticipating Freud's description in 1908 of the 'growing child' who no longer plays but '*phantasies*. He builds castles in the air and creates what are called *day-dreams*'.[29] Elsewhere, too, Stevenson suggested that an exhilarating, instinctual life persisted not only in modern children but also in many adults. In 'The Lantern-Bearers' (1888), for instance, he denied that 'a poet has died young in the breast of the most stolid' and asserted the vitality of the imaginative impulse: 'His life from without may seem a rude mound of mud; there will be some golden chamber at the heart of it, in which he dwells delighted.'[30]

A Child's Garden of Verses (1885), Stevenson's enduringly popular collection of poetry for children, engages with similar issues about play and the childhood imagination. As Michael Rosen has shown, Stevenson intervened consciously in evolutionist debate, but did so, notably, in a volume intended for an audience of children.[31] The verses, mostly spoken in the direct voice of a child, sound 'a kind of childish treble note', as Stevenson wrote to Edmund Gosse in 1885, although in places a didactic or sentimental adult strain interferes.[32] They offer a revitalised Romantic vision of the childhood imagination's transformative power. This debt to Romanticism, incidentally, is suggested by the alternative titles which Stevenson considered for the collection, including *New Songs of Innocence*.[33] The motif of the *Garden* figures childhood as a visionary Arcady; indeed, Stevenson described the childhood holidays which the volume commemorates, spent with cousins at his grandfather's manse, as his 'golden age' or '*Arcadia*'.[34] As much as the poems evoke childhood, though, they represent an adult reconstruction of the past:

Stevenson started writing them in 1881, just as he was rediscovering the world of childhood play with his stepson, Lloyd Osbourne.

The collection explores and animates the workings of the child's creative imagination in ways that resonate with evolutionist child psychology. 'Child's Play' had described the child as 'passionate after dreams and unconcerned about realities', anticipating Sully's later assertion that '[f]or the child, as for primitive man, reality is a projection of fancy'.[35] In the world of A Child's Garden, too, everyday objects are imaginatively transformed. The child-speaker in 'Block City' declares, 'Let the sofa be mountains, the carpet be sea', and in 'Pirate Story' three children 'afloat in the meadow by the swing' imagine the nearby cattle as a pirate 'squadron a-rowing on the sea'.[36] The real becomes the visionary in the space of a line of verse: in 'The Land of Counterpane', toy soldiers march 'Among the bed-clothes, through the hills' (p. 370). Sully's Studies of Childhood uses this poem's 'transformations of the bed-scene' to illuminate how play involves 'the working out into visible shape of an inner fancy'.[37]

At the root of this childhood make-believe is a primitive animism. Describing how 'primitive child-lore, like its prototype in folk-lore', is 'largely mythological', Sully cites the personification of the elements in Stevenson's 'The Wind'.[38] In numerous other poems, such as 'The Dumb Soldier' and 'The Kingdom', the child's playthings are invested with life, and often seem more real, more central to the child's universe, than the mysterious adults who intervene with peremptory calls to tea or bed.[39] The speaker in 'My Ship and I' imagines himself joining 'the dolly at the helm' and becoming the captain of his toy ship (p. 390). The child's imagination opens up other worlds, with smaller dimensions and more congenial inhabitants: in 'The Little Land', the boy has just to 'shut [his] eyes' to sail to 'the pleasant Land of Play; / To the fairy land afar / Where the Little People are' (p. 396). Returning to the adult world brings a sense of spatial dislocation:

> Great big people perched on chairs,
> Stitching tucks and mending tears,
> Each a hill that I could climb,
> And talking nonsense all the time (p. 397).

Adults and children, then, inhabit separate mental spaces: as Stevenson claimed in 'Child's Play', young and old 'visit the same country and yet move in different worlds'.[40] The speaker in 'The Land of Story-Books' notes in a bemused manner that 'Around the fire my parents sit; / They sit at home and talk and sing, / And do not play at anything' (p. 394).

Most evolutionists, of course, saw the transition from childhood fancy to adult rationality as one of progress. Thus Sully contrasted children's 'imperfectly developed brain' and 'susceptibility to powerful illusory suggestion' with adults' 'volitional control' and ability to 'reason away a fancy, and generally to guard ourselves against error'.[41] By contrast, a Romantic and primitivist nostalgia for childhood pervades A *Child's Garden of Verses*. 'To Willie and Henrietta' wistfully describes an adult Stevenson and his cousins resting 'in the elders' seat', and watching 'the children, our successors, play' (p. 407). Speaking to adults as well as children, the volume articulates a yearning for the past, for the lost world of the childhood imagination. The child in 'The Land of Nod' reveals the elusive nature of that terrain:

> Try as I like to find the way,
> I never can get back by day,
> Nor can remember plain and clear
> The curious music that I hear (p. 371).

Yet, although the poem emphasises loss, Stevenson aimed to reanimate these dreams, by stirring the adult's memory of childhood fantasy. One New York reviewer, writing in 1885, described how his 'youth has been renewed' by A *Child's Garden*.[42] Underlying the volume was a hopeful sense that the child's imagination might revitalise a prosaic adulthood: as the child in 'Block City' says of the city he had built with his blocks, 'as I saw it, I see it again [. . .] / And as long as I live and where'er I may be, / I'll always remember my town by the sea' (p. 394).

Despite Stevenson's belief that the childhood imagination was rejuvenating, he was at the same time preoccupied by its morbidity. By the *fin de siècle*, in the context of fears about racial and cultural reversion and imperial decline, commentators increasingly interpreted the nervous child as a symptom of British degeneracy.[43] As Sally Shuttleworth observes, the 'pessimistic psychology of the late century' depicted the child as 'the carrier of [. . .] the attenuated nerves of an overdeveloped civilization'.[44] Stevenson's work resonates with this degenerationist discourse. Even in A *Child's Garden of Verses*, but most obviously in non-fictional and fictional prose including 'Memoirs of Himself' (1912) and *Weir of Hermiston* (1896), he evokes childhood as sickly, nervous, and over-imaginative.

A *Child's Garden* has attracted criticism for what William Archer condemned in 1885 as its 'persistent dwelling on the sunny aspect of childhood, with scarcely a hint of its night side'.[45] Stevenson protested that his childhood was 'full of fever, nightmare, insomnia, painful days and interminable nights', but the critique has endured.[46] For Hugh Cunningham, the poems exemplify the 'middle-class sentimentalizing of childhood'.[47] Certainly, the volume articulates a middle-class perspective, although in places the child-speaker unwittingly undercuts the smug piety of affluence, as in the poem

'System'.[48] But even the prosperous childhood depicted in the collection has its bleaker side. In 'Memoirs of Himself', Stevenson described the 'three powerful impressions of my childhood: my sufferings when I was sick, my delights in convalescence at my grandfather's manse [. . .] and the unnatural activity of my mind after I was in bed at night'.[49] The Arcadian 'delights' celebrated in the poems can perhaps be understood, accordingly, as a release from the travails of the sick-room; Stevenson's portrayal of his mind's 'unnatural activity' also provides a darker reading of the child's imagination as morbid or pathological. Indeed, the dedication to Stevenson's nurse, 'To Alison Cunningham', underlines physical frailty: the once 'sick child' thanks her 'For the long nights you lay awake / [. . .] For all the pains you comforted: / For all you pitied, all you bore' (p. 361). 'The Land of Counterpane', despite its emphasis on the consoling delights of the imagination, revealingly contrasts the child's martial play with his real enfeeblement, 'When I was sick and lay a-bed' (p. 370). Childhood is beset, too, by shadowy 'night terrors'. In 'The Land of Nod', the child faces 'many frightening sights abroad / Till morning in the Land of Nod', while 'North-West Passage' describes his 'heart [. . .] a-beating like a drum' as he imagines 'the breath of the Bogie in my hair' (pp. 371, 388, 387).

'Memoirs of Himself', written in 1880, allowed more space to the fears and suffering which Stevenson largely suppressed in the later *Child's Garden*. 'Memoirs' does celebrate the child's creative imagination, claiming that Stevenson and his cousin 'lived together in a purely visionary state'.[50] But it also emphasises the morbidity of the sensitive child's imagination, recalling 'the most hideous nightmares, which would wake me screaming and in the extremest frenzy of terror' (p. 150). Stevenson's analysis chimes with contemporary medical discourse about 'night terrors', which were often blamed on over-stimulated imaginations.[51] For Stevenson, as for many scientific commentators, childhood neurosis was associated with religion: Sully warned that 'even religious instruction when injudiciously presented may add to the terrors of the dark for these wee tremulous organisms'.[52] Stevenson describes his 'high-strung religious ecstasies and terrors':

> I would not only lie awake to weep for Jesus, which I have done many a time, but I would fear to trust myself to slumber lest I was not accepted and should slip, ere I awoke, into eternal ruin. I remember repeatedly [. . .] waking from a dream of Hell, clinging to the horizontal bar of the bed, with my knees and chin together, my soul shaken, my body convulsed with agony. (p. 154)

Stevenson attributes his 'morbidly religious' nature to his strictly Calvinist nurse, Cummy (p. 158). Under her influence, he agonised over his parents' 'spiritual welfare [. . .] because they gave dinner parties and played cards, things contemned in the religious biographies on which my mind was fed' (p. 154). As this intimates, Stevenson believed that literature exerted a powerful – and often insidious – influence on children's development. His mind, he lamented, was 'defiled' by stories about 'dismal and morbid devotees', instead of being amused by what he deemed 'healthy [stories] about battles' (p. 155).

Stevenson also stressed the vulnerabilities of the only child: 'I was an only child and, it may be in consequence, both intelligent and sickly' (p. 149). Contemporaries increasingly viewed the only child as prone to overstimulation and neurosis.[53] In *A Child's Garden*, the child is often alone, and Sully even cited 'The Unseen Playmate' to demonstrate that the invention of 'mythical companions' was 'common among lonely and imaginative children'.[54]

The nervous and isolated child, schooled in religious morbidity, also figures prominently in Stevenson's fiction. His earlier fiction features intolerant fathers who provoke filial rebellion. The sons in 'Edifying Letters of the Rutherford Family' (written around 1877) and 'The Misadventures of John Nicholson' (1887) reject their fathers' rule, embodied, respectively, in the 'damned wearisome ten commandments' and the 'tight little theological kingdom of Scotland'.[55] Interestingly, in the later, unfinished *Heathercat* (1897) and *Weir of Hermiston* (1896), it is the mothers' religious instruction that is more insidious and destructive. *Heathercat*, a novel started in the early 1890s, is set in seventeenth-century Scotland, during the confrontation between Royalists and Covenanters (Calvinist religious dissidents). The laird's wife, a 'mad, raging, Presbyterian zealot', attempts to perpetuate her fanatical brand of Calvinism through her son, coaching him in a language of hell-fire and damnation.[56]

Weir of Hermiston, set partly in the same fictional Borders country in the early nineteenth century, shows the community unable to escape its heritage of intolerance. Archie's early lessons in religious prejudice shape the tragedy related by the novel – a tragedy precipitated by his conflict with his father, Lord Hermiston, the 'hanging judge'. Following a confrontation with his father over capital punishment, Archie begins a doomed love affair; the novel breaks off as Archie ends the affair, but Stevenson's notes indicate that Archie was to kill a rival who seduced his sweetheart and to be convicted of murder by his own father.[57] Archie's early years ferment the discord, breeding in the child a neurotic antipathy to his father. His mother tells Archie folktales of the Covenanters' persecution 'till their tears ran down', teaching him to fear and despise his father as an irreligious 'persecutor'.[58] Archie's characterisation, like Stevenson's description of himself as a 'snivelling' only child, resonates with the contemporary degenerationist interest in nervous childhood.[59] His psychological morbidity is rendered in physical terms, as an effect of degeneracy and over-civilisation. His mother is 'the last descendant' of her race, and Archie is the 'only child of [a] scarce natural union' (pp. 56, 60). His fate appears ineluctable ('[i]t was in his horoscope to be [. . .] the son of Adam Weir and Jean Rutherford'), chiming with a late-Victorian psychology which, Shuttleworth observes, saw the child as marked by 'familial and racial history' (p. 101).[60] Archie's pathological birthright is written in somatic symptoms, as his 'shivering delicacy', 'inherited' from his mother, prompts a bodily revulsion from his father ('shuddering' and violent impulses) (pp. 70, 91).

Yet, despite this emphasis on the corporeal, Archie's inheritance is cultural rather than biological: as the narrator notes, '[t]he power of ancestry on the character is not limited to the inheritance of cells' (p. 105). The novel's tragic outcome is ultimately caused by Archie's exposure as a child to a narrowly repressive culture: he rebels against his father because he uses 'language that the child had been schooled to think coarse, and [. . .] words that he knew to be sins in themselves' (p. 64). Archie's psychology is shaped by his early diet of biblical and Covenanting stories and traditions. His mother's frequent scriptural allusions, including her visions of the biblical territory of Naphtali in the Pentland Hills, have a 'deep' effect on the 'impressionable child' (p. 63). Naphtali, the name of Jacob's second son in the Bible and hence of his people and their land, was also the title of a celebratory seventeenth-century history of the Covenanters, *Naphtali, or the Wrestlings of the Church of Scotland for the Kingdom of Christ*.[61] The name Naphtali, with its rich cluster of biblical, devotional and Covenanting associations, clearly made a deep – if equivocal – impression on Stevenson. According to '"Rosa Quo Locorum"', the Church of Scotland minister and evangelical writer Robert Murray McCheyne was the 'favourite author' of Stevenson's childhood, and he particularly savoured his lines, 'Behind the hills of Naphtali / The sun went slowly down.'[62] 'The Pentland Rising' (1866), Stevenson's boyhood commemoration of the Covenanters as heroic martyrs, cites reverently *Naphtali*'s testimony of persecution.[63] Yet Stevenson's later work invokes Naphtali's associations to quite different effect. In *Weir*, Archie's mother's exalted dreams of Palestine in the Pentlands are evidently unhealthy. And McCheyne features in Stevenson's 'Memoirs' as a symbol of religious intolerance, one of a 'crowd of dismal and morbid devotees'.[64]

Thus Stevenson exposes the violent psychological effects of devotional literature for both Archie and his autobiographical self. The childhood imagination emerges as vulnerable, at the mercy of piety's distorted view of the world. Recalling his childhood priggishness, Stevenson speculates that '[h]ad I died in these years [. . .] I might perhaps have figured in a tract'. This leads him to wonder whether

> all the young saints of whom I have read and meditated with enthusiasm in my
> early period, suffered from their biographers the same sort of kindly violence, or

had idealised themselves by the same simply necessary suppressions, that would have fitted myself and my career for that gallery of worthies.[65]

Stevenson suggests here that devotional literature's 'suppressions' (its denial of vital aspects of the psyche) radically damages human nature. Children, especially over-imaginative, over-civilised children, are particularly susceptible to its 'kindly violence'.

Stevenson represents the childhood imagination, then, in deeply conflicting ways – as an invigorating savage survival or as pathologically morbid. How can these divergent constructions of childhood be reconciled? In places Stevenson seems to see savagery as an antidote to the modern child's morbid introspection. Thus he intimates that 'something healthy about battles' might have cured him of his childhood nerves.[66] This suggestion chimes with the contemporary belief in the restorative power of 'primitive' cultural forms such as children's fiction, oral culture and adventure novels. The American psychologist G. Stanley Hall warned that if children were not allowed to 'revive the ancestral experiences', at least in a 'vicarious way, by tales of the heroic virtues', these would 'crop out in menacing forms later'.[67] But despite Stevenson's attraction to the idea of the primitive imagination as a psychological tonic, *Weir*'s narrative casts doubt on its revitalising power. Following his first clash with his father, Archie is banished from Edinburgh to the Borders, where his exposure to epic story-telling and expressive vernacular dialect proves briefly invigorating (the narrator describes him as 'profoundly moved, and lapsing into the broad Scots') (p. 166). However, he eventually finds that the traditional, oral culture of the ballad world is decaying, and is unable to provide him with a curative for his morbid solitude.[68]

This hesitancy about the regenerative potential of the 'primitive' imagination – and hence of adventure or romance – has often been attributed to Stevenson's disillusioning experience of colonialism in the South Seas from 1888 onwards.[69] Indeed, *The Ebb-Tide* (1893–4) exposes the affiliations of adventure with brutal, imperialist masculinities. Such doubt about adventure's revivifying force, however, surfaces much earlier in Stevenson's career, informing even *The Black Arrow* (1883), a historical novel set during the Wars of the Roses. Initially, the novel seems to promise an exhilarating return to the delights of the childhood imagination. Stevenson's wife described how it recalled his failing father to youthful animation, dissipating his 'tragic gloom'.[70] In its opening scenes, the hero, Dick Shelton, appears an uncomplicated *Boy's Own* type, a plucky and honourable adolescent: he subscribes to the masculine adventure ethos, displaying a boyish antipathy to 'maids' and exclaiming, '"Give me to hunt and to fight and to feast, and to live with jolly foresters."'[71] Perhaps this is why the story was such a success with the readers of *Young Folks*, the children's magazine in which it was serialised.[72]

But Stevenson, who had sounded ambivalent about being an 'Author of Boys' Stories' as he wrote *Treasure Island*, cast his new novel as thoroughly degenerate: 'Daily the lyre grows dumb and dumber / I leave the Muse for the Penny Number.'[73] The narrative itself evinces a reflexive doubt about the romance code of boys' fiction: even the *Arabian Nights*, which usually symbolised for Stevenson an invigorating childhood imagination, are ironically deployed here, figuring adventure's degeneracy (Dick uses the tale of Ali Baba to deceive a hapless victim). Moreover, while Stevenson's father was rejuvenated by the novel, its hero is gradually released from adventure's spell, and comes to recognise the destructive nature of its primitive forces. Describing how Dick eventually realises the tragic consequences of his desire for glory – 'for the first time [he] began to understand the desperate game that we play in life' – the narrator revalues the idea of the 'game' or play at the heart of the romance code.[74]

As this uncertainty about the curative value of the primitive imagination suggests, Stevenson negotiated debates about childhood psychology with some ambivalence, even in his early work. Far from being 'a boy till the day of his death', Stevenson engaged in sophisticated and self-conscious ways with contemporary understandings of childhood. Depicting the childhood imagination as a 'primitive' survival, he nonetheless questioned the evolutionist emphasis on progress, and hailed instead the endurance of the child's consciousness in the modern adult. Yet this neo-Romantic vision of childhood fantasy's rejuvenating power was undercut by a darker reading of the childhood imagination as prone to nervous pathology. While his essays demonstrate Stevenson's attraction to 'healthy [stories] about battles', his fiction intimates scepticism about the idea that the child's morbidity can be cured by such 'savage' survivals.

CHAPTER FOUR

Stevenson and *Fin-de-Siècle* Gothic

Stephen Arata

We typically associate Gothic writing with excess, but Stevenson's Gothic tales are notable for their restraint. By and large, they avoid the extravagances, both stylistic and thematic, that characterise the horror stories of late Victorian authors such as Bram Stoker, Arthur Machen, Richard Marsh, H. Rider Haggard and Oscar Wilde. His writings instead make full use of the resources of silence and understatement. Like his exact contemporary Sigmund Freud, moreover, Stevenson was fascinated by the psychic mechanisms by which we come to attach feelings of deep discomfort, even terror, to ordinary objects or occurrences. In some circumstances – in a dream, for instance – the most terrifying thing imaginable might well be the sight of an old brown dog lying asleep in a quiet farmyard. In his essay 'A Chapter on Dreams' Stevenson recounts just such a dream. Here is how it ends:

> Something about this dog disquieted the dreamer; it was quite a nameless feeling, for the beast looked right enough – indeed, he was so old and dull and dusty and broken down, that he should rather have awakened pity; and yet the conviction came and grew upon the dreamer that this was no proper dog at all, but something hellish. A great many dozing summer flies hummed about the yard; and presently the dog thrust forth his paw, caught a fly in his open palm, carried it to his mouth like an ape, and looking suddenly up at the dreamer in the window, winked to him with one eye.[1]

In *The Interpretation of Dreams* (1900), Freud calls attention to a fact that all dreamers know already from their own experience, namely that the content of a dream may have nothing to do with the emotions it produces. Innocuous content is often coupled with intense affect; sleepy dogs can somehow become hellish. Freud attributes such anomalies to the work of displacement, whereby latent dream-thoughts – the dream's 'real' contents – are transformed so as to mask their true nature. To unravel the intricacies of a dream is to bear witness to human inventiveness and ingenuity. Freud put dream interpretation at the heart of psychoanalysis because it is in dreams that we most fully reveal ourselves – and work most creatively to avoid knowing it.

Stevenson did not need Freud to tell him that dreaming and artistic work are often closely allied. Nor does Stevenson ever doubt that his relation to the workings of his own psyche is at once intimate and estranged. In 'A Chapter on Dreams' he serio-comically portrays himself as simply the front man ('I hold the pen [. . .] and I do the sitting at the table')[2] for the 'Little People' who run his dream life and there concoct the stories he makes his living by. The Little People are a part of him, but they somehow seem to know more about him than he himself does. They reveal what they know mostly by way of stories or fragments of stories whose meanings seem wondrous but are seldom entirely clear. A cloud of summer flies, an unnervingly dexterous hound (or is it an ape?), a complicitous wink: Stevenson understood as surely as did Freud that dreams tell what they tell precisely by way of such overdetermined images.

Freud the clinical analyst sought to interpret such images in order to get at the dream-thoughts behind them, whose revelation, he believed, could have therapeutic value. Stevenson the artist pursues a different agenda. In 'A Chapter on Dreams' he eventually acknowledges that the dog dream is his own, yet he offers no interpretation of it. 'A Chapter on Dreams' is not a confession or an exercise in self-analysis; it is an exploration of literary technique. For Stevenson, the dog dream may well be interesting for what it reveals about the dreamer. But it is more interesting for the challenge it offers the writer, who through the resources of his craft attempts to reproduce in his readers the precise quality of the horror the dream produced in him. Having conceived the fly-eating, winking hound, the dreamer has no idea what to do next, and so squanders his opportunity. The 'point of interest for me', Stevenson writes, is in the fact of this failure. Proving 'unable to carry the tale to a fit end', the dreamer 'fall[s] back on indescribable noises and indiscriminate horrors'[3] – a disappointing capitulation to the most banal of literary conventions for signalling psychic distress.

The twin topics of 'A Chapter on Dreams' – the inexhaustibly fecund complexity of human consciousness on the one hand, the bracingly astringent challenges of literary composition on the other – were of abiding interest to Stevenson throughout his career. They also correspond to fundamental concerns of Gothic writing. Gothic has been conducive to narrative and stylistic experimentation. To portray human beings 'realistically', Gothic writers seem to say, requires more than the resources of conventional literary realism have to offer. The very nature of Gothic material – human beings in their involuted individuality as well as in the intricacies of their social relations – seems to call forth the stylistic excesses, alogical progressions, fractured narrative structures and multiplication of perspectives that characterise the genre.

The flourishing of Gothic in the last decades of the nineteenth century drew much of its energy from late Victorian culture's fascination with the human psyche. The 1860s and 1870s saw the elaboration of a variety of discourses on consciousness that eventually coalesced into the new discipline of psychology. This was also a period utterly enthralled by the contemplation of psychological limit cases and borderlands. Mesmerism, hypnotism, telepathy, telekinesis, second-sight, somnambulism and other abnormal or paranormal states of consciousness were the subject of scientific inquiry and popular speculation. Such phenomena are frequently central to the plots of late Victorian popular fiction, especially Gothic: consider the various kinds of 'mind control' that figure in works such as Rider Haggard's *She* (1885), George du Maurier's *Trilby* (1894), Arthur Machen's *The Great God Pan* (1894), Bram Stoker's *Dracula* (1897), or Richard Marsh's *The Beetle* (1897). Significantly, though, Stevenson never avails himself of such devices. His Gothic fiction is more concerned to investigate the strangeness of what we like to call 'normal' consciousness. Even tales that include elements of the fantastic, such as 'Thrawn Janet' (1881), 'The Body Snatcher' (1884), 'Markheim' (1885) and most famously *Strange Case of Dr Jekyll and Mr Hyde* (1886), are primarily psychological dramas rather than explorations of the supernatural or the paranormal. In these stories Stevenson highlights the sense of uncanniness and self-alienation that result naturally, as it were, from the operations of our psyches, just as he foregrounds the mechanisms by which we attempt to ward off the self-knowledge we sometimes prefer not to have.

Early readers of 'A Chapter on Dreams' would have recognised in Stevenson's account of his Little People a fanciful if implicit reference to 'unconscious cerebration', a phrase in wide circulation from the 1860s onwards. It is possible that Stevenson was familiar with two essays on unconscious cerebration written by the journalist and reformer Frances Power Cobbe and published in *Macmillan's Magazine* in 1870–1. For Cobbe, unconscious cerebration refers to the many mental activities that occur below the threshold of conscious awareness. Like Stevenson, Cobbe marvels at the creativity of the dreaming mind, and like Stevenson she calls attention to the sense of estrangement we often feel from the workings of our own brains. As Cobbe shrewdly notes in 'Unconscious Cerebration', it seems 'our brains sometimes think without us'.[4]

The similarities between Cobbe's essays and 'A Chapter on Dreams' are instructive, but not nearly so instructive as the differences. Where Cobbe is interested in what dreaming reveals about the physiognomy of the brain, Stevenson is interested in what it suggests about the nature of artistic labour. The tales we tell ourselves in dreams convey only private meanings. The difference between the dreamer and the writer is that the writer knows how to make such meanings public property. This is an insight Stevenson offers with characteristic indirection in 'A Chapter on Dreams' through his humorous

– and thoroughly implausible – assertion that he has been training his unconscious to dream only marketable stories for him.

An essay less about dreaming than about writing, 'A Chapter on Dreams'
provides us with a vocabulary for talking about his specific achievements in
Gothic fiction. Thanks primarily to *Dr Jekyll and Mr Hyde*, Stevenson's name
figures prominently in any discussion of *fin-de-siècle* Gothic, a genre which
recent critics have justifiably defined in terms of its obsession with what Kelly
Hurley evocatively calls 'the ruination of the human subject'.[5] Horrified
fascination with the mutability of human subjectivity, the permeability
of the human body, and the morphic possibilities of both finds expression
in the startling array of monstrous or abhuman figures who inhabit *fin-de-
siècle* popular fiction. Clearly, Henry Jekyll and Edward Hyde belong in this
company.

Stylistically, though, *Jekyll and Hyde* is unlike its compeers. The spectacle
of human ruination in *fin-de-siècle* Gothic typically calls forth a language of
excess. Yet Stevenson's Gothic fiction is difficult to fit within such a paradigm.
His language is seldom extravagant, and he usually avoids stylistic excess.
As he contends in his 1883 essay 'A Note on Realism', the literary artisan
knows that the first rule of writing is to 'suppress much and omit more'.[6] This
commitment to restraint is evident even when the subject matter is most
outrageously Gothic. When Stevenson wants to produce an especially strong
effect, he tends to turn down the rhetorical temperature.

Stevenson often says much less than a particular situation might seem to
call for. He uses the tension between content and style to open up a space
for the uncanny. If readers find the winking dog of 'A Chapter on Dreams'
creepy, that reaction is due in no small measure to the matter-of-factness of
Stevenson's description. Similarly, many early readers of *Jekyll and Hyde* agreed
that the book's most frightening scene is the one in which Poole and Utterson
do nothing more than listen to the sound of footsteps 'going up and down, up
and down, in the quiet of the night' behind the cabinet door.[7] When the two
men violently break into the room, the scene that greets them is not one of
unspeakable horror but instead one of quiet domesticity, placidly described:
'a good fire glowing and chattering on the hearth, the kettle singing its thin
strain, a drawer or two open, papers neatly set forth on the business table, and
nearer the fire, the things laid out for tea' (p. 41). The lifeless body of Edward
Hyde is quickly discovered, but rather than linger on it the narrator follows
Poole and Utterson as they survey the room, which turns out to be remarkable mostly for being unremarkable. The uncanniness of the scene comes not
from the revelation of a grotesquely abhuman body and the disgust it arouses.
Instead it arises from the tension between the hushed domestic setting – 'the
most commonplace that night in London' (p. 41) – and the unnerving truths
that the setting seems both to stand in for and to stand in opposition to.

Stevenson's interest in the uncanny is at once psychological and aesthetic. Here he again anticipates Freud. In an influential 1919 essay, Freud defines the uncanny as 'that class of the frightening which leads back to what is known of old and long familiar'.[8] A sense of the uncanny occurs when a mental state associated with childhood is temporarily reactivated. 'What is known of old and long familiar' are infantile ways of conceiving of one's relation to the world that have been overcome but have left 'certain residues and traces' in the psyche which 'are still capable of manifesting themselves' under the right conditions.[9] For Freud, uncanny experiences thus possess psychoanalytic interest – our psyches seem to be hardwired for Gothic – but he is also aware that they give rise to a separate set of aesthetic questions. Uncanny effects are a feature of Gothic literature, but what strikes us as uncanny in fiction and what strikes us as uncanny in life ultimately comprise distinct (though overlapping) categories. What then, asks Freud, are the conditions for uncanniness in fiction?

In fiction, he suggests, feelings of uncanniness can be produced only within the context of 'the real'. The writer is free to 'select his world of representation so that it either coincides with the realities we are familiar with or departs from them in what particulars he pleases'.[10] If he chooses the latter course and assumes the existence of supernatural beings, he forfeits the uncanny. But the 'situation is altered as soon as the writer pretends to move in the world of common reality'.[11] The potential for uncanniness arises only once readers assent to the fiction as a mirror of reality, since the uncanny emerges from a disjunction between the world as it is known by the rational mind and the world as it is on occasion experienced by the irrational – but not therefore necessarily mistaken – unconscious. Freud's formulation allows us to see that the Gothic almost invariably erupts from within realism itself. *Fin-de-siècle* Gothic often foregrounds the everydayness of the world being depicted so as to set off (in both senses of that phrase) whatever horrors disrupt that world.

Dr Jekyll and Mr Hyde is a good instance of a Gothic work whose episodes of uncanniness emerge from 'the world of common reality'. To find an example, we need only return to Henry Jekyll's cabinet and contemplate, as Utterson and Poole do 'with an involuntary horror', an ordinary cheval glass standing near the tea table. '"This glass has seen some strange things, sir," whispered Poole' (p. 42). The strange things it has seen are precisely the revelations concerning Henry Jekyll that Utterson and Poole have, unwillingly, begun to suspect but have yet to acknowledge even to themselves. The sense of uncanniness experienced by the two men is triggered by the cheval glass, an ordinary object that is felt both to be out of place (it belongs in a home, not a laboratory) and yet somehow to signify the 'secret and hidden' truths about Jekyll.

Here as elsewhere in *Dr Jekyll and Mr Hyde*, uncanniness is not only represented *in* the text but is also an effect produced *by* the text. Just as Freud's uncanny is both a real life phenomenon and a virtual or aesthetic one, so too does Stevenson compel our attention to the way he stages uncanniness while at the same time evoking it in readers. For Utterson the mirror's uncanniness is a sign that what 'ought' to have remained secret about Jekyll is now revealed. For readers, the sense of uncanniness seems tied to the mirror's tantalising status as a hermeneutic key to the story. The mirror presents itself to us as a repository of meaning and affect that have little to do with its literal function in the story. (Jekyll uses it to monitor his transformations into Hyde.) It thus appears to be an index to the 'unconscious' of the story itself – the things the story 'knows' but never explicitly says.

Stevenson was admired by his contemporaries as a writer who took more than usual care to calibrate the effects he strove to achieve. In his Gothic tales, this care is, somewhat paradoxically, often most apparent at those moments when language is suddenly deformed. As Richard Dury has shown in detail, *Dr Jekyll and Mr Hyde* in particular is full of weirdly unidiomatic expressions, unconventional verbal constructions, and slight but decisive skewing of words and phrases from accustomed usages. The overall effect, Dury notes, 'contributes to the general strangeness and indeterminacy' of the text.[12] In his essay on style, Stevenson writes that the goal of the literary artist is to 'restore to [words] their primal energy'.[13] A friend recalled that Stevenson 'seemed to attach great importance to the use of words which from association carried with them a fuller connotation than a mere dictionary one; and to the effectiveness of words and phrases in everyday use when employed in a not altogether usual connotation'.[14] Contemporary readers consistently noted his stylistic precision *and* his fondness for verbal constructions that border on solecism. The result is a prose that takes great pains to sound 'unnatural' on occasion. As Dury points out, the result is 'a feeling of uncanniness' arising from uses of language that 'seem both familiar and unfamiliar'.[15] This productive estranging of language may well be what Gerard Manley Hopkins had in mind when he wrote to Robert Bridges shortly after reading *Dr Jekyll and Mr Hyde* that 'Stevenson is master of a consummate style, and each phrase is finished as in poetry'.[16] Like Hopkins, Stevenson uses 'finish' not to cover over but to bring out the uncanniness of language. Both writers like to dislodge words or phrases from familiar usages in order to revitalise them or to make them available for new purposes, which has in turn the effect of startling readers into heightened forms of awareness.

A careful technician of language, Stevenson produced Gothic fictions that are stylistically unlike those of most of his contemporaries. Looked at from the perspective of content, though, Stevenson's Gothic texts share many concerns with other Gothic fictions of the period. The genre proved useful for addressing questions of gender, sexuality, class and race that vexed the age, as well as questions regarding the implications of research in the natural sciences and in psychology. For Stevenson, these public issues were overlaid with older, more private anxieties and fears traceable to his Scottish Presbyterian upbringing.

With good reason, accounts of Stevenson's Gothic fiction often begin with descriptions of the scarifying Calvinist instruction he was subjected to as a child by his parents and, more spectacularly, by his nurse, Alison Cunningham. One result was the appalling nightmares in which young Louis imagined himself cast into eternal perdition, exacerbated by the skilful storytelling of his beloved 'Cummy', who regaled the often sickly child with tales worked up from the fierce and bloody history of the seventeenth-century Covenanters. The Covenanters were not known for their tolerance of most things secular, an outlook shared by Cummy, who abhorred such soul endan-gering activities as card-playing, theatre-going and novel-reading. That her own stories were often outrageously theatrical in content and delivery was an irony not lost on the adult Stevenson, though as a child his nightmares were that much more vivid. Little wonder that, as he acknowledged in 'A Chapter on Dreams', 'hell gaped for him' (p. 152) so often in his sleep.

When Stevenson turned to Scottish subjects in his fiction, he did so by way of the Gothic. During the summer of 1881 he lived in cottages in Pitlochry and Braemar, his first extended residence in Scotland after his return from California the previous year. The period was one of great crea-tivity for Stevenson. In a matter of weeks he wrote three Gothic tales, all set in Scotland: 'Thrawn Janet', 'The Merry Men' and 'The Body Snatcher'. Jenni Calder calls 'Thrawn Janet' Stevenson's 'first piece of Scottish fiction, in maturity at least, and a story that uses the fears and prejudices of a devil-conscious national imagination with great effect'.[17] Indeed, all three stories foreground the terrors that in Stevenson's view were central to the Scottish national imagination and which derived their power from the Calvinist emphasis on fallibility and guilt. Together, they comprise his first concerted effort to come to terms with a cultural inheritance that put enormous weight on the supposed fact of human fallenness and on the human capacity for wickedness and self-deception.

Stevenson, then, considered Calvinist theology as a Gothic view of the world. In this respect he follows a strong tradition in Scottish writing. As Ian Duncan argues, from the late eighteenth century on, the 'thematic core of Scottish Gothic consists of an association between the *national* and the *uncanny or supernatural*'.[18] The mostly lowland, largely urban and almost exclusively middle-class Scots who comprised the bulk of Scotland's anglo-phone literary culture were nevertheless instrumental in the creation of a phantasmic 'authentic' national identity that was none of those things. The religious, ethnic, ideological and cultural divisions between lowlands and

highlands were recast as a temporal disjunction between Scottish modernity (urban, secular, bourgeois) and a pre-modern Scottishness whose forms
of identity were imagined to align with an organic national culture. The
Scottish writer's relation to that organic national culture was inevitably
one of intimate estrangement: a deep investment in an 'authentic' Scottish
identity was coupled with the recognition that that identity was alienated
from – indeed, was alien to – modern life and corresponded to nothing in the
writer's own identity.

Scottish Gothic constitutes a response to the specific trajectories of
the nation's history after 1707, in which the structures and practices of
Enlightenment modernity are striated by various anti-Enlightenment political
and religious discourses. An eager student of his country's history, Stevenson
was acutely aware of the divisions that Duncan describes. Moreover, he was
sensitive to the way those divisions were experienced as psychic splittings
and fragmentations. His own psyche was, so to speak, exemplary in this
respect. Though a Calvinist sensibility pervaded the Stevenson household,
Louis nevertheless was raised and educated in a manner befitting the son of
a highly successful and scientifically-minded professional man whose aspirations for his offspring – engineering or the law – were conventional in their
worldliness. As a young man, Stevenson was self-consciously cosmopolitan
in outlook, taking his bearings as a writer from trans-Atlantic and European
(particularly French) models. This is the aspect of Stevenson's persona that
Henry James has in mind when he writes: 'If it is a good fortune for a genius
to have had such a country as Scotland for its primary stuff, this is doubly
the case when there has been a certain process of detachment, of extreme
secularization. Mr. Stevenson has been emancipated – he is, as we may say,
a Scotchman of the world.'[19] But James greatly overestimates the extent to
which Stevenson detached, let alone emancipated, himself psychologically
from the 'primary stuff' of his Scottish heritage.

The desire for detachment is apparent in all three Pitlochry tales, which
employ framing devices familiar to Gothic fiction in order to locate readers
at a slight distance from the stories' characters and events. This distancing
is most evident in 'Thrawn Janet' and 'The Body Snatcher', both of which
are set in the past and make use of multiple narrators. After a brief preamble,
the story of the Reverend Murdoch Soulis in 'Thrawn Janet' is turned over
to an unnamed narrator – or, more precisely, the story we read, printed in
Scots dialect, seems to be a composite of many tellings by different residents
of Soulis's moorland parish. 'Now and again [. . .] one of the older folk would
warm into courage over his third tumbler and recount the cause of the minister's strange looks and solitary life.'[20] Those looks and that life are traced
to events that occurred shortly after Soulis took up his ministry fifty years
before, events which culminate in the discovery that Soulis's servant, Janet

M'Clour, has for some time been possessed by the devil. Well before Soulis's arrival, Janet had been 'mair than suspeckit by the best folk in Ba'weary', ostensibly for being a witch and 'sib to the deil' (p. 111) but more mundanely for her reputed sexual promiscuity. Soulis hires her in part as a rebuke to his parishioners' superstitions, but also perhaps in covert recognition that he, like Janet, is not wholly accepted by the Balweary community. In his case the separation is due to his having 'been ower lang at the college' and thus too 'fu' o' book learnin'', which is seen as a poor substitute for a genuine 'experience of religion' and 'a speerit of prayer' (p. 111).

From the perspective of those who later recount his story, Soulis's experience with Janet teaches him that she is in fact what they always claimed, a devil in disguise, and that his scepticism is finally a form of self-deception. Soulis must accept as truth what he once dismissed as superstition: 'it was borne in upon him what folk said, that Janet was deid lang syne, an' this was a bogle in her clay-cauld flesh' (p. 116). For us, though, what is perhaps most striking about the minister's experience is that it makes him an outcast of a different kind. The uncanniness attributed to 'thrawn' (crooked, mis-shapen) Janet attaches itself to Soulis in her wake. The brief preamble to the tale describes the aged minister, a 'severe, bleak-faced old man, dreadful to his hearers', with an eye that is 'wild, scared, and uncertain' (p. 109). Soulis embraces an ostracism that enhances his stature as a preacher by making him an uncanny figure to his parishioners. 'This atmosphere of terror, surrounding, as it did, a man of God of spotless character and orthodoxy, was a common cause of wonder' (p. 110). Stevenson leaves the exact nature of the minister's transformation unspecified. By omitting any account of Soulis's response to the episode with Janet – the narrative concludes abruptly with the 'revelation' of her possession – Stevenson of course leaves ample room for speculation and interpretation. Soulis in old age seems to be suspended between cultures, neither integrated into the Balweary community nor able to return to the beliefs associated with his earlier university training.

'Thrawn Janet' stages a confrontation between 'modern' and 'traditional' societies. For Stevenson's first readers, that confrontation – a staple of Gothic fiction – took on a further temporal dimension, though it is one that is doubly displaced: the distance between Thrawn Janet's story, which occurs in 1712, and its telling in the 1760s is replicated in the distance between that telling and its narration by Stevenson in the 1880s. 'The Body Snatcher' stages a similar confrontation between past and present, though here the time-scale has been shortened so that the story's events are within living memory. Stevenson had long been intrigued by the lore surrounding the infamous William Burke and William Hare, who in the late 1820s plied a brisk trade in corpses. Digging up bodies to sell to medical schools was a growth industry in this period, with demand far outstripping the supply of legally obtainable cadavers for dissection. Showing astute business sense, in 1827 Burke and Hare decided to streamline the process by murdering their commodities. In the course of a year at least fifteen victims were thus dispatched and sold to the anatomy school run by the eminent Dr Robert Knox. The two men were eventually arrested. Hare confessed in exchange for immunity, but Burke was convicted and executed – and then publicly dissected! – in 1829. Knox avoided prosecution, but his reputation was irremediably shattered, and for many people his name became a byword for the dangerous excesses of modern scientific research.

In 'The Body Snatcher' Stevenson casts a very thin fictional veil over his source material. The tale's sole supernatural touch, in which an exhumed body is suddenly revealed to be that of a victim murdered and dissected long before, is interesting only in so far as it throws light on the psychological drama that is Stevenson's main concern. In this relatively brief story, he rings an impressive number of changes on the theme of duplicity, as well as on 'the terrors of the conscience'[21] to which such duplicity gives rise. At the centre of the story is the young medical student, Fettes, whose duties include receiving the midnight deliveries of bodies to the dissecting room of 'Mr K–' without inquiring into their provenance. Stevenson's shrewd decision to focus attention on Fettes sharpens the psychological questions the story raises. Unlike the grave robbers, whose incentives are economic, or Mr K–, whose professional standing depends on a steady source of cadavers, Fettes colludes in illegal activities from motivations that are obscure to himself if not to us. '[I]ncapable of interest in the fate and fortunes of another, the slave of his own desires and low ambitions' (p. 189), Fettes chooses not to acknowledge what he is involved in so that he may enjoy its benefits with a clear conscience. Duplicity is the keynote of his character: 'civil, attentive, and intelligent in the presence of his masters' (p. 188) and careful to maintain the appearance of propriety in his professional activities, Fettes 'indemnifie[s] himself' for his good behaviour in the daytime 'by nights of roaring, blackguardly enjoyment' (p. 189). In living this dual life, though, he is simply mimicking his 'betters': Macfarlane, the smooth young doctor whose off-duty activities leave him open to blackmail, and Mr K– himself, whose strict policy to 'ask no questions' 'for conscience' sake' is presented as the epitome of hypocrisy (p. 190).

With the deaths of Jane Galbraith and then of the blackmailer Gray, Fettes can no longer practise his convenient self-deception, though with the help of Macfarlane he manages to stifle his conscience even yet. The vehemence with which he rejects conventional morality, though, strongly suggests the intense psychological conflict raging within Fettes: 'Hell, God, devil, right, wrong, sin, crime, and all the old gallery of curiosities – they may frighten boys, but men of the world, like you and me, despise them', he rather desperately assures Macfarlane (p. 200). The magical transformation of the corpse of the farmer's wife into that of Gray functions, in a gruesomely literal way, for both Fettes and Macfarlane as a return of the repressed or, in Christian terms, as the very embodiment of their sins. Significantly, though, the two men respond to this revelation in diametrically opposed ways. Fettes, it is implied, collapses under the burden of finally acknowledging the depths of the evil of which he is capable, eventually emerging as the 'stupidly fuddled' (p. 184) drunk of the story's opening frame, while Macfarlane continues on the path of hypocrisy to become a successful London physician. This dichotomy allows Stevenson to stage one of those Manichean confrontations that recur throughout his fiction, with 'bald, dirty, pimpled' and righteous Fettes accosting the sleek and richly dressed London doctor at the foot of a staircase (p. 185). Macfarlane is compelled to look into the face of his own moral degradation, much as Henry Jekyll does when he looks into the mirror to find Edward Hyde.

Like 'Thrawn Janet', 'The Body Snatcher' makes good use of its frame tale, in part to dramatise the eruption of the past, with all its burden of 'Hell, God, devil, right, wrong, sin, [and] crime', into the ostensibly placid present day. The story's theme of untimely 'resurrection' is also played out on the narrative level: the unnamed narrator is proud of 'worming out a story' (p. 188) for our readerly pleasure, which he does by digging up, so to speak, the details of Fettes's sordid past. Stevenson may well have been troubled by the suspicion that with 'The Body Snatcher' he had himself become a 'Resurrection Man' (p. 198) of sorts, who sought to profit by putting into circulation stories of his nation's history that were better left buried.

That sense of guilt is given indirect expression in the third of the Pitlochry tales, 'The Merry Men'. The narrative of 'The Merry Men' traces an arc that is fundamental to both Gothic and Scottish fiction in the nineteenth century. Like the hero of a number of Walter Scott novels, young Charles Darnaway travels from his lowland home to one of the remoter reaches of the Highlands and Islands. As with the Scott hero, or the typical protagonist of a Gothic tale, we are encouraged to see Charles's journey in temporal as well as spatial terms, as a movement from civilised modernity to a rougher, more primitive past. That past is embodied in the figure of Charles's uncle, Gordon Darnaway, a dour and gloomy man who with his 'black fits' and fierce piety puts his nephew in mind of 'one of the hill-preachers in the killing times before the Revolution'.[22] 'The Merry Men' consists of two interwoven narrative strands. The first involves the spectacle of Gordon Darnaway's descent into madness. His collapse is triggered by guilt at having murdered the survivor of a recent shipwreck for the sake of the goods washed ashore, but the ultimate cause of his madness is the sheer pressure of his uncompromising Calvinist worldview. Gordon is wracked by a sense of his own ineradicable sin and of nature's implacable hostility to all human endeavour. His nephew imagines himself immune to such spiritual terrors, but the older man's psychic distress clearly finds an answering echo in Charles's own psyche – as well as in Stevenson's.

Charles acts as Stevenson's eidolon in another respect as well. The obscure sense of guilt awakened in Charles by the spectacle of Gordon's fall into madness is due in part to his recognition that he has come to Aros to do what he finds his uncle has himself been doing, namely scavenge for riches that belong to others. This is the story's second narrative strand. Charles's discovery, while a student in Edinburgh, of documents locating the wreck of a Spanish galleon off the coast of his uncle's property awakens the dreams of wealth that bring him back to Aros. Anxious to 'acquit' himself in his readers' eyes of the charge of 'sordid greed', Charles assures us that he desires riches only 'for the sake of a person who was dear to my heart – my uncle's daughter, Mary Ellen', whom he wishes to marry (p. 9). As the close proximity of the two ideas suggests, however, Charles's plan to abscond with Mary Ellen can be seen as simply an extension of his desire to plunder the island's treasure. From Walter Scott forward, lowland Scottish writers, Stevenson included, were discomfited by the suspicion that they were guilty of enriching themselves by in effect ransacking their country's past. 'The Merry Men' expresses its bad conscience about this state of affairs by aligning Charles's desire for plunder not only with that of his murderous uncle, but also with that of the avaricious 'historian from Madrid' (p. 22), who like Charles is in search of the Spanish wreck. His 'pretended historical inquiry had been but a cloak for treasure-hunting', Charles says indignantly of his rival (p. 51), but the indignation clearly is meant to mask the recognition that the mysterious historian is his double. The horrific deaths of both Gordon Darnaway and the Spaniard can be read as displacements of the punishment that 'rightly' belongs to the other two plunderers of Aros's riches, Charles Darnaway and Robert Louis Stevenson.

The three stories composed at Pitlochry provide us with basic co-ordinates for approaching Stevenson's Gothic masterpiece, *Strange Case of Dr Jekyll and Mr Hyde*. This short novel gives consummate expression to Stevenson's fascination with what in an 1886 letter he called 'that damned old business of the war in the members'[23] – that is, the sense of psychic fragmentation and conflict he had imbibed from his religious training. Where *Dr Jekyll and Mr Hyde* differs from Stevenson's earlier Gothic tales is in its skilful mapping of these older theological concerns onto a range of contemporary cultural discourses. Henry Jekyll's prediction that science would eventually reveal the human personality to be not a unified entity but 'a mere polity of multifarious, incongruous, and independent denizens' (p. 53), for instance, had already been fulfilled by the 1880s. As early as the 1830s, scientists had begun to document cases of what quickly came to be termed 'double' or 'divided' consciousness, in which different personalities seemed to inhabit the same individual. In 1876, the French psychiatrist Dr Eugène Azam produced a sensation with his reports on 'Félida X', who swung back and forth between two diametrically opposed selves who evidently did not share the same memories and were not aware of each other. Nine years later readers were introduced to the celebrated case of Louis Vivet, who moved among five distinct personalities. By the time Stevenson sat down to write *Dr Jekyll and Mr Hyde*, the reality of what Frederic W. H. Myers called 'the multiplex personality' was largely taken for granted. For Myers, as for most late Victorian thinkers, the multiplex personality was not an aberration but a condition common to us all. Investigations into unconscious cerebration, subliminal consciousness, automatic and reflex action, and the like revealed not only that our brains sometimes think without us but that we often act in accordance with a volition seemingly not our own. Edward Hyde gives a bodily form to these insights of Victorian psychology: Henry Jekyll literally stands at a remove from an aspect of his own identity, whose relation Jekyll feels to be at once intimate (Hyde is 'closer than a wife, closer than an eye' [p. 65]) and thoroughly alien ('he – I say: I cannot say, I' [p. 63]).

If Hyde indexes the fragmented psyche, he also discloses the disturbing instability of the human body, which is shown to be permeable, fluid, capable of transformations both sudden and gradual. With his squat, swart, misshapen form, Edward Hyde clearly evokes the malignant beings of traditional folklore and fairy tale. But for late Victorian readers he is also seen to signify more contemporary maladies both physical and spiritual. In the novel itself, Utterson, Enfield, Lanyon and Poole all agree that Hyde 'gives a strong feeling of deformity' (p. 9), yet no one seems able to specify the nature of that deformity. Who or what is Edward Hyde? is a question that troubles everyone who encounters him. What is his class status? his race? his nationality? What are his family ties? his profession? More abstractly, what *kind* of person is he? What are his proclivities? his desires? his tastes? The answers to such questions, it was widely assumed throughout the nineteenth century, ought to be available through the proper interpretation of physical signs such as clothing, manners, deportment, even – or especially – bodily features. Hyde, though, baffles the efforts of others to interpret him. 'I never saw a man I so disliked,' confesses Enfield, 'and yet I scarce know why [. . .] He's an extraordinary-looking man, and yet I can really name nothing out of the way'(p. 9).

Enfield's response has been repeatedly echoed by Stevenson's readers. From the moment of its publication, reviewers and critics have taken *Dr Jekyll and Mr Hyde* as a complex parable. What it is a parable *of* remains an open question. It is an indication of the fertility of Stevenson's conception that the figure of Edward Hyde continues to exercise a hold on the imagination of readers; continues, too, to provoke critical debate of a high order. What Oscar Wilde teasingly claimed of the 'hero' of his own Gothic masterpiece applies to Stevenson's protagonist as well: 'What Dorian Gray's sins are no one knows,' Wilde wrote. 'He who finds them has brought them.'[24] In the case of Hyde, it is more accurate to say that readers have responded with a rich sense of the various cultural discourses that he brings into play. His 'sins' remain for the most part unspecified in the story, encouraging readers to provide their content. Declining a request from a correspondent for the 'key' to his 'allegory', Stevenson writes: 'I have said my say as I was best able: others must look for what is meant.'[25] Many early readers assumed that Hyde's transgressions were primarily sexual and took the story as a warning of the dangers of sexual indulgence. Stevenson rejected so narrow a reading – 'people are so full of folly and inverted lust, that they can think of nothing but sexuality',[26] he complained – not because it is mistaken but because it too quickly forecloses other interpretative possibilities that Stevenson wished to keep open.

As the many stage, film and television adaptations of the past century attest, and as even the most cursory survey of recent criticism confirms, those possibilities have remained wide open. *Dr Jekyll and Mr Hyde* has attracted critical attention across a wide spectrum of media and methodologies pre-cisely because this novel, like its protagonists, is an accomplished shape-shifter. It has proved illuminating – when it has not been troubling – to critics interested in the development of late Victorian ideologies of sexual identity and masculinity;[27] in theories of gender and sexual desire;[28] in ques-tions of atavism and degeneration;[29] and in the cultural construction of race, ethnicity and class.[30] As these and other critics have shown, *Dr Jekyll and Mr Hyde* engages in complex ways with late Victorian debates in psychology, biology, medicine, anthropology, criminology and sexology. Broadly speak-ing, what links these debates, as well as current critical investigations of the period, is an interest in the mutability of human identity under the varying deforming pressures of modernity.

Dr Jekyll and Mr Hyde memorably dramatises the effects of those pressures. Even so, the novel remains haunted by those old, old conceptions of human fallenness that so exercised and appalled Stevenson. Though the novel is set in modern London and peopled solely with English characters, it is, as readers have always sensed, pervaded by the Calvinist atmosphere of Stevenson's Edinburgh youth. This aspect of the story is what G. K. Chesterton had in mind when he wrote in 1927 that 'there is something decidedly Caledonian about Dr. Jekyll'.[31] Indeed, Henry Jekyll is a lineal descendent of Soulis, Fettes and the elder Darnaway, men burdened by their conviction of human-ity's innate depravity and finally broken by the awful strain of trying to keep at bay the devils within themselves.

In the mid-1880s Stevenson began to give imaginative play to the idea that one might find relief by simply succumbing to the attractions of sin. This notion lies at the heart of 'Markheim', a brief and intense tale written shortly before *Dr Jekyll and Mr Hyde*. 'Markheim' recounts a gratuitous murder committed by its title character and the immediate aftermath of that event. The similarities to *Crime and Punishment* are not coincidental: Stevenson was staggered by his experience of Dostoevsky's novel – reading it was like 'having a brain fever', he wrote[32] – and seemed to take from it the suggestion that there might be liberation, even perhaps a kind of redemption, in surrendering to an evil impulse. The bulk of the story is devoted to Markheim's conversation with a shadowy figure who is the Devil (or perhaps an angel) or else a projection of Markheim's own guilty conscience. Markheim in no way attempts to mitigate his own guilt; indeed, it is his recognition not only that 'Evil and good run strong in me, haling me both ways' but that he loves both evil and good that clears a path to genuine self-knowledge. In the dark victory he achieves – 'my eyes are opened, and I behold myself at last for what I am'[33] – Markheim separates himself from the 'devil-haunted' protagonists of Stevenson's earlier Gothic fiction.

It is of course this same recognition that 'evil and good run strong' in him that motivates Henry Jekyll's efforts to give each its proper sphere. 'I saw that, of the two natures that contended in the field of my consciousness,' he writes, 'even if I could rightly be said to be either, it was only because I was radically both' (p. 53). Jekyll opens his 'Full Statement' by stressing that he is exactly like his fellow men in this respect, differing only in his frank acknowledgment that, thanks to this 'curse of mankind' (p. 53), neither half alone is his 'real' self. He is, each of us is, radically both. What makes Jekyll a modern figure is precisely his belief that our innate impulses toward evil cannot in the nature of things be eradicated, nor can they even be effectively repressed for long without great psychological cost. The costs of repression are everywhere evident in the novel, whose broader canvas allows Stevenson to paint a damning portrait of a society defined by repression and its inevitable twin, hypocrisy. The story is filled with men for whom respectability acts as a lid screwed down tight over sometimes illicit, sometimes just vaguely shameful, desires. The opening description of Gabriel Utterson, who drinks gin 'to mortify' his taste for wine and refuses to attend the theatre because he enjoys it too much (p. 5), sets the tone for the entire book. Utterson, Enfield, Lanyon and Poole – the novel's four male characters apart from Jekyll – are continually shown to be skittish about inquiring too deeply either into their own motivations or into the lives of others.

In this context, Jekyll's decision to 'strip off' the shackles of respectability and 'spring headlong into the sea of liberty' (p. 56) is exhilarating. When he is first transformed into Edward Hyde, Jekyll insists that he knew right away that he was 'sold a slave to [his] original evil', but what we are more likely to recall is the sheer joy Jekyll feels at his sudden liberation:

> I came to myself as if out of a great sickness. There was something strange in my sensations, something indescribably new and, from its novelty, incredibly sweet. I felt younger, lighter, happier in body; within I was conscious of a heady recklessness, a current of disordered sensual images running like a mill race in my fancy, a solution of the bonds of obligation, an unknown but not an innocent freedom of the soul. (p. 54).

There is nothing quite like this moment either in Stevenson's earlier work or in the Gothic tradition as a whole. 'I came to myself as if out of a great sickness': it is as if Jekyll has been released from the burden of consciousness, which is to say, released from the burden of the knowledge of sin. Jekyll's claim that Hyde's is not 'an innocent freedom' is unquestionably true, but for a brief moment Stevenson allows himself to imagine the ecstasy of a positively Nietzschean liberation from the shackles of morality.

To posit such a liberation is, of course, immediately to recognise its impossibility. Jekyll's flight from hypocrisy simply leads him to hypocrisy in another form; dualism and duplicity remain closely aligned. Jekyll attempts to put ethical questions to one side in order to indulge a seemingly harmless 'gaiety of disposition' (p. 52) in himself, but the ethics of Hyde's behaviour are never in doubt. 'The Hypocrite let out the beast Hyde', Stevenson wrote with unusual directness in an 1887 letter, 'who is the essence of cruelty and malice, and selfishness and cowardice'.[34] Yet Stevenson never allows *Dr Jekyll and Mr Hyde* become a simple morality tale. Indeed, one reason the tale is so unsettling is that it offers no ready moral at all. In a remarkable letter, Stevenson himself attributed the novel's indeterminacy to an uncomfortable confluence of his 'Scotch Presbyterian preoccupation' with ethical problems and a late Victorian uncertainty about the grounds of ethics:

> What you say about the confusion of my ethics, I own to be all too true [. . .] I have the old Scotch Presbyterian preoccupation with these problems, itself morbid; I have alongside of that a second, perhaps more – possibly less – morbid element – the dazzled incapacity to choose, of an age of transition. The categorical imperative is ever with me, but utters dark oracles [. . .] The Scotch side came out plain in *Dr Jekyll*; the XIXth century side probably baffled me even there, and in most other places baffles me entirely. Ethics are my veiled mistress; I love them, but I know not what they are.[35]

The novel's darkness and pessimism are rooted equally in the Calvinist tradition and in the uncertainties of 'an age of transition'. There is no exit from the situation Henry Jekyll describes at the opening of his 'Full Statement', just as there is no salvation to be found in any of the courses of action open to him. In like manner, Stevenson refuses his readers either the catharsis or the closure typically offered by Gothic fictions. One effect of the novel's multiple narrators is precisely a sense of perpetual anticlimax. The story twice seems about to end only to begin once more, first with Lanyon's narrative and then with Jekyll's. Structurally, ethically, psychologically, Henry Jekyll's 'case' remains suspended and thus unresolved.

CHAPTER FIVE

Stevenson, Scott and Scottish History

Alison Lumsden

In 1866 at the age of only 16 Robert Louis Stevenson wrote an article that was to be published privately by his father. Its title is 'The Pentland Rising' and its subject is a little known Covenanter rebellion culminating with their rout at Rullion Green in the Pentlands. In beginning his literary career in this way Stevenson announces his interest in Scottish history; by choosing a Covenanting theme he aligns himself with Scotland's earlier writers of historical fiction John Galt, James Hogg and most notably Walter Scott. As Barry Menikoff has suggested, however, over time Stevenson has 'lost [his] status' as a writer of 'historical fictions'[1] and on the rare occasions when he is discussed in this way it is often to conclude that his work is operating upon very different principles from Scott's. Jenni Calder, for example, argues that 'Scott clearly intended to provide a narrative of historical interpretation' while 'it is not historical narrative that interests [Stevenson], so much as a cognitive unfolding of personality located in the past.'[2] But Scott is Stevenson's most obvious literary precursor and the two writers may not be as different as recent criticism suggests. In this chapter, therefore, I hope to reassess Stevenson's renegotiation of Scottish historical fiction and, in doing so, his relationship to Walter Scott.

It is hardly surprising that Stevenson himself frequently refers to Scott; when looking for examples from poetry and fiction to illuminate the ideas proposed in his essays he often falls upon the author who is in many respects his literary forefather. There are, for example, numerous references to Scott in his letters and he also features extensively in his essay 'A Gossip on Romance'. Writing about the importance of place in creative inspiration Stevenson suggests that the Hawes Tavern in Queensferry 'seems to wait the coming of the appropriate legend' and continues:

> Americans seek it already for the sake of Lovel and Oldbuck who dined there at the beginning of [Scott's] *The Antiquary*. But you need not tell me – that is not all; there is some story, unrecorded or not yet complete, which must express the meaning of that inn more fully.[3]

More significantly Scott is praised by Stevenson as an example of a writer whose mode is essentially one of romance. Following his now aphoristic statement that 'Fiction is to the grown man what play is to the child' Stevenson points out that fiction which most successfully operates in this way is 'called romance' with Scott being 'out and away the king of the romantics' (p. 61). Qualifying this statement he writes that the strength of the narrative poem *The Lady of the Lake* lies in the fact that 'even after we have flung the book aside, the scenery and adventures remain present to the mind, a new and green possession' (p. 62), while even that 'ill-written, ragged book, *The Pirate*' is for Stevenson 'conceived in the very highest manner of romantic invention' (p. 62). Stevenson also admires *Guy Mannering* because certain moments in the novel provide 'model instance[s] of romantic method' (p. 62). Yet Stevenson is not unequivocal in his praise for Scott, also noting what he regards as the failings of his predecessor with some frustration:

[H]ere we have a man of the finest creative instinct, touching with perfect certainty and charm the romantic junctures of his story; and we find him utterly careless, almost, it would seem, incapable, in the technical matters of style, and not only frequently weak, but frequently wrong in points of drama [. . .] How comes it, then, that he could so often fob us off with languid, inarticulate twaddle? (p. 63)

Stevenson's response to this question is equally ambivalent, for echoing his earlier statement on the relationship between play and fiction he reflects that 'As his books are play to the reader, so they were play to him' and that he is simultaneously 'A great romantic' and 'an idle child' (p. 64).

Stevenson's commentary on Scott in this essay epitomises the ways in which he both aligns himself with Scott and simultaneously distances himself from him. As late as *The Ebb-Tide* Stevenson describes the text he is writing to Colvin as having 'not much Waverley Novels' about it and this pattern of rejecting and emulating Scott is evident throughout Stevenson's approach to historical fiction.[4] It is perhaps this act of distancing that has, in some respects, contributed to a failure to regard Stevenson as a historical novelist in any straightforward sense. While, for example, he praises Scott here for his mastery in the romance mode, romance is itself frequently seen as in binary opposition to history; Scott himself defends his novel *The Tale of Old Mortality* against accusations of historical inaccuracy with the statement that its author was writing 'a romance, and not a history'.[5] Moreover, Stevenson locates his own preference for fiction writing firmly in the romance camp, aligning the mode with a love of 'incident', the passivity of 'circumstance' and, as we have already seen, place. 'There is a vast deal in life and letters [. . .] which does not regard the human will at all, or deals with it in obvious and healthy relations', he writes:

where the interest turns, not upon what a man shall choose to do, but on how he manages to do it; not on the passionate slips and hesitations of the conscience, but on the problems of the body and [. . .] the shock of arms or the diplomacy of life. (p. 54)

Within this aesthetics of passivity, chance and landscape, it is hard to see where Stevenson can engage with the dynamics of historical process. Indeed, 'A Gossip on Romance' almost goes as far as to suggest that the past, and the figures which have peopled Scotland's history, can simply be plundered to flesh out a landscape of romance, and to supply the incident so crucial to Stevenson's romantic aesthetic: 'Give me a highwayman and I was full to the brim; a Jacobite would do, but the highwayman was my favourite dish' (p. 53).

In spite of his admiration for Scott, then, Stevenson's predilection for historical effect over historical process seemingly serves to distance him from him. Georg Lukács, in his seminal work *The Historical Novel* (1937), defines the genre of historical fiction precisely in terms of an articulation of process; writing from an essentially Marxist position he argues that the historical novel operates not by simply depicting historical events, but by demonstrating the ways in which the forces of history operate via violence, rupture and conflict to affect the movement of history. For Lukács, consequently, Scott's work epitomises the genre, since he identifies in it a recurrent paradigm within which Scott, following what we might call a philosophy of Enlightenment stadial development, depicts moments of historical conflict so that he can articulate the negotiation of them towards historical progress. It is, however, hard to reconcile this paradigm with Stevenson's work. If a highwayman is as good (if not better) than a Jacobite, and Stevenson's interest lies in that which is outside of human will, his work would not seem to fit well within a narrative mode which is defined by an interest in historical process and the movement of history.

This lack of historical process or progress lies behind the distinctions made between Scott and Stevenson by modern criticism. Julia Reid, for example, compares Stevenson to Scott directly suggesting that Stevenson replaces Scott's narrative of national progress with one of national tragedy:

Stevenson's sympathies in *Kidnapped* seem to lie with the suffering members of a dying culture. In *Waverley*, the period after the 1745 is depicted as one of national prosperity, and the birth of a new Scotland from the ashes of Jacobite conflict is celebrated with emblematic wedding festivities. *Kidnapped*, by contrast, suggests a much harsher delineation of decaying Highland culture [. . .] Despite its picturesque credentials, then, *Kidnapped* is a bleak novel, charting the often frustrated attempts of the hero, an exile in his own country, to understand an alien culture, and undercutting the meliorist account of Scotland's gradual progress towards civilized modernity. *The Master of Ballantrae* [. . .] renders the same theme of the divided nation in yet more sombre tones.[6]

Jenni Calder observes a similar kind of 'tragic' response to presentation of Scotland in Stevenson's fiction. Examining this via the depiction of Highland landscape in both Scott and Stevenson she argues that they offer very different responses to it and that these encapsulate Scott's optimism at the progressive trajectory of Scottish experience as opposed to the more sceptical and cautious approach that Stevenson epitomises. While Scott, she suggests, offers us a Highland landscape which can still be negotiated and assimilated into a British Union, Stevenson's protagonists find themselves within a landscape that has become alien and defamiliarised: 'The landscape became the possession of the tourist rather than the native' she writes 'and Scott himself helped it to happen'. '[By] the 1880s,' she continues, 'the relationship of human activity to landscape had changed' and it is therefore far harder for Stevenson to be optimistic about that Highland landscape or the consequences of the political and cultural schism which it had come to represent.[7] As a consequence, as William Gray concludes, both *Kidnapped* (1886) and *The Master of Ballantrae* (1888) portray 'a Scottish identity divided against itself', Scott's apparent aesthetics of reconciliation having given way to one of Stevensonian division.[8]

Closer examination of both *Kidnapped* and *The Master of Ballantrae* seems to support these readings of Stevenson's response to Scottish history as one that is essentially tragic and divided. This response to Scotland's violent and disrupted past is in fact pre-empted in his early essay 'The Pentland Rising' when Stevenson suggests that the events he describes are forgotten precisely because they were only the precursor to darker and more tragic events in Scotland's story:

> Two hundred years ago a tragedy was enacted in Scotland, the memory whereof has been in great measure lost or obscured by the deeper tragedies which followed it. It is, as it were, the evening of the night of persecution – a sort of twilight, dark indeed to us, but light as the noonday when compared with the midnight gloom which followed.[9]

Stevenson's use of metaphors of twilight and darkness, day and night are interesting, as they foreshadow a similar kind of rhetorical patterning that recurs in both *The Master of Ballantrae* and *Kidnapped*. The sub-title of the later novel is 'A Winter's Tale' and in 'The Genesis of *The Master of Ballantrae*' Stevenson describes how the novel was conceived on a 'fine frosty night, with no wind and the thermometer below zero' while the family were living in Saranac near the Canadian border. The night was also 'very dark'.[10] Much of the coldness and darkness of the northern winter survives in the text, contributing to its general sense of sterility. On the night of the duel that takes place between the Master and his brother Henry, for example, Mackellar informs us that there was a 'stifling cold' and describes 'some of the spring birds that had already blundered north [. . .] besieging the windows of the house or trotting on the frozen turf like things distracted' (p. 92). By night, he continues, 'it fell dark and still and starless, and exceedingly cold: a night the most unseasonable, fit for strange events' (p. 92). As he returns to the house the presence of free traders necessitates that he extinguishes his candle so that 'blackness fell about [him] groping dark' (p. 105) and of course the frozen ground is evoked again as Alison attempts to thrust the sword into the frozen ground. The end of the novel is also located in a landscape inscribed with images of cold and darkness; as the brothers approach their mutual death we are given an image of Secundra working in the moonlight to dig the Master from the frosty ground.

If images of darkness and cold pervade *The Master of Ballantrae*, so too do images of age and approaching death. While the 'Preface' to the novel is ostensibly by Robert Louis Stevenson, the persona adopted within it is of a man much older than 38, revisiting his native city and 'smitten with an equal regret for what he once was and for what he once hoped to be' (p. xix). His friend too, laments the passing of years, stating that his visit brings back his youth, but 'in a very tattered and withered state' (p. xx). The House of Durrisdeer is also associated with decay, the last lord Henry Durie having died in 1820 and his unmarried sister in 1827, 'not rich' (p. xxi). Similar images pervade Mackellar's narrative, as he describes first of all his own 'white hair' at the time when he writes (p. 1) and the premature aging of the old Master at the time when he arrived at Durrisdeer:

> My old lord, eighth of the name, was not old in years, but he suffered prematurely from the disabilities of age; his place was at the chimney-side; there he sat reading, in a lined gown, with few words for any man, and wry words for none: the model of an old retired housekeeper. (p. 2)

These images of cold and age within *The Master of Ballantrae* reinforce a sense of sterility that is in turn mapped onto the Scotland that Stevenson portrays as a consequence of the historical events that underpin the narrative. While the world of *Kidnapped* is very different from that of *Ballantrae*, it offers images that are potentially equally barren. While much of the action of *The Master of Ballantrae* takes place at night, *Kidnapped* is a novel where events largely occur out of doors and during the day (with the notable exception of David's uncle's attempt to kill him near the opening of the text). Nevertheless, the Scotland that is presented in it is in many ways as sterile as that of the later novel arising from an aridity that comes to encapsulate the Highland landscape.

This formulation of the Highland landscape, as one inscribed with memorials of death and tragedy is again one that Stevenson rehearses (here in a Lowland context) as early as 'The Pentland Rising'. Here he describes the scene on the morning of the battle at Rullion Green:

> The sun, going down behind the Pentlands, cast golden lights and blue shadows on their snow-clad summits, slanted obliquely into the rich plain before them, bathing with rosy splendour the leafless, snow-sprinkled trees, and fading gradually into shadow in the distance. To the south, too, they beheld a deep-shaded amphitheatre of heather and bracken; the course of the Esk, near Penicuik, winding about at the foot of its gorge; the broad, brown expanse of Maw moss; and, fading into blue indistinctness in the south, the wild heath-clad Peeblesshire hills. In sooth, that scene was fair, and many a yearning glance was cast over that peaceful evening scene from the spot where the rebels awaited their defeat; and when the fight was over, many a noble fellow lifted his head from the blood-stained heather to strive with darkening eyeballs to behold that landscape, over which, as o'er his life and his cause, the shadows of night and of gloom were falling and thickening.[11]

This passage moves from a description of a vista – 'the rich plain before them' – to close-up – the figure striving to lift his head from the blood stained heather to behold the landscape, and there is a sense in which this trajectory reflects the varying descriptions of Highland landscape in Scott's and Stevenson's work and the ways in which it operates as a paradigm for Scottish history. The contrast can be easily seen if we compare the opening of Scott's poem *The Lady of the Lake* (commended as romantic by Stevenson in a 'Gossip on Romance') with the 'Flight in the Heather' sections of *Kidnapped*. While in the first the monarch of the glen surveys a Highland landscape from a vantage point ('The noble stag was pausing now, / Upon the mountain's southern brow, / Where broad extended, far beneath, / The varied realms of fair Menteith'),[12] in the second Scotland is seen not from the top of a hill, but with a face pressed into the heather. After enduring many hours baking upon a rock where, rather than the cold of *Ballantrae*, it is heat which causes near death, Alan and David begin to make their way across the heather. David recounts their journey: 'Sometimes, for half an hour together, [they] must crawl from one heather bush to another, as hunters do when they are hard upon the deer'.[13] He continues:

> Some of these had been burned or at least scathed with fire; and there rose in our faces (which were close to the ground) a blinding, choking dust as fine as smoke. The water was long out; and this posture of running on the hands and knees brings an over-mastering weakness and weariness, so that the joints ache and the wrists faint under your weight. (p.155)

As Jenni Calder points out, this is a landscape that has become 'unambigu-ously hostile'[14] – the Highlands that Stevenson presents here in close-up are almost unendurable.

This divergence between the panoramic view of Scotland offered by Scott and the close-up offered by Stevenson is also in many ways representative of the different approaches to history they take in their work, and the implica-tions of historical event which they offer within their texts. Lukács credits Scott with presenting moments of crisis in Scottish history as staging posts towards greater reconciliation and resolution, and in part this is achieved in his work by offering us a vista not only of landscape, but also of time. While *Waverley*, Scott's novel of the 1745 Jacobite rising, is often seen as the quin-tessentially Jacobite novel, it is, in fact, only the first in a series of texts on this historical theme which includes *Rob Roy* and *Redgauntlet*. *Waverley* may be the first to be written but by revisiting the subject in *Rob Roy*, a novel dealing with the 1715 rising, and *Redgauntlet*, set in 1753 and dealing with a fictional attempt at a Jacobite coup, Scott can trace the history of Jacobitism from its earliest manifestations to the point where it largely became an irrel-evance. Similarly, Scott's novels *The Tale of Old Mortality* and *The Heart of Mid-Lothian* both deal with the Covenanting wars which divided Scotland over matters of religious organisation in the seventeenth century and the chronicle structure of *The Heart of Mid-Lothian* again allows Scott to show the trajectory of history over a long span of years. These strategies, arguably, allow Scott the space, and time, to show Scottish history moving towards a process of potential resolution. Stevenson, however, writes far shorter novels and, presenting us a Scotland in close-up, he seems to offer us one that is in fact not healed by moments of crisis, but rather, ravaged.

This is particularly evident in the narrative of *The Master of Ballantrae*. At the opening of the text the Durrisdeer family are faced with a dilemma common to much of Scotland in 1745; to rise for the Stuarts or to remain loyal to the Hanoverian monarchy. They resolve to hedge their bets; seem-ingly adopting a plan which will lead to reconciliation one way or the other after a 'whole day's disputation' they agree to 'steer a middle course, one son going forth to strike a blow for King James, my lord and the other staying at home to keep in favour with King George' (p. 4). Apparently reflecting Stevenson's interest 'not upon what a man shall choose to do, but on how he manages to do it', the family decide to settle the matter of which son will fight by chance; 'Will you stand by the toss of a coin?' asks the Master. This plan seems almost foolproof and one that is designed to mitigate conflict in the wake of the Rising, whatever its outcome. This, however, is not what happens. Rather it becomes the catalyst to a chain of events that sees the brothers locked in a symbiotic conflict that is resolved only by their deaths in the wilderness of America. Rather than producing a historical *process* which leads to resolution, then, Stevenson's novel suggests that this pivotal moment in Scottish history only produces an endless cycle where the two brothers seem doomed to repeat their quarrel until it is ultimately resolved in death.

This lack of historical process is also reinforced by the narrative strategies of the novel that, perhaps more than any of Stevenson's other fictions, leaves readers with no stable ground beneath their feet. As discussed above, the novel is introduced by an editor who claims that he will convey the story 'as it stands' in the packet which he receives from his friend. The narrative is recounted by Ephraim Mackellar, who swears that he will describe events like a 'witness in court' (p. 12) but who, it is quite apparent, is not the most reliable of narrators since he is clearly biased towards Henry, and has already related a 'summary of events' which he can only have gathered from hearsay, or from Henry himself. The narrative is further complicated by the interpolated account of the Master's wanderings by the Chevalier de Burke – what Mackellar calls 'a very varnished version' of what likely took place. At the end of the novel the reader is taken into a narratological as well as a physical wilderness when Mackellar informs us that he will conclude his tale via 'a narrative which [he] has compiled out of three sources' (p. 205). In place of closure or resolution, therefore, *The Master of Ballantrae* offers only fragmentation and uncertainty as the narrative 'splinters off' into indeterminacy.

The narrative structure of *Kidnapped* is far less complex than that of *The Master of Ballantrae*, but it is not unproblematic, as, told from a first person perspective, it too raises questions of reliability and authority. Moreover, like *Ballantrae*, it is far from straightforward in its conclusion. While the final two chapters of the text are entitled 'I come into my Kingdom' and 'Good-Bye' they offer little in the way of closure; while David may comment 'So far as I was concerned myself, I had come to port' (p. 220) he is also left with 'a cold gnawing in [his] inside like a remorse for something wrong' (p. 223) and all the time, he tells us, he is thinking of Alan. Oliver S. Buckton comments that the source of this remorse lies in the fact that 'Alan Breck emerges as the key figure in the novel's historical plot, diverting the narrative away from its concern with inheritance and family and toward a complex engagement with Scotland's Jacobite history.' 'The narrative, and indeed David as narrator,' he concludes 'are "kidnapped" by Alan, the Jacobite who usurps the protagonist's role, determines David's journey, and in his Highland speech contributes the most vital part of the discourse.'[15] In other words, David's novel of quest or *bildungsroman* is 'hijacked' by one of historical significance; while the inheritance plot can be resolved, the discourse of Scottish history remains an indeterminate question, incapable of simple or straightforward resolution, leaving a 'cold gnawing' of something wrong.

These readings of Stevenson's novels demonstrate that his work does not fit comfortably into a paradigm of resolution, reconciliation and historical process or progress, and that in the Lukácsian sense at least this makes his position as a historical novelist problematic. They also imply that if we are to accept Lukács's reading of Walter Scott, he is a very different exponent of the genre from Stevenson. Stevenson, it suggests, offers a more tragic view of the aftermath of the Jacobite Rising than Scott did, writing nearly seventy years before him, and is far more sceptical about the possibility of the progress of history than Scott's work seems to imply. It is, consequently, no surprise that Stevenson should have considered 'The Highland Widow' – arguably the bleakest of all Scott's tales – as his 'masterpiece'.[16] But are these novelists as different in their approach to history as this reading implies?

Scott and Stevenson may indeed have more in common than recent criticism has recognised, not only because it has misread Scott's approach to history and taken Lukács's reading at face value, but, more significantly, because it has also partially misread the ways in which Stevenson's narratives of Scottish history are to be understood. Much of the comparison that is made between Stevenson and Scott is predicated on a strangely outmoded view of the earlier novelist's fiction. In recent years approaches to Scott, often driven by post-structuralist theorising, have acknowledged him as a more complex writer than Lukács's reading comprehends. Several critics have recognised that in spite of what appears to be a dominant trajectory of reconciliation and resolution in his work it is in fact fraught with tensions; while Lukács's reading of Scott may accommodate the bare bones of his narratives there is much within them that resists such straightforward closure.[17] While Scott may appear to validate discourses of progress and historical process recent criticism has identified an emotional residue or excess which spills outside of these to suggest a more complex relationship to Scotland and her troubled past.

Scott himself, in fact, suggests this more complex view of the role of the historical novel on numerous occasions throughout his work, perhaps most significantly in the opening chapter of *The Tale of Old Mortality*. In Scott, opening chapters, dedicatory epistles and prefaces are often significant, this para-textual material functioning as a palimpsest for how we are to read the novel that follows. The preliminary chapter of *The Tale of Old Mortality* is particularly significant since it explores the relationship of text to history and raises the question of how best to commemorate the dead – in this case the Covenanters – and the struggles in which they have fought. The fictional editor of the tale describes how its author Peter Pattieson visits a graveyard; a theme of commemoration is thus introduced from the outset, and the significance of such remembrance articulated:

> [U]pon another two stones which lie beside, may still be read in rude prose, and
> ruder rhyme, the history of those who lie beneath them. They belong, we are

assured by the epitaph, to the class of persecuted Presbyterians who afforded a melancholy subject for history in the times of Charles II. and his successor. In returning from the battle of Pentland Hills, a party of the insurgents had been attacked in this glen by a small detachment of the King's troops, and three or four either killed in the skirmish, or shot after being made prisoners, as rebels taken with arms in their hands. The peasantry continue to attach to the tombs of these victims of prelacy an honour which they do not render to more splendid mausoleums; and, when they point them out to their sons, and narrate the fate of their sufferers, usually conclude, by exhorting them to be ready, should times call for it, to resist to the death in the cause of civil and religious liberty, like their brave forefathers.[18]

The incident recounted here offers a direct link between Scott and Stevenson's essay on the Pentland Rising but it also offers a commentary on the significance of memorial and the purpose of commemoration. This is underpinned when Pattieson encounters the figure of Old Mortality, who has dedicated his life to cleaning the graves of the Covenanters as a kind of 'sacred duty' by which he may '[renew] to the eyes of posterity the decaying emblems of the zeal and sufferings of their forefathers'. Pattieson concludes, however, that 'It is now some years since he has been missed in all his usual haunts, while moss, lichen, and deers-hair, are fast covering those stones to cleanse which was the business of his life.'[19] Pattieson, consequently, chooses to write down the stories that he has heard from Old Mortality and garnered from other sources. The novel which follows thus becomes an act of commemoration in itself, standing not only as a discourse of historical process, but also as a synecdoche for Old Mortality's cleaning of the graves.

As Catherine Jones has identified, much of Scott's work is concerned with different kinds of memory and the ways in which these can impinge upon historical narrative. In the preliminary chapter of *The Tale of Old Mortality* Scott offers his readers an alternative model of historical fiction, one based not on historical process, but rather, on text as commemorative act. This is an impulse which can be found elsewhere in Scott's work, and is in fact his proclaimed purpose for the Waverley Novels; in *Waverley* he writes that he hopes that 'to elder persons it will recall scenes and characters familiar to their youth' while to 'the rising generation the tale may present some ideas of the manners of their forefathers'.[20] But what of Stevenson? If we consider that in addition to an analysis of historical process Scott may also be offering us an idea of the historical novel as an act of commemoration, is it possible that Stevenson's work is also engaging with history upon similar principles? Certainly this at least seems to be a possibility if we again return to Stevenson's first engagement with Scotland's history, 'The Pentland Rising'. Just as Scott's novel opens in a graveyard this essay opens with an epigraph which is taken from a gravestone; an inscription from the monument to the

Covenanting martyrs in Greyfriars' Churchyard in Edinburgh: 'Halt, passenger; take heed what thou dost see, / This tomb doth show for what some
men did die.' The opening of the text, moreover, overtly announces itself as
a memorial or commemoration of sorts, designed to re-inscribe in its readers'
minds the memory of something which has been forgotten: 'Two hundred
years ago a tragedy was enacted in Scotland, the memory whereof has been
in great measure lost or obscured by the deeper tragedies which followed it.'[21]
The text ends with a call to readers to have sympathy for those who have
fallen, urging that they be 'charitable to what was evil, and honest to what
was good about the Pentland insurgents'.[22] However, this is in part disingenu-
ous; if the event has been forgotten, as the writer claims at the outset, it is no
longer contentious. What is most important here is not the response that the
reader may have to the event, but rather that the event itself should not be
forgotten, that it should be commemorated in the act of writing just as it is on
the memorial in Greyfriars' Churchyard.

There has been much theorising of commemoration in recent years. As
Kerwin Klein demonstrates, the concept of 'memory studies' emerged in
the twentieth century in the work of writers like Pierre Nora and is often
seen as offering a critique of historical discourse: 'the emergence of *memory*
promises to rework *history*'s boundaries' he claims, describing how it is often
seen as arising from the trauma of the twentieth century and offering a 'mode
of discourse natural to people without history' thus emerging as 'a salutary
feature of decolonization'.[23] If these explanations of the rise of the concept of
memory are correct, it is hardly surprising that we should see it emerge as a
literary trope in literature dealing with the trauma of the Jacobite Rising and
the eradication of Highland culture that ensued in its wake.

It is also an aesthetic that seems in many ways suitable for Stevenson since
it is consistent with his general philosophy elsewhere. That Stevenson should
reject a version of historical fiction based on process is hardly surprising since
throughout both his essays and his fictional work he offers an approach that
is repeatedly anti-teleological, insisting, rather, on a philosophy of 'travelling
hopefully' rather than arrival. While this philosophy is perhaps most clearly
articulated in the essay 'El Dorado' it in fact imbues much of Stevenson's
writing and is particularly clear in the essay 'Crabbed Age and Youth':

> All opinions, properly so called, are stages on the road to truth. It does not
> follow that a man will travel any further; but if he has really considered the
> world and drawn a conclusion, he has travelled as far [. . .]
>
> Because I have reached Paris, I am not ashamed of having passed through
> Newhaven and Dieppe. They were very good places to pass through, and I am
> none the less at my destination. All my old opinions were only stages on the
> way to the one I now hold, as itself is only a stage on the way to something
> else.[24]

Rather than a philosophy of personal 'stadial development' Stevenson suggests that human experience does not necessarily evolve towards improvement but simply changes; all stages in that journey should be valued – and perhaps remembered – because of what they contribute to the journey.

This philosophy also explains the emphasis that Stevenson places upon the importance of incident in his work since incident in fact offers an alternative to process. In 'A Gossip on Romance' he suggests that the use of incident (along with place) in the romance mode allows the writer to evoke particular images that will resonate in the reader's mind:

> Other things we may forget; we may forget the words, although they are beautiful; we may forget the author's comment, although perhaps it was ingenious and true; but these epoch-making scenes, which put the last mark of truth upon a story and fill up, at one blow, our capacity for sympathetic pleasure, we so adopt into the very bosom of our mind that neither time nor tide can efface or weaken the impression. This, then, is the plastic part of literature: to embody character, thought, or emotion in some act or attitude that shall be remarkably striking to the mind's eye. This is the highest and hardest thing to do in words. (p. 56)

For the Romantic writers of the earlier part of the century the relationship between memory and creativity was of course crucial, memory feeding into creativity, and creativity allowing for the generation of new memories via poetry. It is, similarly, the capacity of romance 'to embody character, thought, or emotion in some act or attitude that shall be remarkably striking to the mind's eye' that makes it so appealing to Stevenson, and it is what he admires in Scott, 'the king of romantics'. It is in effect an aesthetics of remembering, for while, as we can see here, much may be forgotten about a literary text, its purpose, for Stevenson, is to create a kind of emotional residue via the mind's eye that will remain as a commemoration.

If we approach texts such as *Kidnapped* and *The Master of Ballantrae* with this in mind we can begin to see that Scott and Stevenson may have more in common than the paradigm of historical process may suggest. Barry Menikoff has demonstrated that Stevenson took far more care with the production of *Kidnapped* than his positioning of it as 'no furniture for the scholar's library' (p. xi) seems to suggest, arguing that 'sources were [. . .] the lifeblood of his fiction' and that the novel was based on meticulous research. He also acknowledges, however, that Stevenson's great gift is imaginative, so that his historical fiction is 'a statement on the power of art to reclaim the past and reconstitute its victims and its villains'.[25] Stevenson himself acknowledges the imaginative premise of the novel suggesting that its purpose is to 'steal some young gentleman's attention from his Ovid, carry him awhile into the Highlands and the last century, and pack him to bed with some engaging images to mingle with his dreams' (p. xi). While this statement is couched in typically throwaway terms it suggests a desire to commemorate, to ensure that certain episodes in Scotland's past are not forgotten. The artistic purpose of *Kidnapped* is to provide a novel that will resonate in the reader's mind, which will capture the imagination (as indeed it has for so many readers) rather than provide a critique of the historical process of Jacobitism.

Commemoration is inscribed in the very fabric of the novel, for it is one in which David Balfour is made to remember much that he would like to forget. This operates at both a personal and a national level, for the text opens with David's discovery of his own identity – the relationship he bears to the House of Shaws (p. 2). But personal identity soon gives way to national identity and here too David has much to learn. The catalyst for this discovery is, of course, Alan Breck and the chapter 'I Hear of the Red Fox' provides a cat-echism of Scotland's recent past, and initiates a reassessment of what David has believed to be a straightforward division between Whig and Jacobite in Scottish politics. This is enhanced once he finds himself in the Highlands where he encounters people unlike those he had imagined to exist in his own country alongside political dynamics of which he has been unaware:

> They seemed in great poverty; which was no doubt natural, now that rapine was put down, and the chiefs kept no longer an open house; and the roads (even such a wandering, country by-track as the one I followed) were infested with beggars. And here again I marked a difference from my own part of the country. For our Lowland beggars – even the gownsmen themselves, who beg by patent – had a louting, flattering way with them, and if you give them a plack and asked change, would very civilly return you a boddle. But these Highland beggars stood on their dignity, asked alms only to buy snuff (by their account) and would give no change. (p. 101)

While David's journey through Highland landscapes, culture and moral values in the company of Alan forces him to reassess his understanding of his country, its politics, and his naïve assumption that one set of moral or ethical standards can be transferred without question to a different set of cir-cumstances, the reader is left with a sense that to weigh up the evidence and make moral judgments is not quite the point of the text. As Edward Eigner has pointed out, Stevenson is not interested in morally 'separating the sheep from the goats' and this is also true when dealing with Scottish politics.[26] *Kidnapped* is not a text in which we are necessarily asked to sympathise with the Jacobites – Alan Breck is presented far too equivocally for that and this is compounded by the presentation of Jacobites in *Catriona*. Rather, like David, the reader is simply invited to acknowledge this episode in Scottish history. If, as Stevenson hopes, the purpose of fiction is to produce an image in the mind's eye of the reader that will resonate emotionally, the three 'Flight in the Heather' sections clearly achieve this. Remembered by most readers as occupying more of the novel than it actually does, David's gruelling journey pursued by Redcoats serves to remain with the reader as a reminder of this painful episode in Scottish history; for those who already know this history it also serves as a subtle reminder of the trials faced by Charles Edward Stuart following Culloden. The 'remorse for something wrong' that both David and the reader feels at the end of the novel is, consequently, not a remorse which stems necessarily from a sympathy with Alan (or the Stuart cause), but from a sense that we have been awakened to an aspect of Scottish history that we may have forgotten, or even prefer to choose to forget. Stevenson is not encouraging his readers to work their way through the moral maze of Scottish politics, but to journey into the Highlands, and to add to our imaginative story of Scotland the resonant memory of this episode in Scottish life.

If *Kidnapped* operates as a memorial of sorts, however, *The Master of Ballantrae* does so much more overtly. Oliver Buckton notes the ways in which this novel alludes to Scott's historical fiction commenting that 'much of Stevenson's narrative apparatus – the use of "editors" and other figures who mediate between text and reader; the distant historical setting; and the first-person narrator – derives from Sir Walter Scott and represents Stevenson's professional investment in the historical novel'.[27] However, what he does not note is that Stevenson uses this apparatus, as Scott does, to set up his text as an act of commemoration. This is indeed evident in the Preface where the ostensible editor of the text states that he has only a dim memory of the history of the Durrisdeer family, gleaned from tradition and fragments of memoir:

> 'To say truth,' said I, 'I have only seen some dim reference to the things in memoirs; and heard some traditions dimmer still, through my uncle [. . .] My uncle lived when he was a boy in the neighbourhood of St. Bride's; he has often told me of the avenue closed up and grown over with grass; the great gates never opened, the last lord and his old-maid sister who lived in the back parts of the house [. . .] and, to the country folk, faintly terrible from some deformed traditions.' (p. xxi)

The text that consequently ensues can be seen as a kind of surplus to dim memory, filling in the gaps in the fictional historical record. The need for such a record of the past is also inscribed within the text itself. Mackellar, in fact, states this as his aim in writing his memoirs claiming 'I think it is not fit that so much evidence should perish; the truth is a debt I owe my lord's memory; and I think my old years will flow more smoothly, and my white hair lie quieter on the pillow, when the debt is paid' (p. 1). Similarly, upon writing to the Chevalier de Burke so that he can be 'very exact as to the adventures of the Master after Culloden' Mackellar reports that he is 'somewhat embarrassed by his response; for he sent me the complete memoirs of his life, touching only in places on the Master [. . .] he begged [. . .] that I would find a publisher' (p. 27).

These references within the text to the need for commemoration alert us to the fact that the text itself, consequently, may be read as a memorial. While 'The Pentland Rising' opens with an inscription from a gravestone, *The Master of Ballantrae* ends with an inscription on the makeshift tombstone of the two brothers. Mackellar recounts how he himself has arranged for the inscriptions to be 'chiselled on a boulder' in the America wilderness. James's inscription includes the comment that he 'lies here forgotten' (p. 233); Henry's comments on his 'life of unmerited distress' (p. 234). Neither stone makes any mention of the Jacobite Rising that has caused the brothers' initial quarrel. The novel, consequently, stands in place of what the tombstones omit, acting as a commemoration of that event; not so that it can offer a critique of the rights and wrongs of this episode in Scotland's past – the tossing of the coin has removed the text from that sphere – but so that it can rework the boundaries of historical discourse to remind the reader of the pain and division that lie behind Scotland's official narrative of historical progress.

Both *Kidnapped* and *The Master of Ballantrae*, then, suggest that Stevenson's interest in the historical novel lies with a negotiation of what should and should not be forgotten in Scotland's past, his aesthetic of romance providing an imaginative reminder of the significance of 'not forgetting'. This negotiation is also one that can be seen in a far less familiar text 'The Misadventures of John Nicholson'. Written for Cassell's Christmas Annual in 1887 this story takes as its historical framework a far more recent event in Scotland's troubled history; the Disruption of 1843. Essentially involving a quarrel concerning the relationship of the state to the Established Church of Scotland, the Disruption harked back to the struggles of the Covenanters and resulted in 474 ministers breaking away to form the Free Church of Scotland. While involving no bloodshed, the event caused significant schism in Scottish religious and cultural life. 'The Misadventures of John Nicholson' opens by positioning itself within this discourse, describing its protagonist's father as 'enthroned [. . .] on the heights of the Disruption Principles'.[28] This opening to the story suggests that the tale that follows will concern itself with this historical event and a reader familiar with Scottish history might suppose that the 'misadventures' of its protagonist will – like so many others in Scottish fiction – stem from the severity of the father's religious principles and the implications they have for the Scottish psyche. This, however, is not the case. The story that ensues is one of a random series of events leading to a grisly account of John's dilemmas. In the spirit of the Christmas Annual in which it appeared, however, it ends – somewhat artificially – with all former sins of the prodigal being forgotten, his troubles resolved and with marriage to his childhood sweetheart; 'the family' we are told 'was welded once more into a fair semblance of unity' (p. 202). More significantly, the issue of church politics is not referred to again and seemingly disappears from the narrative after its opening pages.

So in what sense does the 'The Misadventures of John Nicholson' operate by an aesthetic of commemoration? The simple answer is that it does not. But by opening with this significant event in Scottish history and then evading it, this tale too offers us a negotiation of the relationship of fictive memory to history. As the narrator tells us in the opening pages, Disruption politics are, in one sense, irrelevant even at the time of the controversy: 'A stranger to the tight little theological kingdom of Scotland might have listened and gathered literally nothing [. . .] there was a vast world outside, to whom Disruption Principles were as the chatter of tree-top apes' (pp. 137–8). There are, this tale seems to imply, some episodes which are best forgotten, which do not need commemoration; *The Master of Ballantrae*, however, was written only a year later and in it Stevenson reminds us of those things which, on the other hand, should not be allowed to pass into oblivion.

Kerwin Klein argues that 'Memory [. . .] figures as a therapeutic alternative to historical discourse' and can 'pour presence back into the past'.[29] While official historiography is bound to encompass all aspects of a national story within it – and perhaps offer a critique of them as elements in a historical process – commemoration can select those events that are most worthy of remembrance. The novel, as Stevenson defines it within his own aesthetics of romance, is uniquely placed to 'pour presence into the past'. It is this impulse for commemoration that links Stevenson to Scott; while Stevenson may apparently differ from Scott in a faith in historical process, he nevertheless learns from this 'great romantic' and 'idle child' that the past is best kept alive through some 'thought, or emotion [or] some act or attitude that shall be remarkably striking to the mind's eye'. His novels, consequently, stand as memorials to Scotland's past, reminding us of what should not be 'lost or obscured' within it.

CHAPTER SIX

Travel Writing

Caroline McCracken-Flesher

Stolen away and then shipwrecked, David Balfour heads for home through unfamiliar lands. The hero of *Kidnapped* is thus an explorer as well as the reader's guide. But given his dual role, it is a question whether he knows where he is going. Stevenson helpfully insisted on a map for David's travels, yet that map fails to place our Davie. Stevenson wrote: 'a red line is to show the wanderings of my hero [. . .] It must be sometimes dotted to show uncertainty.'[1] Nonetheless, generations have rushed to follow in the footsteps of Stevenson's characters, and even of the writer himself.[2] Stevenson's travel writing mapped France, America and the Pacific not just for eager tourists, but for writers in search of appropriate literary style. This chapter asks what route these various imitators follow. Does Stevenson lay a clear path in place, and does he map out a distinct mode of travel writing? We will track the topographical dashes and the stylistic spaces to discover that in the end, our voyage lies not across the land, but across the shifting terrain of Robert Louis Stevenson's mind. Stevenson himself changes through his encounter with unknown places and people, and his involved sensibility reconfigures the literary landscape for travel writing.

Our discussion superficially repeats the opposition between tourist and traveller that arose in the early nineteenth century and was firmly in place by the 1930s – thus bracketing Stevenson. James Buzard recognises an early distinction between the terms in a *Fraser's Magazine* declaration of 1849 – 'he was rather a tourist than a traveller' – and sees them confirmed as opposed values in Evelyn Waugh's 1930 comment that 'every Englishman abroad, until it is proved to the contrary, likes to consider himself a traveller and not a tourist'.[3] Stevenson, we might assume, was a traveller, hacking a trail through hostile geographical and literary landscapes, and – David Livingstone-wise – occasionally disappearing off the map. His imitators would then occupy the Cook's Tour charabanc, following merrily and thoughtlessly behind. However, if we are always travellers, but tourists are those other people, then the split between the exploratory traveller, actively engaged with the landscape, and the tourist supposedly moving across that landscape like a package in transit, is a function of how we see ourselves socially. In fact, situated at the crossover point of money and status – where money gives access to experiences generally reserved for a class not only leisured but entitled – movement in a landscape challenges both geographical and sociological boundaries. It points to an inward journey. Thus, as Judith Adler says:

> the traveler whose activity lends itself to conceptual treatment as art is one whose movement serves as a medium for bestowing meaning on the self and the social, natural, or metaphysical realities through which it moves. Performed as an art, travel becomes one means of 'worldmaking'[. . .] and of self-fashioning.[4]

Which is to say that the literary space between tourist and traveller is always one of the mind. It is this inward landscape, which we too easily obscure behind the oppositions of tourism and travelling, that is mapped by Robert Louis Stevenson. This is the route that his best imitators follow – but on their own behalf.

Stevenson tracked geographical places and literary spaces that were already thoroughly overrun and written about. Nigel Leask and Mary Louise Pratt describe a world caught in the linguistic web of colonialism, curiosity and incipient capitalism. Leask defines the 'Romantic Traveller' in whom curiosity about antique lands meets modernity in the form of the transcendental self.[5] Pratt traces the interplay of developing perspectives: science battles with sentiment; travellers express their colonial and economic power, but simultaneously claim to be suffering in a foreign and hostile space – a space Pratt terms the 'contact zone'.[6] Each encounter, generated by the search for health, commerce, or converts, entertainment or education, spawns a discourse – of exploration or description, science or sentiment, triumph or survival. And each discourse deploys its techniques, such as the aesthetics, dense description and masterly tone of the explorer Richard Burton, the irony of Mary Kingsley – who fled her family to anthropologise elsewhere – the distance and cynicism of the 'flâneur' (languid man about town), or the bathos of a Baedeker – the German guidebook trusted by a generation of European tourists. Stevenson, indeed, journeyed through a France overrun with artists and already depicted in their terms; he travelled in an American west circumscribed by the dime novel; in the South Seas, he followed in the wake of Captain Cook and Herman Melville. As James Buzard says, the experience of travel is 'surrounded and regulated by a variety of guiding texts'.[7] Moreover, authors must 'work within the boundaries mapped out by those prior texts or somehow [. . .] stake out new territories with one's own text'. This was no easy task.

As a Scot, Stevenson occupied an even more troubled literary space. Walter Scott, that trail-blazer across the genres of poetry and the novel, was his compatriot and predecessor: Scott's 1810 poem *The Lady of the Lake* had contributed to the modern tourist industry by converting Scotland's geographical and historical spaces into romantic places. When in 1822 George IV – a fan of Walter Scott – travelled north of the border, attired himself in tartan, and insisted on Scottish dancing, the tourist experience was confirmed as Scottish.[8] Stevenson's 'home' itself was overwritten as 'away' – so much so that Stevenson called his fellows in Edinburgh 'chartered tourists'.[9]

Given these difficulties, Stevenson works in interesting ways to place himself within the discourses of travel. Stevenson was perfectly capable of meeting the genre's different modes. Writing from Scotland's north coast in 1868, where he went to learn about his family's engineering work, the 18-year-old mimics the informational guide book: 'Wick lies at the end or elbow of an open triangular bay, hemmed on either side by shores, either cliff or steep earth-bank, of no great height.' He also turns an anthropological eye on the colourful natives, though still in Scotland:

> The girl here tells me that she was a fortnight in bed of the Wick Revival [. . .] A fearful sermon was given; and a woman near the pulpit began screaming in a dreadful manner [. . .] I asked if she knew any of the people who had made a vow during the period and if there were any change in 'em.[10]

Stevenson's 'Foreign Children' from A Child's Garden of Verses (1885) mocks the superior tones of empire in the language of naïve children:

> Little Indian, Sioux or Crow,
> Little frosty Eskimo,
> Little Turk or Japanee,
> O! don't you wish that you were me![11]

'The Canoe Speaks', from Underwoods (1887), turns to the picturesque and sentimental:

> On the great streams the ships may go [. . .]
> But I, the egg-shell pinnace, sleep
> On crystal waters ankle-deep [. . .]
> I, the unnamed, inviolate,
> Green, rustic rivers, navigate.[12]

And the posthumously-printed 'The Tropics Vanish' privileges nostalgia. Stevenson's wife Fanny noted, moreover, that Stevenson's occasional tendency to the scientific view came to bear in the South Seas: 'He had got [. . . books] on Melanesian languages, books on the origin of the South Sea peoples, and all sorts of scientific pamphlets and papers.'[13] Thus far, Stevenson might seem caught within the conventions of travel writing.

Stevenson seldom, however, used the discourses of travel unselfconsciously. In fact he sensed early on that travel writing brought into question the writing self. Even at Wick, Stevenson's eye turns toward himself as a participant observer. When a carpenter falls off the staging for the lighthouse, he blithely declares, 'I don't think I was ever so much excited in my life', but the momentary voyeurism is replaced by the shock of disconnection: 'I asked him how he was; but he was a Highlander, and – need I add it? – dickens a word could I understand of his answer. What is still worse I find the people here about [. . .] don't understand *me*.'[14] Stevenson begins in the self-absorption of the teenager; his anthropological interest then suggests a distance between himself and the object of his gaze; as a result, he realises the possibility of a return gaze that posits *him* as the oddity in the landscape. Looking back from Edinburgh, this Stevenson goes on to critique his picturesque sensibility, finding his role as nascent author generally suspect: 'I am mad for nature just now,' he notes, but 'I am never satisfied [. . .] I grow delirious over a wooded aisle [. . . with] a utilitarian, Benthamitical desire to take it and hug it and use and make it a part of myself [. . .] What an egotistical brute I am! self! self! self!' And in this growing awareness, faced with Kirkwall Cathedral on Orkney he makes an admission that might usefully be generalised through the travel writing to come: 'I must fairly give up any hope, and my hope from the first has been feeble, to give you any idea.'[15] As Stevenson works to describe using the standard languages of travel, he realises the impossibility of the task. The problem – but also the potential – of travel writing lies in the author. Here we see Stevenson gradually learning that travel writing is at its most challenging, but also its most interesting, when it maps not the landscape, but the way the landscape is perceived by a complex, unpredictable and self-critical viewer.

Of course, Stevenson did not then simply spring into life as a full-fledged travel writer, capable of enacting and reconceiving the genre. In what follows, we will track his maturation, and that of his writing, as his travels brought him into contact with new places, and into collision with the established modes of writing about them. Stevenson often commented from and about his travels in his letters, and we will draw on those to understand his view of his travel writing, but we concentrate on his published narratives, with their interplay of author, place, genre and audience. It is here that we can understand Stevenson's contribution to a literary field.

Through the 1870s Stevenson tested the parameters of the personal and literary problem he had encountered at Wick. In 1873, under doctor's orders he abandoned plans to take the English Bar exam and fled his parents to Mentone in the south of France. This experience produced his first commercially-published essay, 'Ordered South' (1874), which harks back to eighteenth-century travels in search of a cure, with all their embarrassments

and difficulties.[16] Various ambles through France and Scotland turn into
'Walking Tours' (1876). The article echoes a tradition that includes the feats
of the celebrated Captain Barclay (who walked a thousand miles in a thousand hours for a thousand guineas), and the wanderings of Wordsworth and
Carlyle, but was now taking the tone of the flâneur.[17] In these early essays,
the author's perspective is the subject. But such an emphasis oddly separates
the writer and the reader from the landscape. In 'Ordered South', the sufferer
searching for health 'seems to himself to touch things with muffled hands,
and to see them through a veil'.[18] The glib pedestrian of 'Walking Tours' con-
siders the landscape 'quite accessory' in comparison to 'certain jolly humours'
that he carries with him.[19] This traveller is removed from the experience
that surrounds him. All is inward. Yet the reader learns little even about
this authorial persona. The 'sense of distance' that grows upon the speaker
in 'Ordered South', divorced from experience by failing bodily capacity,
extends over us. And we are kept at bay by Stevenson's casual, insulting tone.
The seeker for health is 'like an enthusiast leading about with him a stolid,
indifferent tourist'.[20] For the walker, 'to be properly enjoyed, a walking tour
should be gone upon alone. If you go in company, or even in pairs, it is no
longer a walking tour in anything but name; it is something else and more in
the nature of a picnic.'[21] Granted that Stevenson was himself ill and travelling for a cure when he wrote 'Ordered South', it is nonetheless significant
that two of the common motives for travel – seeking health or entertainment
– fail to translate movement in this landscape into meaningful experience.
Stevenson's personal engagement with places and persons will become the
dynamic force of his travel writing. But here the writer's perspective maintains a distance between him, the landscape and the reader. It actually pre-
vents us from entering either the geographical or the literary landscape.

  Never one to flee a problem, Stevenson wrestled with the relation between
the world, the text and the perceiver as he worked to present his home city
to readers of the *Portfolio* magazine in the essays that became *Edinburgh:
Picturesque Notes* (1879).[22] Edinburgh intensified the difficulty not just
because it was both 'home' and a tourist destination, but because, as many
critics have demonstrated, Stevenson loved yet also hated the place. This
would be a test of Stevenson's involvement in a sense of place and his technique. Now, Stevenson resists placing himself within the city even as he
introduces it to others. An odd pronominal adjustment demonstrates not what
'I' can tell from my experience, but what 'you' see: 'the feeling grows upon
you', and 'there may be seen' – presumably by you – all sorts of sights from
which the narrator seems perversely removed. Yet this official tone of tourist
catalogues and guide books oddly connects us to the narrator. He may stand
aloof, but we literary tourists stand in his shoes: 'To the east you may catch at
sunset the spark of the May lighthouse.' Moreover, those outside look in and

see us. '[P]eople on the decks of ships, or ploughing in quiet country places over in Fife, can see the banner on the Castle battlements', that site where we stand as facsimile locals and therefore touristic artefacts. The Edinburgh author claims little. Instead, he projects the external gaze that constitutes the city from afar:

> It was, I suppose, from this distant aspect that [Edinburgh] got her nickname of *Auld Reekie*. Perhaps it was given her by people who had never crossed her doors: day after day, from their various rustic Pisgahs, they had seen the pile of building on the hill-top, and the long plume of smoke over the plain; so it appeared to them.[23]

Home and away, insider and outsider, are intertwined by the dynamics of the gaze.

Where, then, does our local guide stand? Stevenson places himself outside, using a distinct language of exploration. Colonial travel literature privileged a discourse of survival – through perils unknown, adventurers fought their way home, surviving to tell the tale.[24] Stevenson uses his rare first person to insist on himself as 'a survivor', so we might expect him now to be at home. However, '[O]ne of the vilest climates under heaven', which makes him sick, relocates this narrator among those who 'aspire angrily after that Somewhere-else of the imagination'.[25] Represented as a survivor, Stevenson has escaped the travails usually associated with travel but – counter to the established genre and unlike sufferers from Robinson Crusoe to Richard Burton – into a place that is not home. Aspiring angrily, the writer resists the limitations of place ('home', in particular) and implies his location lies elsewhere. His anger, however, expresses his close relationship with Edinburgh and forges an emotional bond with us literary tourists. It reveals travel with Robert Louis Stevenson to be an uncomfortably inward experience.

It is Stevenson's vexed positioning, using but calling into question the terms essential to travel writing, and being himself affected by those choices, that he gives to the genre in formation. For Stevenson, neither the tourist who supposedly slips along the surfaces of experience, nor the traveller who presumes the luxury of a transparent and authentic connection with geographic and human landscapes, can escape the tensions that are caused by their presence as part of those very landscapes.

The language of nineteenth-century criticism struggled to accommodate this complexity in Stevenson. In terms still echoed today, the *Scotsman* newspaper – perhaps with a hint of Edinburgh chagrin – read across Stevenson's tone the 'cynical humour' of the flâneur: 'a well-bred lounger [. . .] not deeply interested in anything'. Yet the paper wrestled positively and negatively with the phenomenon central to its criticism: Stevenson's role in his own text.

'The faculty is in him,' it mused, 'he has a gift of style; style with a distinct individuality in it, which would be altogether charming if the individuality were less obtrusive.' Perhaps Stevenson needed to be a bit less 'egotistical', this critic suggested.[26] But it was Stevenson's ego, and specifically its entanglements in a landscape, that had already proved crucial in the 1878 *An Inland Voyage*.

In *An Inland Voyage*, Stevenson began to show himself as changed by his outward voyage. With his friend Walter Simpson, Stevenson had spent August and September of 1876 on a canoe trip through north-east France. In his Preface to the resulting book, the author wonders whether 'I might not only be the first to read these pages, but the last as well; that I might have pioneered this very smiling tract of country all in vain, and find not a soul to follow in my steps.'[27] His consequent strategy, however, is not what we might predict. He does not work to sell the book, making no argument for it or for the pleasures of canoeing through Europe. Rather, he places himself in relation to the text: 'The more I thought, the more I disliked the notion [of remaining unread and unfollowed]; until the distaste grew into a sort of panic terror' (p. xvii). This is not the distanced self of *Edinburgh*. Moreover, Stevenson insists the book 'contains not a single reference to the imbecility of God's universe.' It is thus not the work of the cynical flâneur. By contrast, this over-involved speaker 'rushed into this Preface, which is no more than an advertisement for readers' (p. xvii), and shows the intensity of his feelings by a dedication no less anxious than it is elegant. He jokes, rather pathetically, 'To the friend who accompanied me I owe many thanks already [. . .] but at this moment I feel towards him an almost exaggerated tenderness. He, at least, will become my reader' (p. xviii). This speaker requires other figures in his landscape. Without their gaze, he himself may not belong – or worse, he may not make his mark on the genre.

Nonetheless, the geographical and human relationships that place the writer in the landscape may equally undermine him in literature. Afloat on his river trip, Stevenson declared: '[A]n easy book may be written and sold, with mighty little brains about it, where the journey is of a certain seriousness and can be named.'[28] As he wrote *An Inland Voyage*, Stevenson discovered that the relationships invited by travel and its terms might produce a less ordered text, and even name the author anew. The problem looms large from the beginning: four short chapters in, the writer ponders degrees of belonging and thus of identity. We can live happily, he says, where we know nobody, for 'You are content to become a mere spectator'; 'in a place where you have taken some root you are provoked out of your indifference'; '[b]ut in a strange town, not small enough to grow too soon familiar [. . .] you have so little human interest around you that you do not remember yourself to be a man' (p. 19). We are unstable according to our relationships to places and persons. The landscape may shift around us travellers, but it is we who change. Stevenson pushes the point when he meets the driver of the hotel omnibus: 'How he longed to travel! he told me [. . .] "I drive to the station. Well. And then I drive back again." [. . .] Might not this have been a brave African traveller?' (pp. 19–20). We stagger unpredictably between the lure of the foreign and the stasis of belonging.

Stevenson, too, stands subject to the conditions he observes. As British author and 'superior' national and literary subject, Stevenson sometimes tries to take charge of this destabilising landscape. 'Boom,' he sweepingly declares, is 'not a nice place' (p. 4). By their travels, Stevenson and his companion expressed a range of British superiorities: Stevenson was yet again indulging in a luxury easily available only to the middle class and above – getting away from his parents; his travel advertised his family's monied status; the mode of travel (by boat) implied not just disposable income, but leisure time. This Stevenson clearly did not belong – he merely passed through. But within the landscape, often wet, muddy and hungry, Stevenson and Walter Simpson could only be read negatively by the locals. In fact, these scions of British respectability are repeatedly taken for pedlars – people who move between and slip below the social categories defined by belonging in place. The inn at Quartes rejects their patronage with a question not even directed to them: 'These gentlemen are pedlars?' (p. 27). Trying to get lodging at the butchers, they hear again: 'These gentlemen are pedlars?' And 'pedlars' alternates unfortunately with 'the like of you' until Simpson vents: 'Good God, what it must be to be a pedlar in reality!' (p. 74). Meeting actual, well-to-do pedlars does not help, for Stevenson and his companion cannot live up to the type: 'M. Hector was more at home, indeed, and took a higher tone with the world [. . .] on the ground of his driving a donkey–cart' (p. 33). 'Pedlar' turns out to be the watch-word for the sense of self that is constantly adjusted as we move through the landscape.

No traveller, it seems – not even the author – can remain unaltered within the experience they generate. It is this discomfort that allows the great insight of *An Inland Voyage*, and its contribution to the genre of travel writing. Having been turned away from inns, capsized in the torrent, and generally compromised as that dominant figure the British author in an age both of travel and tourism, Stevenson ultimately recognises that 'What philosophers call *me* and *not-me*, *ego* and *non ego*, preoccupied me whether I would or no' (p. 93). And what that means proves surprising: 'There was less *me* and more *not-me* than I was accustomed to expect [. . .] I had dwindled into quite a little thing in a corner of myself [. . .] Thoughts presented themselves unbidden; they were not my thoughts, they were plainly some one else's; and I considered them like a part of the landscape' (pp. 93–4). The outward voyage has broken the barriers between self and circumstance.

The changing self became more and more the subject even as Stevenson's journeys pushed him along more difficult by-ways and further afield. In September to October of 1878, Stevenson took a walking tour through France, assisted only by the donkey Modestine. *Travels with a Donkey in the Cevennes* (1879) intersects with two primary discourses of tourism. James Buzard remembers 'the etymology of "travel" in the word "travail"'.[29] Travel as travail itself harks back to pilgrimage, and Stevenson writes to his friend Sidney Colvin that, '*we are all travellers in what John Bunyan calls the wilderness of this world – all, too, travellers with a donkey*'.[30] But in Stevenson's now complex handling, the travail and the pilgrimage fail to establish either his worldly or his sacred credentials. Stevenson abases himself, but his suffering points to no mighty end.

On his inland voyage, Stevenson had joined the locals to mock a tourist who voyaged in a steamer and 'came ashore at all the locks and asked the name of the villages [. . .] and then he wrote, wrote them down. Oh, he wrote enormously!' (p. 47). Yet he himself was mocked by an old man who challenged the wilful difficulty of his trip: 'it was nothing but locks, locks, locks, the whole way [. . .] "Get into a train, my little young man," said he, "and go you away home to your parents"' (p. 38). Perhaps on the basis of these experiences, Stevenson advertises his trip through the Cevennes as misguided and even ostentatious. But notably, Stevenson's suffering extends beyond silliness into cruelty and culpability, and thus into a much more trenchant consideration of the self that emerges in the matrix of travel and tourism.

Travelling with a donkey, Stevenson depicts himself repeatedly as unable to engage with the situation: he orders the wrong pack for the animal; he loses his way and has to chase reluctant villagers for help. Yet his suffering makes him the centre of every gaze. When he struggles with the donkey's pack 'it toppled and fell down upon the other side. Judge if I was hot! And yet not a hand was offered to assist me.' The local watching him 'told me I ought to have a package of a different shape'. Such trials produce bad behaviour from the author, bringing this traveller uncomfortably into his own eye: 'I suggested [. . .] he might hold his tongue. And the good-natured dog agreed with me smilingly' (p. 154). Modestine, the donkey, in particular poses a test of character that this Stevenson persona conspicuously fails. Stevenson sets out with 'fatuous content' (p. 149), but the donkey's limitations provoke him to violence. The self-satisfied travails of the traveller are thereby displaced onto the truly suffering animal until 'The sound of my own blows sickened me' (p. 153). So the sufferings that should uplift the human abase him below the beast in his own opinion. Consequently, when Stevenson eases Modestine's task by sharing her burden (rather too late to help her), he has become what he prefigured as he set forth, another – but less worthy – pack animal: 'an ox [. . .] to the slaughter' (p. 149). And when Stevenson parts with the donkey he has hurt, his tears that could atone for his behaviour if this was a pilgrimage (though not excuse or undo it), only connect him with her last maudlin yet brutal owner. Thus, Stevenson suggests that a traveller is not just recast by his experiences; he is essential to them – implicated according to the landscape of his own perceptions. The perspective he brings may turn on the blot that he is – and that he must recognise himself to be.

It is important to note, however, that even as Stevenson tested the genre of travel writing, he also wrote in a more conventional mode. His 1884 essay 'Fontainebleau', derived from his early trips to the artist colonies in France with his cousin Bob Stevenson, and later with Fanny Osbourne (both artists), hints at discord among local artists, but it dwells on the picturesque. Stevenson sidesteps his period's lively discussions of artistic perspectives and styles to give a description easily accessible to the bourgeois audience. He leads with 'the vigorous forest air, the silence, the majestic avenues of highway, the wilderness of tumbled boulders'. His tone remains easy, and the author unimpugned, still capable of elegant generalisation: 'No art, it may be said, was ever perfect, and not many noble, that has not been mirthfully conceived.'[31]

Interestingly, when this essay was republished alongside Stevenson's American journey Across the Plains in 1892, the critics demonstrated a clear preference for such a Stevenson.[32] In August 1879, Stevenson had travelled by emigrant train across the continent – no pleasant experience. But the Scottish Leader ignored Stevenson's trials to focus on 'the author's egotistically gossiping style' and remarked on Stevenson's 'self-consciousness' with its 'deliberate posing'. 'Stevenson may have been as limp as possible in that shed on the quays of New York [. . .] but in his account [. . .] he seems [. . .] carefully draped in his shabby garments.' Richard Le Gallienne suggests that Stevenson's 'method is the wayward travel of a gipsy. He builds not, but he pitches his tent, lights his fire of sticks, and invites you to smoke a pipe with him over their crackling. While he dreamily chats.' The Scottish Leader barely noticed the circumstances of Stevenson's tale. It insisted that 'To make a literary effect [. . .] is Mr Stevenson's object [. . .] To him words are what colours are to the painter, and the handling of them in literary fashion is essentially a kind of decoration.'[33] The critics see the Stevenson (more elegantly posed) of 'Walking Tours'. But it is not in fact the Stevenson who travelled querulously Across the Plains.

From the distance of the twenty-first century, Stevenson's adjustments to the travel genre thus far might seem small – gradations of perspective, or of self-criticism – no big excitement in the moment of Henry James, or the run-up to Freud. But the reviewers' obsessive focus on Stevenson's art indicates the degree of Stevenson's innovation. Critics found it hard to accept – perhaps even to register – the meanings that were erupting through Stevenson's realignments of experience and self.

Of course the reviewers were right – up to a point. Stevenson was a self-conscious stylist. And he certainly works within and deploys numerous literary and stylistic expectations, appropriating them for a travel writing that advertises its elegance. For instance, in *Across the Plains* he brings discourses of bourgeois chivalry and adventure together in a moment of American melodrama:

> A little after midnight I convoyed my widow and orphans on board the train; and morning found us far into Ohio. This had early been a favourite home of my imagination [. . .] My preference was founded on a work which appeared in *Cassell's Family Paper* [. . .] It narrated the doings of one Custaloga, an Indian brave, who, in the last chapter, very obligingly washed the paint off his face and became Sir Reginald Somebody-or-other. (p. 108)

But at the same time, Stevenson's joking tone deflates this puffed-up passage.

Increasingly, Stevenson shows his carefully assembled literary modes and their techniques to be inadequate. In fact their disruption shows how far he and his audience have come beyond the limited concerns of the *Scottish Leader*, focused as it was on style and genre. Stevenson laughs at his naïve investment in 'Custaloga', and this moment of humour prepares us for greater conceptual alterations. He admits: 'I had come prepared to pity the poor negro.' But encountering 'a coloured gentleman' waiting on him at table, 'every word, look, and gesture marched me further into the country of surprise' (p. 107). Experience goes against expectation, and even literary convention, for this man 'was indeed surprisingly unlike the negroes of Mrs. Beecher Stowe [. . .] every inch a man of the world, and armed with manners so patronisingly superior that I am at a loss to name their parallel in England.' The ready-made discourse fails: 'I assure you I put my patronage away.' Furthermore, some experiences – such as viewing Wyoming's remarkable scenery from a hot, unsanitary train while suffering a bowel complaint – simply cannot be converted into satisfying literary effect: 'All Sunday and Monday we travelled through these sad mountains, or over the main ridge of the Rockies, which is a fair match to them for misery of aspect [. . .] tumbled boulders, cliffs' (p. 127). And it is perhaps because he had been challenged and changed by such experiences, or because a continent now rose between him and the doyens of style in Britain, that Stevenson at last achieved an insight that broke all categories of place, person and literary convention. In *The Silverado Squatters* (1883), now ostentatiously 'squatting' beside an abandoned California mine (by permission, and against the exalted terms of romance, whether adventurous or chivalric), Stevenson concludes from this wandering geographical and literary experience: 'I think we all belong to many countries.'[34] At last married to the American divorcée he had crossed an ocean and a continent to find, he declares, with shattering frankness: 'perhaps this habit of much travel, and the engendering of scattered friendships, may prepare the euthanasia of ancient nations' (p. 203). Back home, the critics might have been horrified – but they were too (deliberately?) focused on literary effect to notice the swinging of international identity round the carefully composed figure of the suffering author in the landscape.

Perhaps the shift would have been more obvious to the critics had they taken Stevenson's sea voyage, too, and travelled along with *The Amateur Emigrant*.[35] Stevenson's anglocentric friend W. E. Henley had declared as Stevenson set off to America in pursuit of his future wife, Fanny Osbourne, that at worst 'It will end in a book.'[36] But if the critics could recognise only one type of travel book from Stevenson, the author's father was not keen to let them see another. Thomas Stevenson declared *The Amateur Emigrant*, which described Stevenson's August 1879 journey from Scotland to New York, as 'not only the worst thing you have done, but altogether unworthy of you' and paid the publisher to have it withdrawn.[37] What Stevenson the elder disliked may have been precisely what makes this book a substantial contribution to travel writing. As in *An Inland Voyage*, the speaker's identity comes into question. Having fled his parents, and with little money in his pocket, Stevenson travelled cheaply, and notes that his location as a 'gentleman' thus depends on his financial placement with regard to a certain sign on deck (p. 5). He is considered 'a steerage passenger' (p. 4), and recalls his former life as a pedlar (p. 73). But now he is equally taken for 'a mason [. . .] a petty officer in the American navy', and a 'practical engineer' (p. 73). He is thus characterised not so much as different from himself, as the same as everyone else. In this 'iron country' that is the ship (p. 10), a 'little nationality' fuses (p. 17), denying bounds of class and origin. The writer no longer stands apart to gaze; he is no longer simply gazed upon; nor does he gaze upon himself. Rather, the erstwhile flâneur is part of a 'whole parishful of people', connected to 'the web of our corporate human life' (p. 26). Stevenson writes, 'the more I saw of my fellow-passengers, the less I was tempted to the lyric note' (p. 11). Yet the failure of literary effect betokens an access of human sympathy that Stevenson had not yet experienced in his travels. When Stevenson kneels to help a 'black bundle' who turns out to be an elderly man in the throes of illness (p. 46), all bounds of bodies and propriety, self and other fall away: '"Take care of your knee," said I to O'Reilly. "I have got mine in the vomit."' Then the old man 'began to twist in a new way [. . .] I could not imagine what he was at; till suddenly forth came a coloured handkerchief; and he held it out to me, saying "Wipe your knee wi' that"' (p. 49). In the moment of literary naturalism, with its unwavering eye on the ordinary, the unaesthetic and (it was thought) the ugly, the real echoed shockingly in travel writing – a genre manifested through the personality of its author. Small wonder Thomas Stevenson intervened. And small wonder the sick man did not appear fully in print until James D. Hart's return to Stevenson's manuscript.[38] What a loss to the development of travel writing as a genre capable of travelling not just across place, but in inner space, and of adjusting the human relationships within which, Stevenson shows, it exists.

Still, a Stevenson so reoriented toward society, and given therefore to ignoring the usual bounds of identity – a Stevenson capable of kneeling in vomit and talking about it – was not likely to appeal to the critics. The *Athenaeum* had naïvely anticipated that *The Amateur Emigrant* would comprise 'a third set of his charming *impressions de voyage*', no doubt in the style preferred by the *Scottish Leader*, with 'nothing vulgar'.[39] But this new Stevenson, who challenged not only the style but the content and even the meaning of travel writing, no longer set out to charm.

Fanny Stevenson remarked a disturbing move away from the literary and saleable toward scientism in Stevenson's travel writings during their South Sea tour (1888–90). Now based at Vailima, Stevenson read widely and deliberately, and '[i]nstead of writing about his adventures in these wild islands, he would ventilate his own theories on the vexed questions of race and language. He wasted much precious time over grammars and dictionaries [. . .] Then he must study the coral business.'[40] *In the South Seas* (written from 1888 to 1891) promises lyricism enough. Describing a 'first experience [that] can never be repeated', Stevenson gestures to the poetic: 'In the east a radiating centre of brightness told of the day; and beneath, on the skyline, the morning bank was already building, black as ink.' Immediately, however, Stevenson converts the moment to bathos: it 'has inspired some tasteful poetry'.[41] Stevenson was becoming interested in the facts and their critique, more than the image and the literary idea.

Since another essay in this volume will treat *In the South Seas* at length, we will consider only the twists in the telling of travel that arise through this mature Stevenson's encounter with a new kind of otherness, both in his data (the South Seas) and his method. The Stevenson who had learned to question his own relation to and effect upon the landscape when travelling with a donkey brought his comparative gaze, enhanced by his new scientific interest, to the South Seas. Now he was capable of comparing worlds. Here, Stevenson relates himself sympathetically to otherness by his anthropological recognition of Scottish similarity (as opposed, perhaps, to English distinction): 'points of similarity between a South Sea people and some of my own folk at home ran much in my head in the islands; and not only inclined me to view my fresh acquaintances with favour, but continually modified my judgment' (p. 15). Thus 'The grumbling, the secret ferment, the fears and resentments, the alarms and sudden councils of Marquesan chiefs, remind [him] continually of the days of Lovat and Struan' (p. 14). Moreover, the sympathy that Stevenson learns through his boundary-crossing shifts his view of Europe. Describing a woman who had set the kingdom in turmoil, he concludes: 'There are some who give to Mary Queen of Scots the place of saint and muse [. . .] I recommend to them instead the wife and widow of the island conqueror' (p. 214). Iconic Scottishness and royal beauty take a tumble in Stevenson's more fully informed eye.

Equally importantly, Stevenson comes into focus alongside the other – and perhaps alongside his readers. 'A white is a white' (p. 52), he declares, criticising European exclusiveness. However, his view promptly takes a turn into, and then out of, bigotry: 'The Jews were perhaps the first to interrupt this ancient comity of faiths; and the Jewish virus is still strong in Christianity. All the world must respect our tapus, or we gnash our teeth' (p. 52). Willing to be involved in the weave of differences, Stevenson exposes his own biases to an audience he has trained in anthropological comparisons, even as he demonstrates his liberality. The 'scientific' view does not offer us the more precise and objective orientation the reader might expect or desire. Rather, it complicates further the relation between experience, author and reader. Indeed, it may actually make us question ourselves as participants in Stevenson's experience. We too observe; we too have opinions. So we too are implicated. That is to say, Stevenson's developed perspective enhances the uneasiness that lies at the core and generates the energy of his travel writing.

Stevenson's travel writing breaks the rules, whether the bounds between writer and experience, or author and audience. This is all the more clear if we consider that, as he brings together his widening field of data, Stevenson increasingly drops out fine detail. We hear nothing about Fanny Osbourne in Stevenson's frantic dash across the Atlantic to meet her, and little about daily life with her in the islands from Stevenson's text. Nonetheless, within Stevenson's gaps – his apparent failures in the presumably authentic narrative of travel – other authors take their footsteps. Fanny writes a diary that becomes The Cruise of the 'Janet Nichol'.[42] H. J. Moors, Stevenson's neighbour in Samoa, becomes a literary presence through his book With Stevenson in Samoa.[43] Indeed, generations of travellers and literary emulators tramp Stevenson's routes, and try to map his thoughts. But Stevenson's more canny emulators, like Nicholas Rankin, hint at their own inner territory, even as they follow Stevenson's footsteps.[44] The Travel television channel seems replete with self-conscious and self-critical travellers. Yet whatever hordes of travellers, both touristic and literary, follow Stevenson's paths, Stevenson learned from his outward and inward travels yet another route for literature.

The Wrecker (1892), a collaboration with Stevenson's stepson Lloyd

Osbourne, expresses in full the gains of Stevenson's long work in travel writing. Stevenson termed the book 'a machine', but it was a well-oiled machine that brought together the people, the places, the experiences and the literary lessons in manner and matter that had taken approaching a lifetime to accumulate.[45] Ne'er-do-well Loudon Dodd tracks Stevenson from the France of the artists to the Edinburgh of his childhood, then on (back, in Loudon's case) to America and to the South Seas. A flâneur by type – though even more wilting in energy – Loudon is an artist of sorts, with his primary contribution the metaphorically appropriate hot air grating. But he is also allied with the press (that other wind machine) and briefly (and ironically) serves as a tour operator known for his Scottish-themed picnics. Most of all, however, he is a traveller, and thus, punningly, the 'wrecker' of the title. Wherever Loudon goes, complications ensue; he is never central to them, yet often to blame. And back home, the story sold well: Osbourne later claimed it had 'always been in excellent demand, rivalling "Kidnapped", "Master of Ballantrae", and "Catriona", and [continuing] to earn £200 a year with unvarying regularity'. Even the critics loved it. *The Scotsman*, Paul Maixner tells us, thought it 'the best book Stevenson had yet produced, and that it represented a new method and a new concern in that its "motives and sources of interest are drawn from the life of today"'.[46] Apparently, those not quite ready for the rawness of real experience in *The Amateur Emigrant* could accept Stevenson's complex lessons, born from the unpredictabilities of constant movement in landscape and literature, when they fell into the forms of fiction.

   This point is made clear by the reception given Stevenson's analysis of recent Samoa, *A Footnote to History* (1892). In *The Wrecker*, a friend challenged Dodd the putative artist: 'What I can't see is why you should want to do nothing else.'[47] The Stevenson produced by years of travel, and years of coming to understand his implicated role in the landscape through which he moved, now turned dutifully to analysis on behalf of a people he admired. But Stevenson situated the book between 'journalism' and 'history'.[48] While Stevenson may be the journalist, and move through the history, he consequently found no place for himself within these pages. Even where his experience might be first-hand, he holds back. Indeed, he seldom appears in the first person, invoking instead 'my informants', and shows up only to defer knowledge: 'I gather'; 'I may [. . .] exaggerate.'[49] Lacking the authorial personality that Stevenson had taught readers was the crux and problem of experience, his public baulked. Without a Stevenson or a Loudon Dodd whose interactions might construct the dynamic that is the text, Oscar Wilde snapped: 'I see that romantic surroundings are the worst possible for a romantic writer. In Gower Street Stevenson could have written a new *Trois Mousquetaires*. In Samoa he wrote letters to *The Times* about Germans.'[50] Stevenson had changed the literary landscape such that there was no going back – not even for him.

So what kind of traveller, ultimately, was Robert Louis Stevenson? In his 'Walking Tours', young Stevenson invokes Laurence Sterne's wayward *Tristram Shandy*.[51] That novel, presented as Tristram's life story, wanders all over the place – through different stories and modes, genres and styles, and even different languages. Tristram tries to tell his own story, but cannot; because he is not yet dead, he does not know what matters in his narrative trajectory. Thus, everything is a matter of Tristram's shifting perspective. Like Tristram, Stevenson often began his travels randomly, as a flight from death and in search of health and a stable idea of himself: 'DEATH himself knocked at my door,' says Tristram. 'Then by heaven! I will lead him a dance.'[52] And as with Tristram – in his predecessor's decision to describe Calais, though he has never been there – Stevenson's changing view proves the crucial factor in a journey that constantly reconstructs the landscape, realigning self and other, and even self *as* other. But is Stevenson, then, the 'Sentimental Traveller', who Sterne develops in a later novel of that name? The protagonist, Yorick, imagines his 'travels and observations will be altogether of a different cast from any of my fore-runners'. Certainly, Stevenson might echo Yorick, 'I think there is a fatality in it – I seldom go to the place I set out for.'[53]

Stevenson, wherever he went, ended up with himself. Typically, he had commercial prospects in mind: 'I've got thirty quid for it', he sums up his travails with the donkey.[54] Moreover, frequently, Stevenson's travel writing served as a mine for further texts. Researching for his South Seas project, he laid in data and generated prose waiting to 'make a book of it by the pruning knife'.[55] Materials about the artists' community at Fontainebleau inform Loudon Dodd's sojourn in France; windmills admired in 'The Foreigner at Home' appear again in *Catriona*; the tattooed white man of the *South Seas* makes an appearance in *The Wrecker*, as does Wyoming, with its apparently unforgettable horrors of monotony.[56] Yet Stevenson nonetheless made a distinct contribution to travel writing. He developed through his explorations in travel writing, and, in return, he made the genre mobile, a site of exchange between place, persons and perceiver. How did he manage it? Stevenson, in *In the South Seas*, considered Herman Melville blessed with many gifts, but at his christening the fairy godmothers withheld the gift of hearing (p. 28). Stevenson learned to hear. He heard not just the landscape but the people. And he heard the altered echo of himself that came back. At his best, he understood that for better and for worse, he made part of the human landscape.

CHAPTER SEVEN

Stevenson's Poetry

Penny Fielding

In 1883 Stevenson wrote to his friend W. E. Henley: 'You may be surprised to hear that I am now a great writer of verses.'[1] Readers today may likewise be surprised to think of Stevenson, the famous storyteller, as a poet. Or perhaps they may conclude that he was not a poet really, but, as he himself often claimed, a writer merely of 'verses', especially for children. In this chapter, we will see what kind of a poet Stevenson was, and what was the relation of his 'verses' to poetic forms of his day, as well as to his own ideas about aesthetics, travel and time. Stevenson published only three collections in his lifetime: *A Child's Garden of Verses* (1885), *Underwoods* (1887), and *Ballads* (1890). Following his death in 1894, *Songs of Travel* was included in the Edinburgh Edition of his work in 1895, and issued separately the following year. Further poems appeared posthumously in collected editions, and in a volume called *New Poems* in 1918.

Of his poetry for adults, Stevenson's most famous stanza is perhaps this one:

This be the verse you grave for me:
Here he lies where he longed to be;
Home is the sailor, home from sea,
    And the hunter home from the hill.[2]

These lines, the second stanza of the poem 'Requiem', were inscribed (with the addition of '*the* sea' in the third line') on Stevenson's grave in Samoa. Among the many tributes written after Stevenson's death, A. E. Housman composed his own version of 'Requiem', which includes the stanza:

Home is the hunter from the hill:
    Fast in the boundless snare
All flesh lies taken at his will
    And every fowl of air.[3]

Housman requires us to read Stevenson in an unexpected way. The original stanza, with its melodious expression of a longing for home that might finally be satisfied at the end of life, changes to something much darker – the security of death is now expressed ominously as a 'boundless snare' that rapaciously captures life. This poses quite a challenge: contemporary reviewers were apt to use words like 'graceful', 'charming' and 'attractive' to praise Stevenson and few recent critics have challenged this view, leaving the impression of a poet whose works are slight and cheerful. To leave Stevenson's poetry there, however, is to miss the darker, more complex or ambiguous elements conjured up by Housman's elegy. Stevenson often wrote quickly and did not publish all that he wrote, so reading his 'verses' as a complete poetic corpus is not always helpful. But his best work shows us how dedicated he was to poetry as a craft, and how he could use it to express the same tensions as well as hopes that we find in his novels and stories.

Stevenson was writing at a time when there was no obvious single reader-ship for poetry. The long era of Tennyson was coming to an end, with the reading public anticipating his death (it finally took place in 1892). Matthew Arnold's hope that British society would follow the path of 'the idea of beauty and of a human nature perfect on all its sides, which is the dominant idea of poetry'[4] did not seem to be leading to a new, unified poetic tradition. No dominant figure had emerged to fill the space left by Tennyson. After four years of indecision, 1896 saw the appointment as Poet Laureate of Alfred Austin, a writer almost universally thought to be outmoded and undistin-guished. But in any case, many writers were uninterested in the figure of 'The Poet' as a single authority, ostensibly speaking for the whole of society. The late 1880s saw the emergence of poetry like that of 'Michael Field', the joint work of aunt and niece Katherine Bradley and Edith Cooper, or the Jewish, lesbian poet Amy Levy. The ballad was revived as a form of 'unofficial' poetry, by Rudyard Kipling, John Davidson and Stevenson himself.[5] As poetry failed to find a generalised bourgeois readership, it was increasingly published in small print runs, decorative books or specialist magazines.

In these circumstances, it can be constructive actively to consider Stevenson as a 'minor poet' rather than to dismiss him as such. He certainly fits two of T. S. Eliot's suggestions for inclusion in such a category: the few of his poems that are well-known are largely encountered in anthologies, and (to use the terms of Eliot's estimation of Ben Jonson's poetry), '[W]e cannot say [. . .] that the whole is more than the sum of his parts.'[6] But neither of these criteria would have disappointed Stevenson himself. He was writing in a decade in which 'minor' poetry filled a conspicuous gap. Richard Le Gallienne, a popular poet and admirer of Stevenson, lectured on 'The Minor Poet'[7] and was appropriately reviewed as one himself in the *New York Times* (8 Sept. 1895, p. 27) in a review which started 'In these days of minor poets Richard Le Gallienne has pushed his way forward far enough to attract the attention of many literary critics, who would no doubt be glad to engage in the consideration of larger lyric personages. But large poets are not at all numerous at present.' Stevenson called his first adult collection *Underwoods* (borrowing the title from Jonson), to suggest that his poems grew in the shade of his more significant work. But the title also resonates with the state of poetry in general in the 1880s and 1890s as it started to emerge from the long shadows of the great Victorian figures of Tennyson and Browning. New poets did not feel the need to strive to be epic or universal, but were increasingly individualistic, seeing themselves part of small coteries rather than extensive traditions. A large number of the poems in *Underwoods* are very personal, addressed to Stevenson's friends, many of them fellow writers and artists.

It was becoming increasingly difficult for poets to get published and the literary market began to fragment into small-circulation magazines and private presses. Poets began to form small special-interest groups in which they could work out their own criteria for poetry, rather than striving to be part of a continuous, national tradition. The subject of poetry turns increasingly to the ways in which the world is experienced by the individual, rather than ways in which it can be assessed or analysed. In reaction to Arnoldian ideas of the moral responsibility of poetry, many poets turned to what became known as aestheticism – the idea that art should not be any kind of social arbiter, but should be a way of exploring one's own feelings and impulses, set free from social restraints and often in opposition to them. Common themes included visiting prostitutes, taking drugs and wandering through lamp-lit cities at night time (a style of writing often labelled 'decadent'). We can see some of Stevenson's early poetic experiments heading in this direction as he inhabits the voice of the disaffected poet, looking out into a blurred street scene while his 'brain swims empty and light' and he observes from a distance: 'A girl or two at play in a corner of a waste-land / Tumbling and showing their legs and crying out to me loosely' (p. 260) (Stevenson notices quite a few ladies' legs in his early poems). Stevenson did not directly continue this kind of writing in his poetry, although he was to transfer its urban dreamscapes to prose in *Strange Case of Dr Jekyll and Mr Hyde*. But the turn to the aesthetic was always more than the idea that 'art' was largely a life-style choice. In their reconsideration of 'art' as a category, writers like Walter Pater insisted that it should have a vitality that impressed itself on the mind in intense, but fleeting moments that escape rational scrutiny: 'It is with this movement, with the passage and dissolution of impressions, images, sensations, that analysis leaves off.'[8]

Impressionism, the sense that artists and writers should describe what they feel and see, rather than what they intellectually know to be there, links Stevenson's children's writing with his adult poetry. To the speaker of *A Child's Garden of Verses* the world is one of vivid but often impermanent impressions that either defy or forgo analysis. The child imagines the wind as a man riding by and asks 'Late at night when the fires are out, / Why does he gallop and gallop about?'(p. 27). But there is no explanation and the poem never makes the rider a clear simile for the wind. Many single poems are just glimpses of observed or imagined phenomena cast loose of any clarifying context or explanation or reaction:

> The rain is raining all around,
>   It falls on field and tree,
> It rains on the umbrellas here,
>   And on the ships at sea. (p. 26)

Arthur Symons, whose promotion of French symbolist poetry was influential on Yeats and the modernist poets of the next generation, was also an acute spokesman for the poetry of the end of the nineteenth century, and advocates a verse in which 'Description is banished that beautiful things may be evoked, magically.'[9] The meaning or object of a poem is not something that precedes it or that the poem describes, but something that emerges 'magically' from the poem itself. His own early collection *Days and Nights* (1889) uses not only the simple metres of *A Child's Garden* but also the same sensibilities evoked by impressions rather than descriptive statements. In 'The Fisher's Widow' the subject's grief is filtered through her experience of natural phenomena:

> The boats go out and the boats come in
> Under the wintry sky;
> And the rain and foam are white in the wind,
> And the white gulls cry
> [. . .]
> She sees the torn sails fly in the foam,
> Broad on the skyline grey;
> And the boats go out and the boats come in,
> But there's one away.[10]

We might compare this evocation of an adult consciousness with the child of 'Where go the Boats?' whose solitariness is suggested through similar imagery, syntax and vocabulary:

> Green leaves a-floating,
>   Castles of the foam,
> Boats of mine a-boating –
>   Where will all come home? (p. 30)

To set Stevenson in these contexts is to reveal how careful he was as a poet, and how interested in changing ideas about poetic form. Stevenson wrote poetry that was intensely personal, but he also wrote poetry that reads like an exercise in writing poetry itself. In a letter to Le Gallienne he complains of the reading public: 'The little, artificial popularity of style in England tends, I think, to die out; the British pig returns to his true love, the love of the style-less, of the shapeless, of the slapdash and the disorderly.'[11] He is here referring in particular to prose, but his insistence on the importance of 'style' is evident everywhere in his writing. Stevenson's poetic language often works very hard at the craft of poetry – he has a fine control of assonance, internal rhyme and the counterpoint of line- and sentence-structure, and the distribution of different impressions across parts of speech. Even his recommendations for style in prose make it sound like poetry:

> The beauty of the contents of a phrase, or of a sentence, depends implicitly upon alliteration and upon assonance. The vowel demands to be repeated; the consonant demands to be repeated; and both cry aloud to be perpetually varied. You may follow the adventures of a letter through any passage that has particularly pleased you; find it, perhaps, denied a while, to tantalise the ear; find it fired again at you in a whole broadside; or find it pass into congenerous sounds, one liquid or labial melting away into another.[12]

These techniques are everywhere in Stevenson's poetry. In the following example verbs ('gloomed') and nouns ('missile') as well as adjectives do the work of description, and the poem uses internal rhymes ('laggard'/'haggard') and assonance ('scowling town') as a kind of aural impressionism to evoke his sense of the city in winter:

> In our wild climate, in our scowling town,
> We gloomed and shivered, sorrowed, sobbed and feared [. . .]
> The belching winter wind, the missile rain,
> The rare and welcome silence of the snows,
> The laggard morn, the haggard day, the night,
> The grimy spell of the nocturnal town. (pp. 189–90)

If this reads like an exercise in writing poetry, it paid off. Much of Stevenson's best verse shows this very tight control of rhythm and metre, as a frame to carry his more imagistic language. Stevenson was writing at a time when many poets were testing form and imagery, and critics were formulating ways of thinking about art as an end in itself. The mere subject matter of a poem, argued Walter Pater, was 'nothing without the form, the spirit, of the handling'.[13]

Stevenson himself moves restlessly between different poetic forms: blank verse, sonnets, ballad quatrains, free verse, the complex Scottish metre of Burns and the eighteenth century, and a number of song-like forms. But much of his verse, rather than letting existing forms determine the measurement of sense, focuses instead on the relationship between word and sound, the fine local control of rhythm and metre, and the way a poem's shape describes a line of thought. A good example of this is 'Skerryvore: the Parallel'. The puzzling title refers to Stevenson's house in Bournemouth, which he named after a lighthouse constructed by his father and uncle and which summons up his recurrent anxiety that he has not lived up to the expectations of the Stevensons, engineers and lighthouse builders. But the poem itself does not address these concerns directly, rather allowing them to emerge through its careful placing of words:

> Here all is sunny, and when the truant gull
> Skims the green level of the lawn, his wing
> Dispetals roses; here the house is framed
> Of kneaded brick and the plumed mountain pine,
> Such clay as artists fashion and such wood
> As the tree-climbing urchin breaks. But there
> Eternal granite hewn from the living isle
> And dowelled with brute iron, rears a tower
> That from its wet foundation to its crown
> Of glittering glass, stands, in the sweep of winds,
> Immovable, immortal, eminent. (pp. 96–7)

The parallel of the title is played out in the poem. The soft, doughy 'kneaded brick' of the Bournemouth Skerryvore contrasts strikingly with the 'brute iron' that runs throughout the lighthouse. The poem consists of two sentences, hinging on the mid-line break which leads into the spectacular contrast between the mutable Bournemouth home and the lighthouse of 'Eternal granite'. And this itself forms a contrast with early run-on lines like 'his wing / Dispetals roses' where the graceful precision of the bird in flight momentarily holds up the line so that we notice the delicate action of removing the petals of the flowers. The internal half-rhyme ('dowelled'/'tower') drives the poem forward during the long second sentence, building up to the delayed verb 'stands', until it comes to halt with the three words 'Immovable, immortal, eminent' occupying the entire line as if to preclude anything more being said on the subject because the lighthouse itself justifies its own existence. As Pater had suggested, the form itself is the 'spirit' of the poem.

The very precise image of the gull's wing that 'Dispetals roses' is quite typical of Stevenson, who often constructs verbs in this way, with prefixes that suggest change or movement. In 'The Woodman', which I discuss later in this chapter, an 'inarboured' ravine suggests one that has become taken over by forest, rather than just a wooded, or 'arboured' place. The environment of Stevenson's poetry is one of impermanence, instability, loss and constant change. There are few fixed points in time or space from which the poet can contemplate a static object. Stevenson was particularly fond of using 'dis-' as a verbal prefix, a technique which conjures up this sense of a world in which things could easily split up, change form, lose shape or disappear altogether. This is a world never quite present before the viewing subject, but always slipping out of focus, or losing pieces of itself. Again in 'The Woodman', the 'dislustred leaves' (p. 196) carry a ghostly echo of their former sheen, and in a poem to his sister-in-law, he writes: 'The unfathomable sea, and time, and tears, / [. . .] Dispart us' (p. 79) where the verb 'dispart', means not just to part, but to part in opposite directions.

In a poem to W. E. Henley, Stevenson imagines Henley's own art surmounting the sanatorium where he was at the time confined:

> the gaunt ward
> Dislimns and disappears, and, opening out,
> Shows brooks and forests, and the blue beyond
> Of mountains. (pp. 84–5)

To 'dislimn' is a particularly interesting word, and one that Stevenson evidently liked. Its meaning of 'to obliterate the outlines' carries echoes of the verb to 'limn', originally meaning to illuminate mediaeval manuscripts but in its modern sense more usually applied to the painting of watercolours. Stevenson uses it in a way that draws attention to closeness of works of art and intense states of feeling. In the novel *St Ives* he uses it to express the sense of the narrator's loss of security in his own identity as someone watches him: 'My face seemed to myself to dislimn under his gaze.'[14] In a letter of November 1883 Stevenson wrote of his feelings on the death (which he found very troubling) of his friend from student days, Walter Ferrier: 'I feel as if the earth were undermined, and all my friends have lost one thickness of reality since that one passed. Those are happy who can take it otherwise: with that I found things all beginning to dislimn.'[15] Dislimning, then, is the sense that the world is not itself solid or stable – the world is a text itself, like a limned manuscript, that has different layers, or 'thicknesses', of reality. Even when Henley's artistry 'dislimns' the sanatorium ward, it is to 'open out' on a new backdrop, like a stage set.

The French symbolist poet Stéphane Mallarmé (1842–98) argued that poetry should engage the eye as much as the ear, and that rather than offering song-like resolutions with regular rhythms and end-rhymes, the verse form should be free to use complex syntax or line formations that might require the reader to look both forward and backwards in the poem. 'Skerryvore: the Parallel' works like this, moving our attention between nodal points in the two sentences, and driving the sense across the line-endings without coming to a rest. Poetry, according to symbolist ideas, should not contain unitary feelings, or sum up single ideas, but should allow infinite suggestion. Rather than delivering a single mood that might be contained in the language of the poem, symbolist poetry allows language to throw up different meanings during the course of a single poem, and to suggest new meanings from the relations of different parts of the poem.

A great deal of Stevenson's poetry is written to appeal to the voice (a good example is the stanza from 'Requiem' that I quote in the first paragraph of this chapter). But much of it complicates the aural aspect of poetry by exploring the intricate verse forms that were emerging at the time in France. Two consecutive poems in *Underwoods* testify to the different styles he could use and the way his poetry looks both forwards and backwards in literary history, and will help us understand Stevenson's position in the history of poetry. A poem to his friend, the American artist Will H. Low is written in a by-then outworn late Romantic tradition, with some routine rhymes and metre, diluted pastoralism and stock imagery which calls to mind William Sharp's criticism that Stevenson was sometimes guilty of 'infringement of Keats's literary patent':[16]

> Youth now flees on feathered foot,
> Faint and fainter sounds the flute,
> Rarer songs of gods; and still
> Somewhere on the sunny hill,
> Or along the winding stream,
> Through the willows, flits a dream. (p.79)

But if Mr Low's poem is uninspired, his wife's is completely different. 'To Mrs. Will H. Low' starts:

> Even in the bluest noonday of July,
> There could not run the smallest breath of wind
> But all the quarter sounded like a wood;
> And in the chequered silence and above
> The hum of city cabs that sought the Bois,
> Suburban ashes shivered into song. (p. 80)

This strikes the reader as much more modern. The 'winding stream' of Mr Low's poem becomes an impressionist city-scape, and the sound of Pan's flute changes into the noise of cabs (still horse-drawn at this point, but their wheels humming mechanically). Rather than nature taking the role of a lost idyll, the natural and urban worlds melt into each other so that the noises of Paris are 'like a wood'. The imagery rejects the easy choice of the willow-flitting dream of the William Low poem, and instead becomes a complex painting of the urban scene that works through comparisons, coalescences and differences. The 'chequered silence' and the ashes that shiver into song is an example of synaesthesia, crossing the sense of sight and hearing and allowing the experience of the poem to emerge through analogy rather than direct statement. The poem is 'suburban' not just because it describes the suburbs, but also because it questions, in a speculative way, the relationship between the city and nature. Rather than the natural world acting as a retreat from the artifice of the city (a common Romantic motif), nature here seems almost an image for the city, where bodily activities (humming or shivering) describe an urban experience. In a manner that is usually associated with literary modernism, the outer and inner worlds of perceived and affective life blend almost seamlessly together. (Linda Dowling calls this *fin-de-siècle* mode 'urban pastoral').[17] Arthur Symons wrote, 'I think that might be the test of poetry which professes to be modern: its capacity for dealing with London, with what one might see there, indoors or out',[18] and although Stevenson's verse is perhaps more associated with rural scenes, it is surprising to note how many of his poems are about the city.

The relationship between the two Low poems asks us to address the charge that Stevenson's poetry can be nostalgic, affected or even sentimental; categories that have not been greatly valued since Stevenson's death. Reading his poetry in the twenty-first century, his use of poetic archaisms can seem jarring in a line that is otherwise strikingly modern. But this was quite common in the poetry of the period, and not merely a mechanical resort to 'poetic' language. Tracing such a tendency in poetry to Walter Pater's interest in Euphuism (self-consciously high-flown literary language), Linda Dowling has argued that it marks the feeling that poetry should be aware of its own past, and can be seen as 'assiduous attention to the complex linguistic textures of old and new, archaism and neology'.[19]

The charge of nostalgia nevertheless demands some serious attention. A great many of Stevenson's poems are about the loss of home (one original meaning of 'nostalgia' is home-sickness) and of childhood. Modern critics are quick to leap on late-Victorian culture as betraying a whimsical idealisation of simpler states of existence to compensate for complex and painful social realities. But much of Stevenson's poetry suggests the unavailability of the kind of shared assumptions that nostalgia tends to promote. His period was noted not only for what we now see as sentimental longing for the past, but also a renewed scientific interest in the functions of memory. As Linda M. Austin and Cairns Craig have, in different ways, shown, late nineteenth-century literature is bound up in such questions as how memory works, whether it has a bodily origin, how images relate to each other in the mind, whether memory is active or passive.[20] Stevenson's apparently nostalgic writing is part of this inquiry.

Despite the way he circles around familiar addressees, seeming to appeal to mutual experiences, much of Stevenson's poetry turns inwards to a close scrutiny of the individual, unshared memory. The children of *A Child's Garden of Verses* play by themselves, or with the child's own shadow which abandons him at the end of the poem, or in the company of an imaginary 'Unseen Playmate'. This poem opens with the strange image of even a plurality of children playing 'alone': 'When children are playing alone on the green' (p. 47). The culmination of 'A Good Play' is the absence of a playmate: 'But Tom fell out and hurt his knee, / So there was no one else but me'(p. 29).

These simple poems are in fact quite complex, inhabiting a strange and multiple temporality of human experience that John Hollander sums up perfectly: 'a complex dialectic of projected adulthood and recollected childhood'.[21] It is never quite clear whether the speakers of the poems are children rehearsing for adulthood, or the adult poet ventriloquising his lost past. There are numerous examples of this doubled stance, and Hollander gives one of the best from the poem 'Travel', where the child adventurer imagines coming upon an abandoned city in the desert: 'All its children, sweep and prince, / Grown to manhood ages since' (p. 28). As Hollander puts it: 'The child reaches in his journey the house of childhood to find nobody home.'[22] We might also note 'My Bed is a Boat' where the relations of bed and boat are not quite clear – on the one hand the bed is transformed in the child's imagination into the ship of an exciting adventure, but on the other the bed carries associations of not only sleep but death in which the child shuts his eyes to 'sail away / And see and hear no more' (p. 41). The child of this poem takes to bed with him a rather curious item:

> And sometimes things to bed I take,
>   As prudent sailors have to do;
> Perhaps a slice of wedding-cake,
>   Perhaps a toy or two. (p. 41)

Generally speaking, neither children nor sailors routinely take wedding cake to bed with them. The status of this 'thing', as the child puts it, is not apparent; the child is at once charmingly naïve to the grown up writer, and strangely anticipatory of an adult world which is both 'prudent' (an unchildlike word) and sexual. The temporality of human life in *A Child's Garden of Verses* is not linear or incremental, and in a later poem, Stevenson expresses a shocking version of this. On his last visit to the near-death Thomas Stevenson, Louis sees his father as a 'changeling', just as his father is being invited to recognise his own son:

> 'Look!' said one
> Unkindly kind, 'look up, it is your boy!'
> And the dread changeling gazed on me in vain. (p. 200)

Stevenson's children do not often comment on their feelings, which can make it difficult to establish the relation between the child speaker and the adult poet. It is not quite clear what we should make of the relativistic joke of 'Foreign Children' where various 'races' are asked 'Don't you wish that you were me?':

> You have curious things to eat,
> I am fed on proper meat;
> You must dwell beyond the foam,
> But I am safe and live at home. (p. 38)

As with William Blake's children (the *Songs of Innocence and Experience* was an influence on *A Child's Garden*) it is difficult to tell quite how knowing this child is and thus how far we should take the poem as a satire on imperialist attitudes.

The tension in this poem between the insular security of 'home' and its alternative relativity is very common in Stevenson's poetry. A great traveller himself, he was one of the first modern writers to explore the sense of dislocation and rootlessness that globalisation could arouse. A good example of this is a poem in *Songs of Travel* addressed to 'S. C.', Sidney Colvin. The poem follows Stevenson's progress and thoughts as, kept awake by the sound of the sea, he wanders round the island of Apemama during a stormy night and remembers Colvin's residence in the British Museum in London where he was keeper of prints and drawings. Stevenson imagines himself back there:

> there again
> In the upper room I lay, and heard far off
> The unsleeping city murmur like a shell;
> The muffled tramp of the Museum guard
> Once more went by me; I beheld again
> Lamps vainly brighten the dispeopled street; (p. 191)

The poem, to use Stevenson's favourite term, dislimns the contours of place, blurring both the separate geographical locations of London and Apemama, and the distinction between experience and memory. Like a great deal of Stevenson's work, this poem meditates on the idea of 'home' and Stevenson sent Colvin a copy with a letter discussing his thoughts on the subject: '[n]ow that my father is done with his troubles, and 17 Heriot Row no more than a mere shell, you and that gaunt old Monument in Bloomsbury are all that I have in view when I use the word home.'[23] 'Home' is a word that Stevenson used a great deal, sometimes repeatedly in the same poem as if trying to establish its reality by dint of repetition (as in 'Requiem'). Here it becomes an empty signifier, a word that can be 'used' in certain contexts, rather than possessing its own, felt meaning. Like the Stevenson family's former house in Heriot Row, Edinburgh, it is a 'shell', a word Stevenson picks out of the poem, in which the 'unsleeping city murmur[s] like a shell'. The city, which Stevenson wants to be made palpable through his memories, becomes increasingly blurred as it merges both with the island, and with Stevenson's own mind. Much as he tries to make the content of his memories of the city (the sound of traffic or birdsong) real to him, he finds the city acting as a sea-shell, an empty container that produces phantom sounds. 'Dispeopled' (one of Stevenson's 'dis-' words) conjures up a sense of the spectral city; the word summons the uncanny shadows of absent people.

As the poem progresses, Stevenson imagines Colvin going to work in the Museum and another reversal takes place. Colvin passes two statues brought to London from Polynesia:

Far-voyaging island gods, begrimed with smoke,
Sit now unworshipped, the rude monument
Of faiths forgot and races undivined:
Sit now disconsolate, remembering well
The priest, the victim, and the songful crowd,
The blaze of the blue noon, and that huge voice,
Incessant, of the breakers on the shore. (p. 192)

Increasingly both the 'home' of Britain and the 'foreign' Pacific islands melt into each other. Like the dispeopled street, the unworshipped statues are haunted by the absent figures of their original society, and here, to use William Sharp's phrase, Stevenson infringes Keats's literary patent to good effect. The poem explicitly echoes Keats's 'Ode on a Grecian Urn' where Keats contemplates a similarly decontextualised scene of religious sacrifice, but Stevenson transposes its classical relation to a colonial one. Where Keats's poem offers at least some sense of continuities between the aesthetic values of the classical past and present, Stevenson is even more ambivalent. Removed from their Pacific context, the statues are monuments to 'faiths forgot and races undivined', bearing witness to the colonising society's inability to accept that colonised peoples have independent histories. Here Stevenson makes it difficult to distinguish between his own memories of London, and the statues' memories of their island. The statues in London remember the islands, and Stevenson, in the islands, remembers the statues remembering the islands. The sounds of the 'breakers on the shore' with which the poem opened become more vivid in the statues' memory than in Stevenson's direct experience. The poem questions which is more real, the imperial 'home' of London or its supposed global peripheries, the site of myths and exoticism. We are reminded of Stevenson's novella *The Ebb-Tide*, in which one of the destitute Western adventurers washed up on the beach imagines himself back in London, the imperial centre, as an insubstantial fantasy and 'home' as an absurd memory.

Ann Colley notes that Stevenson's 'nostalgic' writing is not a simple act of idealisation, or patriotism, or mourning for a lost childhood, but an intricate response to the structure of recollection, the interplay of past and present, of object and feeling. His nostalgia, Colley argues, is always ambivalent, caught between longing for past states and places and a contrary impulse that recognises why he left them in the first place.[24] These ambivalences are heightened by the Pacific settings of the later poems. In the poem to Colvin, the statues refuse to act as clear objects in the past to be recalled by the remembering mind of the colonising Stevenson.

The island locations of his Pacific travels allow Stevenson to explore forms of geographical location, or dislocation. A poem, for Stevenson, is almost a geographical space itself in which objects from the past can be brought together. The philosopher of place, Edward S. Casey, writes that 'any given place serves to hold together dispersed things, animate or inanimate; it *regionalizes* them, giving them a single shared space in which to be together'.[25] Stevenson's poetry tends to highlight the difficulty of this exercise. We have already seen in 'To S. C.' how the relation of the remembering mind and the thing remembered becomes unclear when they cannot exist together in one space.

Stevenson moves continually between literal and metaphorical models of global space. The possibility that one might physically be at any point on the globe often arises in his poetry. Even the small child is routinely aware of global time and a world mapped by temporal zones:

And when at eve I rise from tea,
Day dawns beyond the Atlantic Sea;
And all the children in the West
Are getting up and being dressed. (p. 39)

One of Stevenson's very best poems, 'The Tropics Vanish', explores this dislocated world where a modern consciousness of entire, global space gives rise to the recognition of the relativity of our experience of it. The speaker of this poem, as his immediate surroundings on a Pacific island fade away, imagines his gaze moving north through Scotland until he arrives at Edinburgh, both his first home and the grave of his ancestors. At first this seems like a straightforward act of cartography. Ann Colley has commented on Stevenson's sense of the past as a map: 'Stevenson composed his fiction so that he could vicariously wind his way through the landscape of home. To do this he relied upon the abstracted space of maps.'[26] In 'The Tropics Vanish' Stevenson's spatial imagination travels 'From Halkerside, from topmost Allermuir, / Or steep Caerketton' (p. 190). He lists these Borders place-names as if trying to enclose them within a precise cartographic space, their repeated sounds (the consonant k and the phoneme al) seemingly giving them a natural relationship. But the poem does not sustain such acts of containment. The focus expands and then contracts again, dizzily drawing the reader across vast ocean spaces, and closing in on the solitary child. The swing of the verse, with its long sentence, delayed verbs and echoing vowels, draws the reader to the phrase 'in vain', emphasising the fallibility of global reckonings of spatiality. External measurements, like the tropics, 'vanish', leaving an internal memorial space:

> Continents
> And continental oceans intervene;
> A sea uncharted, on a lampless isle,
> Environs and confines their wandering child:
> In vain. The voice of generations dead
> Summons me, sitting distant, to arise,
> My numerous footsteps nimbly to retrace,
> And all mutation over, stretch me down
> In that denoted city of the dead. (p. 191)

The poem does not contrast Stevenson's doubled locations as much as it makes the space between them incommensurable. Distance is no longer the interval between two points: the points seem to merge into each other, as we saw in 'To S. C.', the poem which appears alongside 'The Tropics Vanish' in Songs of Travel. The poem proposes an elevated position from which we can see global phenomena (continents and oceans), but far from assuming a navigable globe that one might easily cross, the poet's spatial imagination is dizzyingly variable. The huge, generalised movements of the land masses and oceans, as they 'environ' and 'intervene', fail to pin down the tiny point of the 'wandering child'. The sea is 'uncharted', unmapped. In Stevenson's ambivalent ending, it is only the precision of the Stevenson family (the 'artificers' whose engineering finesse seems to extend to their own tombs), that can measure place in the 'denoted', or spatially fixed city of the dead.[27]

One of Stevenson's longer (and stranger) poems brings many of these ideas together. It is a work far from the better-known and anthologised poems such as 'Requiem', 'I Will Bring You Brooches' or 'Blows the Wind Today'. The metre of 'The Woodman' recalls Andrew Marvell, and in other ways too it updates Marvell's seventeenth-century wrangling with the relation between art and nature. Stevenson, now living in Vailima, decides to clear a path up the hill behind his house, but encounters the immensity of the natural world:

                                   The green
Inarboured talus and ravine
By fathoms. By the multitude,
The rugged columns of the wood
And bunches of the branches stood:
Thick as a mob, deep as a sea,
And silent as eternity. (p. 195)

The difficulty of cutting through the natural growth mirrors the task of turning it into poetry. The woods are silent and the scene cannot easily be measured. They form a uniform 'green' which threatens to obscure the geographical distinctions of the scene and (as in Marvell's poetry) merge the images of land and sea, and the speaker has to impose poetic tropes upon it with repeated similes.

Stevenson casts around for a narrative that will substitute for this profound sense of alienation. Late Romantic ideas of natural places haunted by nature spirits desert him. Forms of 'nature worship' were becoming popular in literature at the end of the century, and to see how distinctive Stevenson's writing is we can briefly compare it with 'Tree Worship' by Richard Le Gallienne (which appeared in the same volume as Le Gallienne's not very good elegy for Stevenson himself). For Le Gallienne, the structure of the poem is straightforward, and starts somewhat like 'The Woodman'. He notes the impenetrability and alien feeling of natural growth: 'Knotted and warted, slabbed and armoured like the hide / Of tropic elephant; unstormable and steep'.[28]

But the tree soon becomes the index of popular history: it is the 'dread haunted palace of bat and owl' of early superstition and the scene of grisly executions in the eighteenth century. More importantly, there is a direct relation between the tree and speaker who asks, 'I seek a god, old tree: accept my worship, thou!'[29] and links the force and vitality of the tree to his own desire for life and potency. Stevenson's poem is very different in its refusal of these kinds of links and continuities. In 'The Woodman' Stevenson's labourer has fled, believing the woods to be haunted, but the poet cannot insert himself into any mythological continuity and the woods remain 'Unmeaning, undivined' (p. 196). The gods of the poem are 'disinvested' (p. 196), another 'dis-' word, suggesting not only that they have lost their formal investiture as gods, but also that no one is investing faith in them any more. Where Le Gallienne's poem slips neatly into its history lesson and nature worship, Stevenson's grows almost as out of control as the undergrowth, although he remains in command of his careful metre. There is no clear distinction between 'vegetable king and priest / And stripling' (p. 196), and the profusion of life and energy seems indistinguishable from death and killing:

Stevenson is like a 'beast' killing the plants which themselves fight for life as 'the green murderer throve and spread' (p. 197). In its effort to make narrative sense of the experience the poem circles round possible mythic, literary and historical analogies without ever alighting on any of them. It ranges from the mediaeval poem *Gawain and the Green Knight*, through the 'Black Hole of Calcutta', to a very modern (and rather un-Victorian) despair of war and imperialism in which 'pale battalions' of potential soldiers trample over London Bridge without caring if they live or die (p. 197), and clerks consign children to death 'with a diligent pen' (p. 198).[30]

In a long letter to Colvin, Stevenson describes the nature of the undergrowth. One of his chief vegetable enemies in the poem is 'the toothed and killing sensitive' plant:

> I found a great bed of *kuikui* – sensitive plant – our deadliest enemy. A fool brought it to this island in a pot, and used to lecture and sentimentalise over the tender thing. The tender thing has now taken charge of this island, and men fight it, with torn hands, for bread and life. A singular, insidious thing, shrinking and biting like a weasel; clutching by its roots as a limpet clutches at a rock.[31]

The poem, which uses the shrinking and biting image, omits the detail that the plant has been brought from outside the island, that it is potentially an image for Stevenson himself as coloniser ('The Woodman' was to lead to Stevenson's novella of imperial disenchantment, *The Beach of Falesà*). But the poem already warns us not to sentimentalise Stevenson. Its speaker is someone who cannot be part of his surroundings, either geographical or historical, a much darker and more desperate figure than we commonly read in his poetry. Stevenson, himself a 'sensitive plant' who had come to Samoa to escape the Scottish climate, depicts himself as a destroyer of his own environment, evoking Housman's later version of him: 'All flesh lies taken at his will / And every fowl of air.'

CHAPTER EIGHT

Stevenson and the Pacific

Roslyn Jolly

Almost one-third of Stevenson's career as a professional writer was spent in the Pacific. Within this vast oceanic region, bounded by the New World societies of the Western United States and Australasia and by the coasts of south-east Asia, are scattered a multitude of islands whose people, cultures and landscapes were unlike anything the Scottish author had previously known or seen. This chapter explores how Stevenson's imagination was possessed by, and attempted to possess, the island world in which he lived from 1888 to 1894. It explores his literary relation to various social environments of the Pacific: to traditional indigenous societies; to the contact zone of trade and informal colonialism; and to the political structures which, in an age of empire, regulated relations between Pacific nations and world powers. No less challenging to his imagination and productive for his writing were the natural environments of the Pacific: its island landforms, tropical climate and vegetation, and the ocean for which the region is named. In his late fiction, Stevenson combined various aspects of these natural and social environments to create specific and very different Pacific worlds. This chapter 'maps' the geographical and cultural co-ordinates of some of these worlds through readings of *The Wrecker*, 'The Beach of Falesá' and *The Ebb-Tide*.

In travelling to the Pacific, Stevenson eagerly took up the challenges to his imagination and his understanding presented by encounters with societies unlike any he had previously known. He was going among people who, although his contemporaries, were 'as remote in thought and habit as Rob Roy or Barbarossa, the Apostles or the Caesars'.[1] The opportunity to observe ways of life so ancient and so alien powerfully attracted one whose writings reflected a long-running quarrel with modern civilisation.

This quarrel seems to have been the expression of a temperamental antipathy, rather than the product of a learned system of ideas. In his early essays and travel-writing Stevenson cultivated the persona of a social misfit, who was constantly straying from the paths of civilisation, and always seeking a more complete escape. In these writings the modern world is represented by a series of synecdoches: 'business habits', 'Burgessry', 'offices and the mercantile

spirit'.[2] Stevenson's attitude towards the sum of artificial repressions represented by these things was one of 'protest', 'social heresy' and free-thinking
dissent, the avatars of which in his writings were strolling players and gypsies,
pedlars and, occasionally, savages.[3] In *Travels with a Donkey* an epiphanic
night in the open air led him to exult that he had 'escaped out of the Bastille
of civilisation' and to speculate that, in finding the natural world to be 'a
gentle habitable place', he 'had rediscovered one of those truths which are
revealed to savages and hid from political economists'.[4] But until he went to
the Pacific, Stevenson's understanding of the 'truths which are revealed to
savages' was largely theoretical, extrapolated from his distrust of 'the thing
we call civilisation', rather than having been gained from direct observation
of traditional societies.[5]

With his first Pacific landfall, in the Marquesas in July 1888, came the
opportunity to test his theories. Stevenson immediately became involved
in the question of the relative merits of civilisation and savagery, *the* topic
for Pacific travellers since the voyage literature of the eighteenth century
had prompted the French *philosophes* to make the Pacific islands – in
particular, Tahiti – a touchstone for their critiques of European civilisation.[6] Stevenson's early perceptions of the Pacific were influenced by the
Romantic primitivism of writers such as Herman Melville and Charles
Warren Stoddard, who created images of island life as more natural and in
many ways more benevolent than the artificial constraints of modern civilisation. Exposure to an archive of Pacific representations, as well as his own
temperamental leanings, thus primed Stevenson to adopt a primitivist position, and despite some initial uncertainty this became his confirmed stance.
In September 1890 he wrote: 'our civilization is a hollow fraud, all the fun
of life is lost by it, all it gains is that a larger number of persons can continue
to be contemporaneously unhappy on the surface of the globe'; in Samoa,
by contrast, one could see 'a healthy and happy people'. In 1892, Stevenson
again wrote dismissively of 'civilisation, if you take any store in that fraud,
which I do not. I always thought I didn't; now I know.' Overall, his attitude
was summed up in the succinct judgment: 'Civilisation is rot.'[7]

Yet Stevenson's intellectual curiosity about the traditional societies he
encountered in the Pacific was not satisfied by this judgment, nor contained
by the civilisation/savagery dichotomy on which it was based. He became
increasingly interested in investigating Pacific societies on their own terms,
rather than merely positing them as havens from the ills of modernity. For
this task, a new organising structure of ideas was needed, which Stevenson
found in the realisation that traditional Pacific islanders were considerably
more 'remote in thought and habit' from his own modern world than even
Caesar and the Apostles; that their 'ideas' and 'manners' indeed dated 'back
before the Roman Empire'; and that in coming to know them, he would

see 'what men might be whose fathers had never studied Virgil, had never been conquered by Caesar, and never been ruled by the wisdom of Gaius or Papinian'.[8] A second stage in his thinking was to link Pacific cultures, in their freedom from the shaping force of Roman civilisation, to the similarly 'unromanised' Celtic culture of the Scottish Highlands.[9] In many respects, he believed, the Samoans and other Pacific islanders were 'the contemporaries of our tattooed ancestors who drove their chariots on the wrong side of the Roman wall'.[10] The 'Highland comparison', which helped him to establish a 'sense of kinship' with people of the Pacific by matching every 'savage custom' or 'superstitious belief' with 'some trait of equal barbarism' from his own ancestors,[11] became an important tool for analysing clan-based societies, which Stevenson understood to be patriarchal in their structures of authority and communistic in their economic organisation.

Stevenson's comparison of Pacific and Highland cultures, and his contrasting of both these with the modern, Western civilisation that had developed under the influence of the Roman Empire, became the key to his understanding of traditional Pacific societies. Although he continued to decry modern civilisation, he did not merely posit Pacific 'savagery' as its antidote; rather, he developed an increasingly complex and critical understanding of Pacific societies as alternative models of civil organisation. With this, his focus shifted from the evaluative (which is better, 'civilisation' or 'savagery'?) to the functional (how does a custom or institution function within a society, and to what effect?). Romantic primitivism gave way to a kind of functional anthropology, as Stevenson sought to unravel the closely entwined strands of law, custom and religion in island life, and to understand the functions in civil society of religious and legal institutions such as the *tapu* and the principles of gift-giving and reciprocity.[12]

But when Stevenson came to the Pacific, the *tapu* system had in many places been dismantled or driven underground by European missionaries, while indigenous principles of communal ownership and reciprocity had been distorted by the introduced institution of private property. Everywhere he travelled Stevenson saw evidence of the breakdown of indigenous structures of social order under the pressure of modern, Western ideas, whose impact upon Pacific societies was secured by the lure of commerce, the prestige of Christianity, and, in some cases, the power of imperial governments. In the Gilbert Islands (now Kiribati), Stevenson found that the ruthless, vigilant King Tembinok' of Apemama had maintained his kingdom in a state of 'social quarantine' from the modern world.[13] But Apemama was an exception. Most of the Pacific in the late 1880s and early 1890s was a vast contact zone, 'a no man's land of the ages, a stir-about of epochs and races, barbarisms and civilisations, virtues and crimes.'[14] Ancient modes of life existed side by side with the most modern technology; native pastors preached the gospel

while their brother priests practised traditional 'devil-work'.[15] Mixed styles
of speech and of dress, like the emergence of compound systems of government and belief, revealed the mutual influence of local and global forces in
contemporary Pacific culture. It was a realm of the hybrid and the dialogic, of
an intense and productive transculturation.[16]

The life-blood of this contact zone was trade. The exchange of material
goods between members of different societies was the central mechanism
governing virtually all aspects of the Pacific life Stevenson recorded in his
writings, from the ritualised first encounters of islanders and travellers, to
the rhythms of daily life on 'the beach', to the operations of global trading
networks which tied the region into the economic and political concerns of
faraway Europe and America. Tropical products – coffee, cacao, copra (dried
coconut meat), pearls and shell – flowed out of the islands; manufactured
goods – cotton 'print', jewellery, metal tools and machines – flowed in. These
exchanges were accompanied by others, less definable: of ideas, attitudes,
manners, points of view.

The most infamous trade conducted in the nineteenth-century Pacific
was the 'labour trade', also known variously as 'recruiting', 'blackbirding',
'kidnapping', or 'slaving'. This traffic in labouring bodies encompassed a
range of practices from indenture, an often harsh but legal contract between
labourer and employer, to the effective enslavement of unwitting victims.
The labour trade caused the expatriation of thousands of islanders, devastated
entire communities, and cast a shadow over relations between islanders and
whites throughout the Pacific. Stevenson saw traces of it almost everywhere
on his Pacific travels, and it came to his back door when runaways from the
German plantation on Upolu turned up on his property at Vailima. It was the
attempt to regulate the labour trade, and thus avoid its worst features, that
led to Britain's official involvement in the region as a somewhat reluctant
colonising power.[17]

The political institutions regulating relations between Pacific nations and
world powers produced the third social environment with which Stevenson
was engaged during his years in the Pacific. Perched above the damaged
yet enduring systems of traditional island life, and the messy, vital region
of exchange where that traditional life was locked in irreversible contact
with the modern world, sat the superstructure of European imperialism.
Stevenson's first exposure to this phenomenon was in French Polynesia,
whose administrative and disciplinary structures he criticised in *In the South
Seas* and wove into the background of *The Ebb-Tide*. In 1888 he wrote privately of France as 'a nation that is not beloved in certain islands, – and it does
not know it! Strange: like ourselves, perhaps, in India!'[18] It was a crucial realisation for this once-staunch supporter of the British Empire. Now, although
Stevenson befriended some colonial administrators, such as the French

Resident Donat-Rimarau in Fakarava, and wrote sympathetically of others, such as the German official Brandeis in Samoa, his attitude towards United States and European colonialism in the Pacific was broadly critical. From 1890 to 1894 Stevenson was closely involved in debates on public policy in his adopted home, Samoa, where three 'Great Powers' (Britain, Germany and the United States) ran an incompetent quasi-colonialist regime. Although on occasion he advocated a British Protectorate of Samoa as the least of evils that might befall a Pacific nation in an imperial age, his preferred position was that the Samoans should be left alone to govern themselves according to their 'natural constitution'.[19] His critics dismissed his views as the fancies of a romantic novelist and the prejudices of an incurable primitivist.[20] Stevenson, on the other hand, argued that he derived his opinions from a careful study of indigenous legal and political institutions, and a depressing familiarity with the failures of the government imposed on Samoa by foreign powers.[21]

These were the three types of society to which Stevenson was exposed in the Pacific: traditional, indigenous societies; the contact zone of interaction between whites and islanders; and the realm of colonial administration. The stimulus these social environments provided to Stevenson's intellect and imagination is the key to his transformation as an author during his Pacific years. In 1887, when he left Europe, Stevenson was known as a writer of romances and historical adventure novels. Now, new challenges led to new kinds of writing. Responding to Samoa's political crisis, Stevenson experimented with non-fictional forms: A Footnote to History (1892) was an account of recent events in Samoa, which sat generically somewhere between modern history and investigative journalism; a series of public letters to The Times combined Stevenson's talent for narrative with a new interest in political analysis. In the South Seas (1896) represented a serious attempt to understand the structures of indigenous Pacific societies, which made the work more like an anthropological study than the romantic travelogue Stevenson's public expected. Meanwhile, his fascination with the effects of the dislocation, juxtaposition and cross-contamination of cultures on the ships, ports and beaches where Europeans and islanders met produced a marked turn in Stevenson's fiction towards the realistic depiction of modern life. Indeed, in works such as 'The Beach of Falesá' (1892) and The Ebb-Tide (1894) Stevenson questioned and subverted the categories of adventure and romance in which his earlier fiction had so heavily invested. In the 1890s, critics began to talk of 'a new Stevenson', barely recognisable as the romancer of the previous decade.[22]

In registering Stevenson's responses, as a writer, to the social environments of the Pacific, it is important not to overlook the impact of an even more primary stimulus to his imagination: the natural environment. The abundance of tropical vegetation, the beauties of marine life, the heat, the light, the sudden deluges of tropic rain, the different landscapes of coral and volcanic islands – all are represented in his writings, providing a sensory framework for his exploration of ways of life and states of mind. The natural world does not merely supply 'background' in Stevenson's Pacific writings; rather, it may function as a set of determining conditions, as an agent in the plot as important as any character, or as a source of powerful symbols.

During his two years of voyaging (June 1888 to July 1890) Stevenson was to be, as a fortune-teller had predicted in his youth, 'much upon the sea'.[23] He came to know many aspects of 'that ill-named ocean, the Pacific'[24] and his responses to it were as variable and contradictory as the ocean itself. In a letter of October 1888 he called the sea 'a horrible place, stupefying to the mind and poisonous to the temper'.[25] Yet in April 1889 he wrote:

> I cannot say why I like the sea; no man is more cynically and constantly alive to its perils; I regard it as the highest form of gambling; and yet I love the sea as much as I hate gambling. Fine, clean emotions; a world all and always beautiful; air better than wine; interest unflagging: there is upon the whole no better life.[26]

The tropical climate and sea air were like a tonic to Stevenson after years of ill health, and there is a strong element of the autobiographical in the sentiments he ascribed to Loudon Dodd, protagonist of *The Wrecker*:

> One thing I am sure: it was before I had ever seen an island worthy of the name that I must date my loyalty to the South Seas. The blank sea itself grew desirable under such skies; and wherever the trade-wind blows I know no better country than a schooner's deck. (pp. 190–1)

But the Pacific Ocean could also be a place of terror. On his first voyage, on the yacht *Casco*, Stevenson experienced storms of a violence he had never known in his crossings of the Atlantic or the English Channel; they called forth a *mélange* of emotions, which he explored in the storm scenes of *The Wrecker* and *The Ebb-Tide*. These are Loudon Dodd's reactions to a storm weathered on the *Norah Creina*:

> By dinner I had fled the deck, and sat in the bench corner, giddy, dumb, and stupefied with terror. The frightened leaps of the poor *Norah Creina*, spanking like a stag for bare existence, bruised me between the table and the berths. Overhead, the wild huntsman of the storm passed continuously in one blare of mingled noises; screaming wind, straining timber, lashing rope's-end, pounding block and bursting sea contributed [. . .] It seemed incredible that any creature of man's art could long endure the barbarous mishandling of the seas, kicked as the schooner was from mountain-side to mountain-side, beaten and blown

upon and wrenched in every joint and sinew, like a child upon the rack. (p. 201)

The morning broke with sinister brightness; the air alarmingly transparent, the sky pure, the rim of the horizon clear and strong against the heavens. The wind and the wild seas, now vastly swollen, indefatigably hunted us. I stood on deck, choking with fear; I seemed to lose all power upon my limbs; my knees were as paper when she plunged into the murderous valleys; my heart collapsed when some black mountain fell in avalanche beside her counter, and the water, that was more than spray, swept round my ankles like a torrent. (pp. 202–3)

Scenes such as these exemplify Stevenson's longstanding narrative interest in 'brute incident' as distinct from 'character or thought',[27] but the Pacific Ocean also provoked a more intellectual response in his writing. Months at sea taught Stevenson that the ocean is not, as it might seem, in *The Wrecker*, a 'blank' (p. 190), but a surface inscribed by weather, rock and the hand of man, with an ever-changing array of meanings – a field of subtle challenges to the faculty of interpretation. In his Pacific fiction islands are fished out of the sea – not, as in Polynesian myth, by the god Maui, but by a process of 'reading' the seascape. This is how Attwater's secret island is discovered in *The Ebb-Tide*:

The sky shaded down at the sea-level to the white of opals; the sea itself, insolently, inkily blue, drew all about them the uncompromising wheel of the horizon. Search it as they pleased, not even the practised eye of Captain Davis could descry the smallest interruption [. . .]
    'Who sang out land?' asked Davis. 'If there's any boy playing funny-dog with me, I'll teach him skylarking!'
    But Uncle Ned contentedly pointed to a part of the horizon, where a greenish, filmy iridescence could be discerned floating like smoke on the pale heavens.[28]

From variations in light above the apparently featureless sea the Hawaiian sailor, Uncle Ned, infers the presence of a lagoon and therefore of the uncharted island on which the action of the novella's second half unfolds. In *The Wrecker*, similarly subtle visual clues combine with auditory evidence and wildly unstable glimpses through binoculars to reveal, emerging from the 'waste' of ocean, the island and wreck that are the focus of an intense desire for meaning:

Nares went below, fetched up his binocular, and fell into a silent perusal of the sea-line; I also, with my unaided eyesight. Little by little, in that white waste of water, I began to make out a quarter where the whiteness appeared more condensed: the sky above was whitish likewise, and misty like a squall; and little by little there thrilled upon my ears a note deeper and more terrible than the yelling of the gale – the long, thundering roll of breakers. Nares wiped his night-glass on his sleeve and passed it to me, motioning, as he did so, with his hand. An endless wilderness of raging billows came and went and danced in the circle of the glass; now and then a pale corner of sky, or the strong line of the horizon rugged with the heads of waves; and then of a sudden – come and gone ere I could fix it, with a swallow's swiftness – one glimpse of what we had come so far and paid so dear to see: the masts and rigging of a brig pencilled on heaven, with an ensign streaming at the main, and the ragged ribbons of a topsail thrashing from the yard. (p. 204)

'[T]o draw near to a new island, I cannot say how much I like', Stevenson wrote to Henry James in March 1889.[29] He regarded every new island as a new world, whose particular physical features stimulated his imagination just as much as did its social features. Stevenson understood the geography of Pacific islands in terms of a broad distinction between 'high' (volcanic) and 'low' (coral) islands, representing utterly different natural environments. 'The Himalayas are not more different from the Sahara,' he declared in *In the South Seas*.[30] His first Pacific landfall was at a high island, Nuku-hiva in the Marquesas. Here, in the picturesque scenery of Anaho Bay, Stevenson found all the ingredients of a South Sea idyll: at night, 'the air temperate and scented' beneath a sky 'bright with stars'; by day, relief from the tropical heat in shady arbours of *purao* and palm, while the air was refreshed by the constant stream of the trade-wind. Further inland, the scenery was ruggedly mountainous, with a solemnity and gloom that reminded Stevenson of Scotland and suggested the sublime rather than the picturesque.[31] It was on another high island, Upolu in Samoa, that Stevenson chose to live in 1890. Letters from his home, Vailima, express his delight in its mild climate, lush verdure, and mountain and forest scenery.

A 'low' island is a coral atoll, the archetypal tropical island of modern tourism: 'a ring of glittering beach and verdant foliage, enclosing and enclosed by the blue sea'.[32] Stevenson saw his first atolls in the Paumotus (also known as the Low or Dangerous Archipelago) in French Polynesia. From the sea such islands could seem infinitely desirable, with their almost magical beauty; one, Taiaro, appeared to Stevenson as 'a ring of white beach, green underwood, and tossing palms, gem-like in colour; of a fairy, of a heavenly prettiness'.[33] In his fiction, atolls (such as Midway in *The Wrecker* and New Island in *The Ebb-Tide*) are consistently associated with desire and its deceptions. For, once landed on an atoll, Stevenson became aware that the island was a mere 'thread of residence', no more than a 'narrow causeway' within 'the outrageous ocean'. The insecurity of the situation, combined with its improbable beauty, haunted his imagination intensely, as he recorded in *In the South Seas*: 'I lay down to sleep, and woke again with an unblunted sense of my surroundings.'[34] Compared with high islands, where food was abundant, the atoll's capacity to sustain human life was poor: little grew there that could be eaten, and the diet (Stevenson was to learn both in the Paumotus and, later, in the Gilbert Islands) was meagre and unvarying. Yet of life useless or even harmful to human beings there was a 'profusion of vitality' that could be 'shocking'.[35] Mosquitoes and flies filled the air; the lagoon was full of beautiful, poisonous fish; and to the undersides of rocks clung fat, pink worms. He wrote:

> It adds a last touch of horror to the thought of this precarious annular gangway in the sea, that even what there is of it is not of honest rock, but organic, part alive, part putrescent; even the clean sea and the bright fish about it poisoned, the most stubborn boulder burrowed in by worms, the lightest dust venomous as an apothecary's drugs.[36]

This twinning of beauty and corruption, desire and horror, suggested to Stevenson by the atolls of the Paumotus, underwrites the conception of Attwater's island in *The Ebb-Tide*.

Other aspects of the atoll environment were also amenable to symbolic construction. The flatness and narrowness of the ribbon of land that made up an atoll, and its thin vegetative covering, meant that such islands offered little refuge from storm, heat or light. In descriptions of the atoll of Apemama in the Gilbert Islands (now Kiribati), Stevenson recorded his sense of extreme and undefended exposure to the elements:

> [T]o wade out on the reef during the day is blinding and giddifying to the last degree: a vast, wrinkled, unbearable, glory spreads all about, and just below a little steel sun (reflected in the water) stares up at you with an eye of fire that you do everything to avoid and find inevitable.[37]

A similar atmosphere is evoked at the climax of *The Ebb-Tide*:

> It was close on noon, there was no breath of wind, and the heat was scarce bearable [. . .] The isle shook before them like a place incandescent; on the face of the lagoon blinding copper suns, no bigger than sixpences, danced and stabbed them in the eyeballs; there went up from sand and sea, and even from the boat, a glare of scathing brightness; and as they could only peer abroad from between closed lashes, the excess of light seemed to be changed into a sinister darkness, comparable to that of a thundercloud before it bursts. (p. 242)

The physical exposure of the characters in this location matches their moral exposure as they confront each other in an ultimate scene of 'death and judgment' (p. 243). Unprotected by social convention or self-delusion, they walk, morally, in 'a glare of scathing brightness' which lays bare their deepest motivations and allegiances, and for which the light of the noonday beach provides an appropriate objective correlative.

If the physical geography of Pacific islands suggested such things to Stevenson's mind, their human geography, too, supplied material for the novelist's imagination to work upon. On his travels, Stevenson was struck by the distinctive patterns of settlement on low islands. '[T]he life of an atoll,' he observed, 'unless it be enclosed, passes wholly on the shores of the lagoon; it is there the villages are seated, there the canoes ply and are drawn up; and the beach of the ocean is a place accursed and deserted, the fit scene only for wizardry and shipwreck, and in the native belief a haunting ground of murderous spectres.'[38] In his short story 'The Isle of Voices', Stevenson made the deserted sea-shore of a low island the setting for a struggle between the protagonist, Keola, and a troupe of 'invisible devils' (p. 116) who, in a twist on local legends of sea-shore sorcerers, represent the unseen and inexplicable powers of international trade.

High islands also had their deserted and mysterious places. In the Marquesas Stevenson noticed that the local people could 'never get their houses near enough the surf', and in Samoa he wrote confidently of 'the beach where islanders prefer to live'.[39] If the beach was the setting for the ordinary business of daily life, in Stevenson's Pacific writings the interiors of islands – consisting of 'bush', 'forest' or 'jungle' – are always associated with activities that are transgressive or *tapu*. 'In the crypt of the wood', in 'the twilight of the forest' on Nuku-hiva, he saw the remains of a cannibal 'high place', a theatre for ritual human sacrifices; in Stevenson's imagination it was a place of past fear and horror, now 'the haunt of spirits'.[40] In Samoa he heard reports of wars and preparations for war taking place 'in the covert of the woods' or 'under the cover of the forest',[41] beyond the gaze and the jurisdiction of white settlers and colonists; in the Samoan war of 1893, heads would be taken in the forest, signalling a reversion to savagery that Stevenson found deeply repugnant.[42] Meanwhile, he absorbed the local legends which made the bush the haunt of *aitus* and *aitu-fafines*: devils and spirits, more or less menacing, and antagonistic to social values.

Stevenson's property at Vailima included around three hundred acres of such jungle, for he had chosen to live, not on the beach, but 'some six hundred feet above the sea, embowered in forest'.[43] This natural environment played powerfully upon his imagination in two ways. First, the overwhelming fertility of tropical nature, on which the settler struggled to make a mark, gave concrete form and dramatic expression to the Darwinian theory of the struggle for existence. Stevenson wrote from Vailima of his attempts to clear the bush around his house:

My long silent contests in the forest have had a strange effect on me. The unconcealed vitality of these vegetables, their exuberant number and strength, the attempts – I can use no other word – of lianas to enwrap and capture the intruder, the awful silence; the knowledge that all my efforts are only like the performance of an actor, the thing of a moment, and the wood will silently and swiftly heal them up with fresh effervescence [. . .] the whole silent battle, murder and slow death of the contending forest – weighs upon the imagination.[44]

At a natural level, the forest preached to Stevenson a kind of 'Darwinian Sermon'[45]– to use a phrase he employed in a different context – about the violent competition for existence between life-forms, which found expression in his poem 'The Woodman'. At a supernatural level, the physical properties of the forest combined with the local legends about it to produce emotions of irrational fear and 'horror', which Stevenson also explored in his letters about clearing the bush.

The horror of the thing, objective and subjective, is always present to my mind; the horror of creeping things, a superstitious horror of the void and the powers about me, the horror of my own devastation and continual murders. The life of the plants comes through my fingertips, their struggles go to my heart like supplications.[46]

A strange business it was, and infinitely solitary: away above, the sun was in the high tree tops; the lianas noosed and sought to hang me; the saplings struggled, and came up with that sob of death that one gets to know so well; great soft, sappy trees fell at a lick of the cutlass; little tough switches laughed at and dared my best endeavour. Soon, toiling down in that pit of verdure, I heard blows on the far side, and then laughter. I confess a chill settled on my heart.[47]

Stevenson ascribed the same responses to Wiltshire, the protagonist of 'The Beach of Falesá', in a powerful evocation of 'the high bush', its atmospheric gloom, its animal and vegetable vitality, and its disturbing impact upon the lone human intruder (pp. 51–2). In this environment Wiltshire is drawn, against his will, to thoughts of local legends of bush-spirits, which he had previously dismissed as merely 'native talk' (p. 51). He comes to realise that nature and culture cannot be divorced, and that the human geography of a place is as real as its physical geography. 'It's my belief a superstition grows up in a place like the different kind of weeds', he concludes, validating the indigenous sense of the bush as an uncanny space (p. 52).

Between ocean and shore, high and low islands, indigenous and European society, Stevenson encountered not one Pacific, but many. The diversity of natural and social environments he observed in the course of his travels is reflected in his letters and non-fictional writings, while his novelist's imagination combined different aspects of his Pacific experiences to create a number of radically different fictional 'worlds'. Every student of Stevenson's life and writing knows the map, drawn to illustrate *In the South Seas*, which shows his three Pacific cruises: the routes of the *Casco* (1888) and the *Equator* (1889) dissecting the ocean in bold, straight lines, the 'very devious course'[48] of the *Janet Nicoll* (1890) weaving in dotted zig-zags among the islands. What follows here is an attempt to 'map' three of Stevenson's Pacific fictions – *The Wrecker*, 'The Beach of Falesá' and *The Ebb-Tide* – to show how variously the Pacific was organised as a mental as well as physical space in these works.

The prologue and epilogue of *The Wrecker* unfold in actual Pacific island settings that Stevenson knew from his travels: Tai-o-hae in the Marquesas, which he visited on the yacht *Casco* in July 1888, and Manihiki (now part of the Cook Islands), where he stopped in May 1890 during the voyage of the steamer *Janet Nicoll*. These were contact zones, the realms of traders and beachcombers, Christianised islanders and indigenised Europeans. The motley culture of such places is symbolised by 'the famous tattooed white man' of Tai-o-hae (p. 2), whom Stevenson had seen in 1888 and described in *In the South Seas*.[49] In the prologue to *The Wrecker* Stevenson imagined the thoughts of this strange figure, stranded between worlds, as a collage of incommensurable images and 'broken fragments of the past':

> brown faces and white, of skipper and shipmate, king and chief, would arise before his mind and vanish; he would recall old voyages, old landfalls in the hour of dawn; he would hear again the drums beat for a man-eating festival; perhaps he would summon up the form of that island princess for the love of whom he had submitted his body to the cruel hands of the tattooer, and now sat on the lumber, at the pier-end of Tai-o-hae, so strange a figure of a European. Or perhaps, from yet further back, sounds and scents of England and his child-hood might assail him: the merry clamour of cathedral bells, the broom upon the foreland, the song of the river on the weir. (p. 2)

These thoughts of the tattooed white man, 'as he dodged in and out along the frontier line of sleep and waking' (p. 2), epitomise the contact world in which 'the frontier line' between races and cultures is equally unstable.

But in the narrative proper of *The Wrecker*, this world disappears. Instead, the novel depicts a Pacific that is home to no one, indigenous or settler, but merely a network of ports, where goods are loaded and unloaded, and dollars exchanged. It is a field for the circulation of international capital in the global 'dollar hunt' (p. 426) which Stevenson found most characteristic of his age. The investors who drive this system of trade and finance care nothing for the region in which it operates, or for the inhabitants of that region; all they want is 'speed between ports', as Captain Nares observes (p. 200). The ports, indeed, define the region, so that the geographical reference points in

The Wrecker are Melbourne (p. 195), Sydney (p. 223), Hong Kong (p. 415), 'Calcutta and Rangoon and 'Frisco and the Canton River' (p. 216). This is not really the Pacific, but the Pacific Rim, within which the ocean, which carries the shipping of international trade, is far more important than the islands those ships pass.

Apart from 'metropolitan' Hawaii (p. 246) – where a tourist may watch 'a *hula-hula*' after dinner and cocktails (p. 259) – the only Pacific island setting in the main narrative of *The Wrecker* is the tiny island of Midway, in the north Pacific. In both parts of *The Wrecker*'s double narrative – which encompasses both the events on the ship the *Currency Lass*, and the story of Dodd's attempts to uncover those events – this island is the focal point of interest as the site of the wreck for which Dodd and his business partner Pinkerton have paid so much money, and the scene of terrible crimes. The island is a mere speck of land within 'vast and solitary waters' (p. 370); it is a 'ring of foam and haze and thunder' (p. 205) within an 'empty world of cloud and water' (p. 246). The island lies so low in the sea that on approach Dodd can see no land at all; to his eyes 'the wreck stood between sea and sky, a thing the most isolated I had ever viewed' (p. 204). 'In that huge isolation, it seemed [to the murderers] they must be visible from China on the one hand and California on the other' (p. 375). Again, the island seems to have no context but that of the great ports and markets of the Pacific Rim. At times Midway is covered with millions of sea-birds, which create a 'vortex of winged life', within which the obscured island is merely the 'focus of centrifugal and centripetal flight' (p. 206). This suggests the way that, in the international world of *The Wrecker*, the Pacific island exists only as a focus of dynamic forces expressing 'the unrest and movement of [the nineteenth] century' (p. 425) rather than as a substantial presence in itself.

Very different is the world of 'The Beach of Falesá', which is set on a populous, native-ruled island at the heart of the Pacific region. The island is imaginary, but its depiction accurately reflects scenery and societies Stevenson had encountered over his years in the Pacific. It is not Samoa, but words and place-names used in the story are similar to Samoan ones, and in writing it Stevenson drew heavily upon his knowledge of Samoan folklore, manners and customs. He also made use of anecdotes and observations from his Pacific travels. The beachcomber looking for a 'soft job', whom the Stevensons met in Manihiki, supplied the keynote for Uma's mother's husband in 'The Beach of Falesá'.[50] The story of the death of Underhill, buried alive with the complicity of a native missionary, was an anecdote from the island of Penrhyn.[51] The infamous marriage certificate, whereby Uma is married to Wiltshire 'for one night' with the groom reserving the option to 'send her to hell next morning' (p. 11), was sighted by Stevenson at Butaritari in the Gilbert Islands.[52] At Funafuti in the Ellice Islands the Stevensons met a trader with a shady past who proved a devoted family man, refusing to leave his indigenous wife and half-caste children;[53] he was the model for Wiltshire's behaviour at the end of the novella. Visits to Maraki in the Gilbert Islands on both the *Equator* and *Janet Nicoll* cruises supplied stories of murderous rivalry between white traders and power struggles between missionaries, traders and local leaders, including the *tapu*-ing of an outsider, 'so that he could neither trade nor be traded with' – the mainspring of the plot of 'The Beach of Falesá'.[54]

As this suggests, trade is vital to the story, but here Stevenson is concerned with traders resident in the islands, not transients speeding between ports in America, Asia and Australia, as in *The Wrecker*. Within the narrative of 'The Beach of Falesá', most geographical references are to places in Polynesia and Micronesia. Uma comes from the Line Islands, a group of atolls near the Equator (part of modern Kiribati). Wiltshire has also come to Falesá from 'a low island near the line' (p. 3). Case's wife is from Samoa; Uma's term for a blackguard is a 'Tonga-heart' (p. 32). The 'flash towns' of Apia and Papeete are mentioned but not seen. Wiltshire and Uma send their son to school in Auckland, showing that New Zealand was then, as now, a centre for Pacific education. This is as far as the narrative moves from the island world with which it is concerned. We do not believe, and neither does Wiltshire, that he will ever return to England to run the 'public-house' (p. 71) of which he used to dream. He may fix up his store 'Sydney style' (p. 17) and 'Bristol fashion' (p. 14), but these comments belong to a metropolitan frame of reference that has little reality within the story. When Wiltshire wants to dazzle Uma with the glamour of urban authority, he quotes the title page of her bible to her: '*London: Printed for the British and Foreign Bible Society, Blackfriars*' (p. 60). Wiltshire tries to argue that from its seat in Blackfriars, London, the Bible Society can protect him from *aitus* in the bush above Falesá, but Uma is unconvinced. Her belief that international powers and metropolitan institutions have no bearing on local, island problems has already been expressed in her argument that Wiltshire must stop relying on geographically distant sources of authority and start paying attention to local power structures. When Wiltshire evokes Queen Victoria as his protectress, Uma concedes that Victoria is a 'big chief', but argues that the English queen is 'too far off' to help Wiltshire in Falesá; it is the local leader Maea, she insists, who, although a 'small chief', can 'make [Wiltshire] all right' (p. 48).

In order to understand both the uncanny power of the bush and the concrete politics of the village, Wiltshire must heed Uma and acknowledge the priority of local conditions over imperial or global forces.[55] It is only when he begins to engage with local beliefs and local society that he gains the knowledge and help he needs to overthrow his rival, Case. The novella's insistence on the importance of these systems of knowledge and authority matches its immersion in an island world that has little to do with distant continents and polities, a world where relations between whites and islanders are played out on the ground of particular social, historical and environmental conditions that are specific to the Pacific region.

The Ebb-Tide involves another imaginary Pacific island, but this time its imaginariness is emphasised within the text. Attwater's island is the 'New Island' Stevenson found intriguingly described in Alexander Findlay's *Directory for the Navigation of the South Pacific Ocean* as an entity of 'doubtful' existence, 'totally disbelieved in by South Sea traders' (p. 185). In the story the island emerges like a mirage from an empty ocean; on the sailors' chart it represents an unmarked point 'in the midst of a white field of paper' (p. 184). It is as if the island appears because the three adventurers want it to, so that it is nothing but the manifestation of their desire. As such, it belongs to a long literary tradition of fantasy islands created by the inscription of European desire upon the unmapped Pacific 'wilderness of waters'.[56]

However, whereas most works in this tradition were written by people who had never seen the Pacific, The Ebb-Tide is intimately connected to Stevenson's Pacific travels. Attwater's island is a composite of features taken from islands Stevenson visited on his three cruises. The figure-head on the beach – symbolic perhaps of justice, perhaps of destiny – came from Penrhyn, which Stevenson visited on the *Janet Nicoll* in 1890.[57] On the same voyage he stopped at Suwarrow, which supplied both the general atmosphere of a once-thriving, now deserted settlement and the specific detail of the romantic jumble of salvage in Attwater's store-house.[58] The glaring noonday scene in which Attwater subdues an antagonist by firing terrifyingly accurate near-misses with his Winchester rifle replays a scene staged by another island despot, King Tembinok' of Apemama, which Stevenson witnessed on the voyage of the *Equator* in 1889.[59] Herrick's enraptured response to the beauty of the island and its lagoon upon arrival mirrors Stevenson's response to Fakarava in the Paumotus, when he came there on the *Casco* in 1888. Indeed, he referred the illustrator of the novel to his 'photographs of Fakarava' for an accurate representation of 'Attwater's settlement'.[60] His remark in *In the South Seas* that at some hours Fakarava, with its palm canopy and neat alleys, resembled a 'public garden by night'[61] was repeated and amplified in Herrick's fancy that Attwater's island 'wore an air of unreality like a deserted theatre or a public garden at midnight' (p. 220). The theatricality of the island – Attwater compares his veranda to 'a lighted stage with all heaven for spectators' (p. 214) – becomes important to an understanding of how deceptive are the desires on which it is founded. On this island, things are not what they seem.

Attwater's island is a pearl island, and the fortune that Attwater has amassed, and which the adventurers want to steal, is a fortune in pearls. Pearls suggest a purity, almost a transcendence, quite unlike the grossly material copra which is the chief article of trade in 'The Beach of Falesá', and seemingly untouched by the corruption obviously attached to the opium trade in *The Wrecker*. But these pearls are not pure, and Attwater's treasure does not transcend the material conditions of its production. For the pearls are products of a regime of effective slavery. While the task of Attwater's partner Symonds was to 'collect' (kidnap) labourers from all over the Pacific and bring them to the island (p. 215), Attwater's job was to 'run' them, extracting their labour by whatever means necessary (p. 216). His violent methods belie the veneer of civilisation he has imposed on the island, which is represented by the church, the neat appearance of the settlement, and the display of sophistication and civility at his dinner party.

Attwater calls his island a 'colony' (p. 204), which links it to the other Pacific setting in the narrative, Tahiti. The Tahitian capital, Papeete, is represented in the early chapters of the novella as Stevenson saw it in 1888, as the seat of a well-established French colonial administration. This colonisation by the state contrasts with Attwater's personal colony, in having a legitimacy, in European eyes at least, which the Englishman's illegal operation lacks. Yet the two colonies mirror each other as manifestations of European power gained through violence. Both are represented primarily as disciplinary structures: Herrick and his companions shelter in the old prison at Papeete, and fear being sent to the penal colony at Noumea; Attwater tells of the regulations, punishments and even executions by which he maintains his authority over his unwilling island subjects. The material conditions of European power are insisted upon in Stevenson's double representation of official and unofficial Pacific colonisation.

With its emphasis on power, economic greed and racial exploitation, *The Ebb-Tide* invites the kind of post-colonial reading that has been so productive in bringing about a revaluation of Stevenson's Pacific work in recent years. But post-colonial criticism cannot uncover the whole story of Stevenson and the Pacific. Stevenson presents a case unique in literature in English of a writer transplanted, in middle age and mid-career, into an environment so alien and new to him as to constitute a perpetual challenge to his intellect, imagination and senses. '[T]he interest, indeed, has been *incredible*,' he wrote in 1888. 'I did not dream there were such places or such races.'[62] The strangeness, beauty and at times sheer terror of the physical environment affected his literary response to the Pacific as strongly as did the new cultural and political conditions he observed and interpreted. The variety and particularity of his encounters with place and race, nature and society, account for both the astonishing range of genres in which he wrote about the region, and the very different 'Pacifics' realised in his writings.

CHAPTER NINE

Stevenson and Henry James

John Lyon

One of the earliest of the consumers of the great globe in the interest of the attraction exercised by the great R.L.S. of those days, comes in, afterwards, a visitor at Vailima and [word lost] there and pious antiquities to his domestic annals.

These final and faded remarks all have some interest and some character – but this should be extracted by a highly competent person only – some such, whom I don't presume to name, will furnish such last offices. In fact I do without names not wish to exaggerate the defect of their absence. Invoke more than one kind presence, several could help, and many would – but it all better too much left than too much done. I never dreamed of such duties as laid upon me. This sore throaty condition is the last I ever invoked for the purpose.[1]

That Robert Louis Stevenson is, amidst an anxiety over the presumption of naming, the last person named – although even that is to stretch his initials – in the opaque, fragmenting but wonderful cadences of what has become known as Henry James's deathbed dictation is evidence of the two men's importance each for the other. Yet it is evidence only of a kind, and of a kind representative of the difficulty of bringing particularity and explanation to the nature of their relation. Here James himself seems to caution against interpretative presumption: 'all better too much left than too much done'. More generally, there is ample testimony to the fact of how greatly James and Stevenson mattered to each other, both as men and as artists. Yet they remain writers of very different kinds with very different lives. It may well be the case that these differences freed the relation of rivalry and opened the way for close personal friendship and mutual professional admiration. So, if one is to move beyond the fact of Stevenson's and James's important interrelation, one moves, by and large, into the area of the cautiously speculative.

It is thus a cautionary tale that, when James and Stevenson first met, neither man seemed to have recognised the interest they would come to hold for one another. In the summer of 1879, James, aged 36, had lunched, probably at the Savile Club in London, with Stevenson, then 28, Edmund Gosse and Andrew Lang. The others present at that luncheon were significant and representative. Both Gosse and Lang (though the latter was literally a Scot) might be described as English men of letters, literary middle men negotiating the complex world of writers and publishers in an age of transition between the Victorian and the Modern, an age which saw radical changes in an (increasingly mass) readership, in the workings of publishers, and in the style and content of literary writing. Gosse and Lang were at home in this complex, shifting literary world in ways that both Stevenson and James were not. Yet Stevenson and James were each intent on making a name for themselves as writers before an increasingly unpredictable readership, and unsure of how best to present themselves to it.[2]

The result seems to have been an uneasy first meeting, a faltering attempt on the part of two young writers to fit in. James, himself playing too much the proper and genteel Europeanised American he often portrayed critically in his own writings, found Stevenson to be 'a pleasant fellow, but a shirt-collarless Bohemian and a great deal (in an inoffensive way) of a *poseur*'.[3] There seems no specific evidence of Stevenson's reaction to James on this particular occasion, but early in the relationship Stevenson reciprocally detected something insubstantial, superficial or phoney in James: 'a mere club fizzle [. . .] and no out-of-doors, stand-up man whatever'.[4] (This is especially damning from a writer who valorised the romance of 'clean, open-air adventure'.)[5] Two years later, Stevenson summed James up in a letter to his friend, W. E. Henley: 'Henry James in the Savile. I'll give you his song: "I have been to Yurrup".'[6] And Stevenson, ever the Anglophobe, did go on to give Henley Henry James's song, lampooning James – not least James's willingness to take English money and his seeming equivocation over his nationality – in verse:

H. James:
Not clad in transatlantic furs,
    But clinking English pence,
The young republic claims me hers
    In no parochial sense.

A bland colossus, mark me stride,
    From land to land, the sea,
And patronise on every side
    Far better men than me.

My books, the models are of wit
    And masterworks of art,
From occident to orient flit
    And please in every part.

Yet I'm a sentimental lot;
    And freely weep to see
Poor Hawthorne and the rest, who've not
    To Europe been, like me.[7]

Stevenson's dislike of James at this point may have been based as much on his reading of James as on his one less than clubbable personal encounter. In 1879 James had published his study of his American literary forebear *Hawthorne* in Macmillan's *English* Men of Letters Series. (The added italics make the double solecism already clear, one American writing about another American writer in a seemingly inappropriate context.) It is a work which is famous or notorious for its catalogue of what was lacking in American provincialism to feed the artistic imagination. The seemingly damning and seemingly unending Jamesian list of nos, given in abbreviated form here – 'No State [. . .] No sovereign, no court, no personal loyalty, no aristocracy, no church, no clergy, no army [. . .] no Oxford, nor Eton, nor Harrow; no literature, no novels, no museums, no pictures, no political society, no sporting class – no Epsom nor Ascot!'[8] – may nonetheless conceal a degree of American wonder and American pride but these Jamesian nos made the hackles of the Scot, loosely but distinctively educated in Edinburgh rather than at Eton or Oxford, rise, and tempted Stevenson to embark on a romantic adventure:

> Received James's *Hawthorne* on which I meditate a blast [. . .] [I]t is very clever, very well written, and out of sight the most snobbish and (in his own word) provincial – provincialism inside out – thing in the world: I have dug up the hatchet; a scalp shall flutter at my belt ere long.[9]

Their friendship once established, James was to return Stevenson's accusation here – of James's provincial internationalism – as a compliment: 'Mr. Stevenson has been emancipated: he is, as we may say, a Scotchman of the world.'[10] The hatchet which Stevenson threatens in 1880, when it finally emerged, was disguised as 'A Humble Remonstrance' (1884). Yet the terms in which Stevenson figures his challenge to James here are remarkably telling, since Stevenson presents himself as a Native American, a scalp-hunting Chingachgook, emerging from the pages of the American romance writer James Fenimore Cooper, whose works had themselves emerged, as it were, from the writings of Sir Walter Scott. Moreover, James's account stung Stevenson since the latter had a particular admiration for Hawthorne, whom he contrasted with the realist novels of the day:

> The purely critical spirit is, in most novels, paramount. At the present moment we can recall one man only, for whose works it would have been equally possible to accomplish our present design: and that man is Hawthorne. There is a unity, an unwavering creative purpose, about some at least of Hawthorne's romances, that impresses itself on the most indifferent reader; and the very restrictions and weaknesses of the man served perhaps to strengthen the vivid and single impression of his works.[11]

In fact, both Stevenson and James, in expressing mutual suspicion and sensing falseness each in the other, were describing, in pejorative terms, a difficult struggle that they had in common – a struggle, involving the adoption of roles, affectations and mannerisms, to establish their identities as artists. Both were literally foreigners in the world of London art in the latter part of the nineteenth century, where the relation between great fiction, on the one hand, and popular and lucrative fiction, on the other – a relation that has never been easy – was fraught and becoming increasingly so as the world moved towards the twentieth century and the fracture of Modernism. Both James and Stevenson struggled under the burden of famous families, each family with a 'serious' history remote from what Stevenson feared might be seen as his choosing 'To play at home with paper like a child' or what James once described as 'the madness of art'.[12] Both families were oppressively over-solicitous, reluctant to allow each writer the autonomy and independence of literary adulthood as something apart from the familial and familiar roles each had been assigned. In short, the Stevensons built lighthouses; the Jameses were philosophers, and had a place, albeit a comparatively minor one, amongst the great families of America. Each son was financially dependent on his family long into adulthood. Neither family was easy. In religious terms, each was marked by religious crisis, despair and blackness. Both families were marred by illness, both physical and mental. Though his elder brother, the philosopher and psychologist William James, had died in 1910, William's widow, Alice, fulfilling her promise to her husband, arrived to look after Henry in his final illness: Henry remained even at the point of his own death, merely – but fondly – the younger brother. In turn, at Bournemouth, Henry James had been quick to see the oppressiveness of the Stevenson parents' presence on Louis. In pursuing identities as writers, names were important for both James and Stevenson. Henry (or Harry) James Junior had no name of his own until his father's death when James was nearly forty. The distinguishing title of 'The Master' must have been especially welcome in James's later years. Stevenson was born Robert Lewis Balfour Stevenson, the names of his paternal grandfather enclosing those of his mother's father. He became Robert Louis Stevenson around 1868–9. But from childhood onwards – 'Names, bare names, are surely more to children than we poor, grown-up, obliterated fools remember,' Stevenson once wrote – he rejoiced in a riot of other names: Smout, Lou, Signor Spruckie, Baron Broadnose, Velvet Coat, Robert Ramsay Fergusson Stevenson . . . and eventually, in Samoa, Tusitala.[13]

A further curious instance of names at play in the relation between these two writers occurs when, in December 1886, in a post script, Stevenson's friend, W. E. Henley writes to Stevenson of Henry James: 'I hear that Henrietta has gone to Florence for the winter. I hope she will not get into any trouble, I'm sure.'[14] Stevensonian correspondence naming Henry James as

'Henrietta' is likely to accord with recent biographical speculation regarding both writers and sexuality. It accords too with the readings which queer theory has brought to some of Stevenson's and James's best known works. However, it seems to the present writer that the naming of James as 'Henrietta' involves a sharper, more particular and more literary joke which goes to the heart of the enduring quarrel, good-naturedly conducted, between the two writers. James is named 'Henrietta' in the context of a trip to Italy, and this is then immediately followed by the curious formulation 'I hope she will not get into any trouble, I'm sure.' Why does Henley need to 'hope' if he is 'sure'? It is because James is being identified with Henrietta Stackpole, the American in James's own novel, *The Portrait of a Lady* (1881) who sails through Europe, and Italy in particular, untouched and unthreatened by it because she simply does not 'get' Europe. Henley is here returning to Stevenson the James whom Stevenson had sent Henley in his lampooning poem. Moreover, Henley is returning this less than fully admired James by reference to James's *The Portrait of a Lady*, a novel which Stevenson especially disliked, perhaps because it is among the most realist of James's works, and, in terms of plot, the most defeatist. In *The Portrait of a Lady* the central character is overwhelmed by life, defeated by its narrative plot and the plottings of other characters within that plot. By contrast for Stevenson, author of adventure stories and romances, it was always the role of the plot to attempt to imprison, kidnap or destroy his protagonists but, at the moment of defeat, the tropes of romance – doubling, escape and transformation – were to effect a rescue. The probability of the way things happen was to be countered by the imaginative alternative possibility. Henley's implicit remonstrance of James here is one which the champion of romance and escape would have especially relished.

It was illness, a trait of both families, that brought James and Stevenson, initially wary each of the other, together as friends. Louis's own illness had forced him, with his wife Fanny, to Skerryvore, a house in the English south coast resort of Bournemouth. James had brought his invalid sister, Alice, to the same seaside resort in 1885. The two writers met and enjoyed each other's company. James gave the Stevensons a mirror. A special chair was kept for James at Skerryvore, and both the mirror and James were celebrated in Stevenson's verse. When Stevenson sailed from Europe in 1887 for what was to be the last time, Henry James was there, with a case of champagne, to see the Stevensons off. The friendship continued in letters until Stevenson's death in 1894, a death which devastated James.

Were James and Stevenson mutual influences on each other's *creative* works? Critics have made cases but the evidence by and large goes no deeper than similarity.[15] Thus, for example, James's *The Princess Casamassima* (1886) has things in common with Stevenson's *The Dynamiter* (1884). Stevenson's trait of 'doubling' characters may lie behind James's late tale, 'The Jolly

Corner' (1908), where Spencer Brydon returns from a life in Europe to confront the ghost of the man he might have been had he stayed in New York. Curiously, just prior to his marriage to Fanny Osbourne, Stevenson had written in *Virginibus Puerisque* (1881) about the limitations of marriage, not least for the artist: 'Once you are married, there is nothing left for you, not even suicide, but to be good.'[16] James had noted that Stevenson's books were 'for the most part books without women' and argued that Stevenson gave 'to the world the romance of boyhood'.[17] So it is certain that James added Stevenson's example to his catalogue of writers who had married. Most particularly, in the teasing story, 'The Lesson of the Master' (1888), which explores the possibility that marriage, and not least the economic demands it makes, may be 'fatal to the quality' of an artist's work, James certainly had the example of Robert Louis Stevenson, among others, in mind.[18] Indeed in his essay on Stevenson of 1888, James had asked rhetorically: 'Why should a person marry when he might be swinging a cutlass or looking for a buried treasure? Why should he waste at the nuptial altar precious hours in which he might polish periods?'[19]

Yet, if one is to be more persuasive about the creative relation of Stevenson and James, one has either to deal in in-jokes, the largely private nods and winks of naming, or one has to speak in altogether more general terms. In the names and initials of Edward Hyde and Henry Jekyll, and in the brothers, James and Henry, in *The Master of Ballantrae* is Stevenson telling us something Jamesian? Or is he merely and more privately sending Henry James a gesture of greeting? More generally it is the ghastly and the ghostly, the monstrous that James's and Stevenson's works have most in common – the depiction of 'the capacity for evil' James was so quick to recognise in *Strange Case of Dr Jekyll and Mr Hyde* – but this is to speak very generally indeed.[20]

Fortunately we have one encounter which does allow specificity. It is a great initiation of a lifelong friendship. It also appears, initially at least, a great missing of minds and, as such, exposes realism, the dominant mode of literary expression in nineteenth-century prose, however defined, to be under a pressure from which it would never persuasively recover. Henry James not merely came to 'Yurrup'. He settled in England, and settled into emulation of George Eliot, not least in his most Eliotic novel *The Portrait of a Lady* (1881). Here the romantic narrative voice pleads in vain for its heroine, Isabel Archer, who is nonetheless punished by harsh Eliotic realism in the workings of the novel's plot, 'ground in the very mill of the conventional' and left imprisoned in a Jamesian sterile marriage.[21] It is unsurprising that, as we have seen, Stevenson had an especial dislike of *The Portrait of a Lady* and that his characteristic epistolary gesture, when considering George Eliot herself, is one of rejection. In 1856, around the time that the child Stevenson was beginning to play with Skelt's Juvenile Drama and a barely teenaged

James was travelling with his family in 'Yurrup', George Eliot could proclaim a confidence in realism, a belief that 'our social novels profess to represent the people as they are' and that 'Art is the nearest thing to life'.[22] Yet this sophisticated and late starter wrote herself into difficulties over realism once she embarked on the creation of fiction. Even the realist manifesto in favour of 'the faithful representing of commonplace things' which interrupts *Adam Bede* (1859) is making concessions; 'The mirror is doubtless defective; the outlines will sometimes be disturbed; the reflection faint or confused; but I feel as much bound to tell you, as precisely as I can, what that reflection is, as if I were in the witness-box narrating my experience on oath.'[23] As a writer of fiction, Eliot, however, was then led not into the witness box but into 'the obscure underside of the imagination', the Gothic nightmare world of 'The Lifted Veil' (1859), itself an uncanny anticipation of Stevenson's and James's celebrated excursions into the Uncanny.[24] She awoke, as it were, to a recognition, famously expressed in an uncharacteristically poetic way in *Middlemarch* (1871–2), that there were limits and limitations to realism: 'If we had a keen vision and feeling of all ordinary human life, it would be like hearing the grass grow and the squirrel's heart beat, and we should die of that roar which lies on the other side of silence.'[25]

The critic George Levine has identified the dilemma of realism. He sees it typically defined against idealism and romance, having 'a primary allegiance to experience over art' but going in fear of the nature of that experience:

> The impelling energy in the quest for the world beyond words is that the world be there, and that it be meaningful and good; the persistent fear is that it is merely monstrous and mechanical, beyond the control of human meaning. Realism risks that reality and its powers of disruption.[26]

Hence when James came to address 'The Art of Fiction' in 1884, his insistence, in his title, on 'art' was already at odds with any insistence on 'realism', and any claims for realism, or even claims to define realism, were under altogether greater strain than they had been for Eliot in 1856. James was joining a debate initiated by the novelist and public figure Walter Besant, chairman of the Society of Authors, and another of those English men of letters, like Gosse and Lang, adept at moving in the shifting London literary world of the 1880s.[27] However, James was using Besant's lecture as the occasion to attempt to rise above that world, and Stevenson was to join James in the attempt, each making different and contradictory claims for writing but both claiming prose fiction as a high art in contrast to the jobbing writing of the London literary world. Besant's lecture afforded James the opportunity of a public platform to set out a Jamesian view of fiction and address or create a Jamesian audience. James has much to say but here, anticipating Stevenson's contrary position, our interest lies in how James situates himself in relation to realism and to the Eliotic 'witness-box'.[28] From his first sentence, James is finding his essay 'wanting in any completeness'; he seeks to resist making any apology that fiction is mere '"make believe" [. . . and] shall renounce the pretension of attempting really to compete with life'.[29] On the contrary, 'The only reason for the existence of a novel is that it *does* compete with life.'[30] Here 'compete', a word upon which Stevenson seizes, proves slippery, pointing in one of two ways: with fiction, as James seems to intend, attempting to equal and represent life; or with fiction, as Stevenson might have seen it, in opposition to life. Hence in revising the essay for book publication James changed 'attempting really to compete with life' to 'attempting really to represent life' and '*does* compete with life' to 'does attempt to represent life'.[31] But it is when James comes to resist Besant's advice that the aspiring young novelist should write only out of experience, out of what she or he knows, that James seems torn between imaginative freedom and accurate representation, and we see realism unravel, even as he attempts to defend it. James begins by taking a cautious step back: 'It goes without saying that you will not write a good novel unless you possess the sense of reality; but it will be difficult to give you a recipe for calling that sense into being.'[32] Here we have an instance of what rhetoricians call apophasis: to have to say something that 'goes without saying' suggests an uncertainty about what is being said. 'Reality' has loosened to 'the sense of reality' and objective reality is already being eroded by the subjectivity of the human mind. James continues:

> Humanity is immense and reality has a myriad forms [. . .] It is equally excellent and inconclusive to say that one must write from experience [. . .] What kind of experience is intended, and where does it begin and end? Experience is never limited and it is never complete; it is an immense sensibility, a kind of huge spider-web, of the finest silken threads suspended in the chamber of consciousness, and catching every air-borne particle in its tissue. It is the very atmosphere of the mind; and when the mind is imaginative – much more when it happens to be that of a man of genius – it takes to itself the faintest hints of life, it converts the very pulses of the air into revelations [. . .] If experience consists of impressions, it may be said that impressions *are* experience, just as (have we not seen it?) they are the very air we breathe. Therefore, if I should certainly say to a novice, 'Write from experience, and from experience only,' I should feel that this was rather a tantalising monition if I were not careful immediately to add, 'Try to be one of the people on whom nothing is lost!'[33]

What does it mean to be someone 'on whom nothing is lost'? Is James not in danger here of hearing the grass grow and the squirrel's heartbeat, the death-dealing roar on the other side of silence? Or – to change from Eliot's figures to James's own metaphor – is he not in danger of being caught, fly-like, in the elaborate silken web of his own making? 'The sense of reality', 'experience', 'sensibility', 'consciousness', 'imaginative', 'revelations', 'impressions' – the terms of the argument merge and blur, shifting between the world out there and the workings of the human mind. It is thus emblematic of the essay as a whole that the potential nebulousness of James's often quoted dictum that the novel must have 'the air of reality' has to be relieved by the immediate glossing, in parenthesis, of this phrase as '(solidity of specification)'.[34]

When, later in this ever complicating, unsettled and unsettling exploration – an essay in the truest sense – James pauses to admire 'the delightful story of *Treasure Island*', he gives Stevenson his opportunity of reply.[35] For, however admiring, James is still intent on privileging realism, in its all-entangling definition or lack of definition, over romantic adventure and so, beyond initial delight, James finds nothing more to say of *Treasure Island*. He explains such silence: 'I have been a child, but I have never been on a quest for a buried treasure.'[36]

The retort was sharp:

> Here is, indeed, a wilful paradox; for if he [James] has never been on a quest for buried treasure, it can be demonstrated that he has never been a child. There never was a child (unless Master James) but has hunted gold, and been a pirate, and a military commander, and a bandit of the mountains; but has fought, and suffered shipwreck and prison, and imbrued its little hands in gore, and gallantly retrieved the lost battle, and triumphantly protected innocence and beauty.[37]

This is unanswerable, except, as James himself answered Stevenson's essay, with a warm and courteous letter of appreciation, initiating, not further debate as Stevenson himself had hoped, but a long literary and personal friendship.

Though never humble, Stevenson's 'A Humble Remonstrance' was more generally generous to James and intent on pursuing a debate with a writer who had as uncharacteristically high an estimate of the art of fiction as Stevenson himself. Stevenson sets himself in opposition to James, and sets his own view of art in opposition to life, to a world 'whose sun we cannot look upon, whose passion and diseases waste and slay us'.[38] Stevenson's is a pessimistic philosophy of the overwhelming chaos of the world:

> Life is monstrous, infinite, illogical, abrupt, and poignant; a work of art, in comparison, is neat, finite, self-contained, rational, flowing, and emasculate. Life imposes by brute energy, like inarticulate thunder; art catches the ear, among the far louder noises of experience like an air artificially made by a discreet musician.[39]

The Stevensonian artist, intent on an 'air artificially made' must therefore 'half-shut his eyes against the dazzle and confusion of reality' (contrast

James's nebulous but more benign 'air of reality') and half-close his ears to the thunderous roar that lies on the other side of silence. Stevenson's engagement with James here is intense, as can been seen in the precise detail of the altered verbal echoes. And so, in contrast to the Jamesian ever-complicating pursuit of the ever-complicated, Stevenson declares that the novel is 'not a transcript of life, to be judged by its exactitude; but a simplification of some side or point of life, to stand or fall by its significant simplicity'. He concludes looking beyond the particulars of the art of his own age to the great artists of all and any time: 'simplification was their method, and [. . .] simplicity is their excellence'.[40]

James and Stevenson are united in the high value they place on the art of fiction. For Stevenson that art is continuous with the art of romance and of poetry, and the abstraction of music. By contrast, James wrote no poems, and his increasingly poetic prose nonetheless continues to look nostalgically and complicatingly back to the prosaic world of high Victorian realism. (Both Peter Brooks and Victoria Coulson, refining our views of a changing James, argue that, even as James's style becomes ever more artful, he retains to a degree a stubborn commitment to the real.)[41]

However, it is very early in 'A Humble Remonstrance' that the most astonishing moment of Stevenson's and James's encounter occurs. Stevenson instantly recognised that a writer, such as James, intent on being someone on whom 'nothing is lost' was himself in danger of getting lost.

> Mr. James utters his mind with a becoming fervour on the sanctity of truth to the novelist; on a more careful examination truth will seem a word of very debateable propriety, not only for the labours of the novelist, but for those of the historian. No art – to use the daring phrase of Mr. James – can successfully 'compete with life'; and the art that does so is condemned to perish *montibus aviis*.[42]

Bizarre though it seems to say as much, Stevenson here anticipates a novel that Henry James had already written (and published in 1875) but a novel which it is likely that Stevenson did not read until November 1887. In 'to perish *montibus aviis* [among pathless mountains]' Stevenson is alluding to one of Horace's Odes, but he is also retelling the end of Henry James's novel, *Roderick Hudson*. Roderick is a young American sculptor of inordinate ambition, as given expression in one of his earliest works, a naked youth drinking from a gourd, entitled 'Thirst'. Brought to Europe through the patronage of Rowland Mallet, Roderick appears initially to be realising his potential as a sculptor in, for example, the creation of an Adam and an Eve. But his art becomes more intermittent and decadent just as, in his life, thirst turns to intoxication and debauchery. Europe, and Italy in particular, proves too much for Roderick, and he meets his death in the midst of a storm, falling from a mountain in the Alps. In death, Roderick 'was singularly little disfigured', 'strangely serene', 'beautiful'.[43] In this, Roderick is at odds with the disfiguring deaths – in James, Stevenson and Oscar Wilde – which were to succeed it in the history of fiction. *Roderick Hudson*'s ending was to dissatisfy the older Henry James because of its precipitateness and implausibility, its being too melodramatic and romantic, but the novel came to delight Stevenson reading it at Saranac Lake in 1887. It was Stevenson who was to die the early, sudden and – in the extraordinarily audacious words of Henry James writing to Stevenson's widow – 'romantically right' death.[44] James did not emulate Roderick Hudson's fate and James, competing with life, avoided the perishing to which Stevenson appears to condemn him.

Stevenson ended his 'A Humble Remonstrance' with a plea for simplicity and simplification. So far this account of the debate between the two writers has itself been a simplification, a simplification intent on bringing out what was at issue in their disagreement over the nature of the world and about how fiction should or should not address it. Of course James was right in his immediate response that 'we agree, I think, much more than we disagree'.[45] Stevenson was never dismissive of realism *tout court* but rather his arguments must be situated in the literary-critical time of their making, where the presumption in favour of the maturity of realism and the dismissal of the frivolity or childishness of romance were to be resisted by Stevenson. 'A Humble Remonstrance' has thus a polemical aim and is broadly consistent with Stevenson's equally polemical remarks elsewhere. Stevenson was always cautious about naming, about any realist claim for a mapping of the given world and language. For example, in 'A Note on Realism' Stevenson had complained musically of contemporary novels: 'Our little air is swamped and dwarfed among hardly relevant orchestration; our little passionate story drowns in a deep sea of descriptive eloquence or slipshod talk.' He complained too of the realist's 'insane pursuit of completion'.[46] By contrast, considering 'Victor Hugo's Romances', Stevenson argues that the art of romance

> is working far ahead of language as well as of science, realising for us, by all manner of suggestions and exaggerations, effects for which as yet we have no direct name; nay, for which we may never perhaps have a direct name [. . .] Hence alone is that suspicion of vagueness that often hangs about the purpose of a romance.[47]

And in 'A Gossip about Romance' Stevenson had argued that the words of even the weakest of storytellers 'may be nourished with the realities of life, but their true mark is to satisfy the nameless longings of the reader, and to obey the ideal laws of the day-dream'.[48] However, the commonplace regarding

Stevenson's development as a writer remains true – that, as Stevenson in later years wrote in exotic climes, his writings moved more thoroughly towards realism, the need to name and describe a world given rather than alternative worlds created by the imagination. (This may be understandable since Stevenson, who had hitherto always made the world strange for his readers, may finally have felt the pressure to render his exotic locations more familiar to, and assimilable by, his English-speaking readers.) However, as a writer, James changed too.

Both writers knew – Stevenson from the first, James only gradually and reluctantly – that realism was naming and shameful. Peter Brooks argues that in the 1890s James went though 'a kind of epistemological anguish, the anxious difficulty of figuring out what one knows about other people and the world, and how to know it'.[49] Brooks argues that James's year in Paris in 1875–6, when at the time James resisted the examples of French writers and artists, returned with these same cultural figures now as more positive influences, moving James beyond realism. However, Brooks concedes that other matters, including 'the loss of [. . .] Robert Louis Stevenson' were in play in James's transformation.[50] Certainly, in the first decade of the twentieth century, when James was planning the great New York Edition of his works, the twenty-eight volume Edinburgh Edition of Stevenson (1894–8) was one of his models. James wrote prefaces for his New York Edition, prefaces which taken together constitute the fullest elaboration of James's thinking about fiction. In the Preface to *The American*, for example, James came to invoke Stevenson's name and to define and, to a degree, to defend romance in ways which would have pleased Stevenson: romance is 'experience liberated [. . .] experience disengaged, disembroiled, disencumbered, exempt from the conditions we usually know to attach to it and [. . .] drag upon it'. In romance, buoyed up by the 'balloon of experience' we sail in 'the more or less commodious car of the imagination'.[51] In the Preface to the *Lesson of the Master* (a gathering of James's tales of the life of the artist) James spoke out *against* the probable, the stuff of realism, in favour of 'the possible other case, the case rich and edifying where actuality is pretentious and vain'.[52] (This shift in Jamesian emphasis is anticipated in 1888 in James's praise for the 'the improbable' and 'the extraordinary' in Stevenson's *Strange Case of Dr Jekyll and Mr Hyde*.)[53] James now inveighed against 'all the stupidity and vulgarity and hypocrisy' of the world and argued for art as romance, idealism and escapism, asking rhetorically: 'How can one consent to make a picture of the preponderant futilities and vulgarities and miseries of life without the impulse to exhibit as well from time to time, in its place, some fine example of the reaction, the opposition or the escape?'[54] Here at last James seems to have found an inner child prepared to quest for buried treasure, gallantly to retrieve the lost battle, and triumphantly to protect innocence and beauty. The horrors of the First World War were to confirm for James Stevenson's view that life was 'monstrous, illogical, abrupt [. . .] inarticulate thunder', and that reality was unspeakable and unbearable.[55] Hence James's last great engagement with a fellow writer, H. G. Wells, who had lampooned the 'copious emptiness' of James's late style, was in defence of an 'art that *makes* life, makes interest, makes importance [. . .] and I know of no substitute whatever for the force and beauty of its process'.[56]

Perhaps the reason that Stevenson has remained, until comparatively recently, on the margins of critical discussion of nineteenth-century fiction is that the struggle over realism was a struggle in which, from the first, Stevenson chose never to engage. Our times are more sympathetic to Stevenson's refusal and Stevenson is now more studied and acclaimed. For James, Stevenson the man, long lost from Europe, came to seem the archetypical figure of romance – 'wholly of the stuff that dreams are made of', he tells Stevenson in an echo of Shakespeare's great romance, *The Tempest*.[57] When Stevenson died, Henry James, writing to Edmund Gosse to express his devastation, invoked the idiom of the romantic closure of *Roderick Hudson*, Stevenson's favourite of James's works. So James tells Gosse he feels 'as if suddenly *into* that place there had descended a great avalanche of ice' but James is also echoing the words of the butler in Stevenson's *Strange Case* which James, in his 1888 essay on Stevenson had singled out to describe the reader's experience of that novel – 'it went down my spine like ice'.[58] As James himself lay dying in 1916, recalling for whatever reason 'the great R.L.S.', experience generally in the form of the First World War and experience, more particularly, of the vulnerability of his own physical body were finally mastering the Master. A realisation of the ghastly and monstrous came reluctantly and grudgingly to James. Stevenson, by contrast, although he had lost his religious faith, lived always with the pessimism of his Calvinist inheritance. Perhaps Stevenson had always been – in the commonplace, non-literary sense of the term – the more 'realistic' of the two writers. Tusitala's writings never sought to compete with life. Instead they offer compensation for it, 'a poor penny world; but soon [. . .] all coloured with romance'.[59]

CHAPTER TEN

Stevenson's Afterlives

Alex Thomson

Writing thirty years after Stevenson's death, G. K. Chesterton already felt the need for a reassessment of his work that would be strong enough to distance itself from both 'the Victorian whitewashers and the Post-Victorian mudslingers'.[1] Chesterton's comment does more than reflect the critical turbulence which has accompanied Stevenson's enormous posthumous celebrity from its inception: his choice of words hints at a childish petulance on both sides; and he slyly suggests that Stevenson's reputation suffered in the larger turning of an epoch, in which his writing was taken to embody the Victorian spirit by both its defenders and detractors. This is an astute observation, and much of the smoke that still clouds our view of Stevenson's work comes from the flames to which a professedly modern school of thinking about literature consigned its immediate predecessors. Indeed Stevenson's position may even be exemplary. Edwin Muir suggested in 1931, a few years after Chesterton's book, that 'in the general eclipse of Victorian reputation no one possibly has suffered more than Stevenson'.[2]

Critics of Stevenson were reacting in part to the hyperbole of his admirers, two of whom in particular were to become synonymous with that impressionistic approach to literature repudiated by the moderns. To put in context Arthur Quiller-Couch's notorious declaration 'Put away books and paper and pen. Stevenson is dead. Stevenson is dead, and now there is nobody left to write for':[3] Quiller-Couch was no hack – he was a critic who commanded the attention of a wide public and went on to be a respected academic – yet not only did he write six concluding chapters for *St Ives*, both the manuscript and serial publication of which had been interrupted by Stevenson's death, but he also published *Dead Man's Rock* (1887) a romance novel overtly indebted to *Treasure Island*. Nor is it difficult to see how the very sentiments with which Walter Raleigh eulogised Stevenson in an 1895 lecture to the Royal Institution could turn into insults at the hands of less charitable readers. For Raleigh, Stevenson was 'a finished literary craftsman [. . .] playing with his tools', whose power over romance stemmed from the fact that 'his childhood never ended'.[4] This seems curiously literal, as if success in writing for children must depend on the failure or the refusal to commit to full adulthood. It is also a notion of literary art which might look evasive or worse in the light of the European catastrophe of the 1914–18 war.

Raleigh comments on the 'happy privilege of making lovers among his readers' and the personal and directly emotional impact of Stevenson's writing, which remains a key component of his wider reception to this day, was another prompt to critical suspicions.[5] Even before his death, there was an established market for articles and memoirs describing encounters with Stevenson, particularly once he was ensconced in the Pacific. He was to be paid posthumous tribute in numerous memorials and reminiscences, not only from friends and relatives, but from acquaintances of imperfect familiarity, and even from those merely touched by his writing. It seemed as if everyone had met him, and everyone who had, had been moved by him in some way. An authorised biography by a family friend (1901) followed lightly-bowdlerised collections of correspondence published in 1895 and 1899 – 'all the book is manly' proclaimed Quiller Couch in his review of the former[6] – and numerous editions of the works, in both expensive collectors' formats and in more affordable readers' editions. As the republication of Stevenson's work was good business for booksellers, his reputation was worth a great deal to his family, who continued to rely on the royalties, and there was a certain amount of rallying amongst his friends to ensure that this investment was secure.

If we take *Eminent Victorians* (1918), Lytton Strachey's scathing attack on the preceding generation's cultivation of heroic exemplars, as typical of the modernist mood, and set it alongside the scientific aspirations of academic literary criticism in the 1920s and 1930s, the backlash against a writer whose personal cult seemed to exert such power over the reading of his works will seem inevitable. Yet the pattern had actually been set much earlier, when W. E. Henley, a former friend of Stevenson's, attacked what he saw as 'this Seraph in chocolate, this barley-sugar effigy of a real man', the legend that had so swiftly supplanted the life.[7] In 1922, Maurice Hewlett described Stevenson in *The Times* newspaper as a man whom 'local renown and the zeal of his friends have tilted out of his place in the scheme of things'.[8] That this did lasting damage to our sense of Stevenson as a writer is attested by Janet Adam Smith in her 1948 study of the relations between Stevenson and James. She echoes the latter's warning that Stevenson's persona would supersede his reputation as an artist: 'Stevenson the serious writer was eclipsed by Stevenson the picturesque character – the imaginative child, the rebellious Edinburgh bohemian, the Tusitala of the last coloured South Sea years.'[9] This suggests that a displacement from the works to the writer was present from the beginning.

Stevenson the man has continued to eclipse Stevenson the writer, and broadly sympathetic biographical studies continue to appear far more frequently than one might expect for a writer of his era. Even more distinctive is the continuing vogue for works concerned to retrace Stevenson's various travels: take for example Richard Holmes, self-professed 'Romantic Biographer', who followed his journey in the Cevennes *sans* donkey and uses the journey as the prompt for his own recollections and self-analysis; or John Cairney, an actor who had played Stevenson on stage and who finishes his own 2004 study *The Quest for Robert Louis Stevenson* by declaring 'I have thought myself so vividly into the life of Robert Louis Stevenson that he lives in my imagination like an old friend.'[10] Nicholas Rankin's *Dead Man's Chest* is the best of the genre, because he recognises that the power of Stevenson's work depends upon the author's absence, and that the attempt to derive the art from the life threatens to become a reductive attack on art itself.[11] The intensity of the personal response to Stevenson by readers and other writers and artists has done much to warn away academic critics.

More considered critical appraisal has also stumbled against the great celebrity of Stevenson's most enduring characters and stories, whose fame is matched only by the speed with which they were absorbed into popular legend; so much so that their literary origins, and even the name of their creator, have often been forgotten. Nowhere is this more obvious than with *Strange Case of Dr Jekyll and Mr Hyde* (1886): within two years of publication numerous dramatic productions were being staged on both sides of the Atlantic and rival adaptations were petitioning Stevenson for his blessing. Major film versions of the novella have been produced regularly since *The Duality of Man* (1910). The common currency of Stevenson's work is also suggested by the fact that, as Scott Nollen points out, his characters were available for topical comic reference, and 'burlesques' reached the stage even before the serious adaptations – *The Strange Case of a Hyde and Seekyl* (1886) first in a long line of plays and films to pay tongue-in-cheek homage to Stevenson's original, including the inevitable pornographic *Dr Sexual and Mr Hyde* (1971).[12]

Treasure Island (1882) may not have been dramatised until after Stevenson's death, and the popularity of the book was not as immediate as that of *Dr Jekyll and Mr Hyde*, but there is a convincing case to be made for it as the definitive reformulation of pirate lore for the twentieth century. The popular celebration of the ambiguous figure of the pirate has been continuous since the golden age of piracy itself at the beginning of the eighteenth century, almost immediately passing from street ballads and sensational trial reports into the stock types of the developing novel form in the work of Daniel Defoe. Stevenson's prefatory poem pays due tribute to his predecessors, but in contrast with Walter Scott's *The Pirate* (1822) or Captain Marryat's *The Pirate* (1836), Stevenson's book continues to be read to this day. The novel has attracted both prequels and sequels, and so enduring has been its myth that modern historians of piracy frequently begin by distancing their own work from such appealing fictions. *Treasure Island* too has been adapted on numerous occasions: first filmed as a one-reeler by Vitagraph in 1908, more than forty film versions have been made since in several languages.

This apparent affinity between Stevenson's most popular works and the cinema and television suggests further reasons for critical suspicion. Peter Keating has suggested that the enormous proliferation of genres in the novel at the end of the nineteenth century is closely related to the birth of a mass reading audience.[13] One of the consequences was a widening of the field of polite letters, particularly as it intersected with the burgeoning market for print journalism, through the incorporation of a range of sensational, lurid and shocking tales which had previously been treated as below the level of the serious writer. Yet the pulp fiction and melodrama of the turn of the century would in turn be the seedbed for the subsequent explosion in the visual media, and the concomitant marginalisation of the printed word within popular culture. Stevenson seems to have recognised the extent to which all story-telling recycles cultural images. Yet just as he re-used material already familiar to his readers from pirate lore, so his most well-known stories have been absorbed into the wider culture. As Brian A. Rose notes, later adaptations refer as frequently to the innovations made in earlier versions, now cultural commonplaces, as to Stevenson's original texts.[14] This suggests that a study of the afterlife of his works in other media would tell us more about the concerns and anxieties of the world through which they have passed than about the original works themselves.

If the test of the true invention is that we cannot imagine the world as it was beforehand, the consequence for the inventor may be to risk being seen as the mere conduit for that which would have been discovered anyway. The passage of one's creatures from literature into popular imagination tends to devalue the artist's cultural stock. Combined with the over-enthusiasm of his early admirers, the subsequent ubiquity of *Treasure Island*'s Jim Hawkins, Long John Silver and Benn Gunn, of *Kidnapped*'s David Balfour, and of Dr Jekyll and Mr Hyde, quickly obscured specifically literary qualities of Stevenson's art, and has narrowed subsequent critical perceptions. Stevenson has been treated as the romancer he is thought to have been rather than the Man of Letters he aspired to be. Edwin Muir also points this out: 'Stevenson has simply fallen out of the procession. He is still read by the vulgar, but he has joined that band of writers on whom, by tacit consent, the serious critics have nothing to say.'[15] In the aftermath of war, a renewed emphasis on artistic seriousness in both the republic of letters and academic literary study, required a stricter enforcement of limits than could have been anticipated in the last decades of the nineteenth.

So within a generation of his death in 1894, early hagiography had ceded to the self-consciously modern fashion for critical debunking and Stevenson's despondent comment in his last letter to his friend Sidney Colvin seemed to have come true: 'I am a fictitious article, and have long known it. I am read by journalists, by my fellow-novelists, and by boys; with these *incipit et explicit* my vogue.'[16] Yet it would be wrong to take this attitude as characteristic of Stevenson's true sentiments, which were put sharply in an aside in his early essay on 'The English Admirals': 'The best artist is not the man who fixes his eye on posterity, but the one who loves the practice of his art.'[17] If by the 1920s Stevenson's name had become a byword for the posthumous collapse of literary credibility, as Leonard Woolf suggests, we should remember that his own criteria were not those of his subsequent judges. As the Latin tag in his letter above suggests, Stevenson's consciously literary style – 'thin', 'artificial', 'nothing to say' gloats Woolf[18] – was sustained by a sense of inherited tradition that was about to come under prolonged attack in the name of a generational revolt. On the basis of his passing remark that he had played the 'sedulous ape' in his early years, Stevenson was attacked as a mere stylist, a slavish copier of other men's work, and his reputation for style was inverted, seen as a weakness of imagination. But what Stevenson was in fact drawing attention to was his conception of writing as a craft, which requires practice and development rather than inspiration alone, and a sense of tradition that was unavailable to the generations to follow.

Stevenson's great concern with pattern, with the formal shape of a text, of the fit of words to the thought expressed in them, is not a reactionary regression to the eighteenth century, but the logical outcome of an aestheticism that refused to topple over into the expressive excess of symbolism. It is this abiding concern with literature as a craft – kept in check, as Stephen Arata has argued, by a distrust of the profession of letters – which makes sense of the apparent hyperbole of Quiller-Couch's comments above.[19] He celebrates Stevenson the writer: consummate stylist, not moral arbiter. Moreover, in context there is a distinctly ambivalent moral tone to his remark, as the reassertion of the 'selfish instinct' rising in the wake of the more genuinely altruistic feeling of 'sorrow'.[20] But stylishness has proved double-edged: critical revulsion against Stevenson's personal cult and popular appeal has been joined by the charge that his style was merely a poetic means to a rather prosaic end, a studied eloquence which gave a mere illusion of profundity. If both sides have agreed on the fact of Stevenson's style, while disagreeing on its value, there has been less said about the nature of his style, and in particular of the interaction between the problem of style, his sense of romance form and his abiding concern with morals.

In his review of Chesterton's Stevenson book, T. S. Eliot, at that time the most authoritative critic writing in English, called for a 'critical essay showing that Stevenson is a writer of permanent importance, and why.'[21] As

Christopher Ricks points out, Eliot asserts rather than questions Stevenson's significance.[22] Yet looking back with the benefit of another eighty years of hindsight, it is clear that nothing of the sort has yet been written. Indeed, the absence of such an essay suggests our continuing confusion about the idea of literary importance, and about the purpose and ambition of criticism. Eliot insists on literary *importance* – as opposed to popularity, or influence, or notoriety. But this distinction has become hard to maintain. One of Stevenson's recent biographers comments: 'No-one would now claim that Stevenson is a great writer. But that he is important, and a crucial part of literature's development in the latter part of the nineteenth century, cannot be doubted.'[23] So by 1982 'importance' had become what we might call 'circumstantial' – a function less of having made a mark in history than of being an interesting example of the tendencies of an age.

Recent critical work on Stevenson has largely continued to avoid the question of 'the practice of his art', which is why early admirers such as Chesterton and Raleigh remain sound guides. It has become common to treat Stevenson's writing as an anticipation of 'modernist' or even 'postmodernist' literary trends. But this is to derive the value of his work from what is taken to be the established authority of other literary fashions. Not only does the modern critical rehabilitation of Stevenson fail to get beyond the frame of reference in which the moderns looked back on the Victorians, but the recent explosion in critical studies of Stevenson can at times look like a continuation of earlier attempts to tie the art to the artist, combing the archives for biographical or historical sources for his work. This is most marked in relation to *Dr Jekyll and Mr Hyde*, in which Stevenson is repeatedly said to be dramatising something which he cannot write about overtly – masturbation, homosexuality, cocaine abuse or alcoholism – and the story itself is reduced to the symptomatic expression of its particular historical occasion.

Yet Stevenson's enduring popularity suggests that he cannot be considered merely a product of his time: what persists is testimony to the fact that a successful artwork is more than the product of its historical circumstances, and contains a reserve of power on which future writers and readers can draw. At the start of *Treasure Island* Jim gives as his reason for withholding the exact co-ordinates of Skeleton Island a motto which might stand over the afterlife of Stevenson's work: '[T]here is still treasure not yet lifted.'[24] In the remainder of the chapter I return to Eliot's question as to Stevenson's importance, based on the premise that to avoid critical short-sightedness we need to do our best to understand Stevenson's work in its own terms, in contradistinction to those of the Victorians or the moderns. Moreover, if treating Stevenson as the originator of distinctive modern myths does him some justice, we should be careful to return to the source on the grounds that what is most characteristic of his writing may be that which resists being translated into other forms.

Stevenson's legacy to the twentieth century novel in English – or the lack of it – is especially revealing. Throughout the century following his death, standard accounts of the history of the novel in English have revolved around the development of 'realism', often contrasted with alternative possibilities which might be described as 'modernist' or 'experimental'. The term suggests more than merely technical resources. For both author and critic the term 'realism' implies a moralistic suspicion of imaginative writing as a form of escapism, combined with the demand for naturalistic, psychological or historical explanation of social phenomena. Indeed, twentieth-century novelists in English have tended to turn away from anything that suggests allegory or fable, and sought to appeal directly to their readers' experiences of everyday life. Anything more sensational has tended to be suspect, the property of popular genre fiction as opposed to literary writing – a distinction which was less rigorously enforced in Stevenson's day than at any point before or since. The posthumous circulation of Stevenson's fiction could be taken by critics as confirmation of the essentially juvenile or immature nature of his work.

A second problem in evaluating Stevenson has been his retrospective assimilation with a host of minor Victorian propagandists, jingoistic advocates of imperialism and a virile masculine individualism. Where exceptions have been made and Stevenson's stories have been judged acceptable to an age which – like his own – sees itself as morally cleansed, this has been attributed to an underlying realism, as in the case of his grimy South Seas stories, in which colonial adventure contaminates all concerned with death and disease. But there is little evidence of a major shift in his style or attitudes. 'Realism' and 'romance' are compatible both for Stevenson, who sees a combination of the 'realistic and ideal' as the key to successful art, and for his contemporaries.[25] One reviewer at the time praised the 'healthy realism' of *Treasure Island*[26] but for many recent critics the novel remains tainted by the ideological associations of the form: 'a kind of popular romance much admired by conservative apologists for the novel.'[27] The failure to appreciate Stevenson's understanding of 'romance' has been crucial to his rejection as a literary model.

In 'A Gossip on Romance', an essay whose title suggests the informality of a fireside chat, Stevenson is open about the artistic principles behind his fiction. At the centre of a story which successfully enthrals the reader's imagination lie dramatic and forceful images: 'the threads of a story come from time to time together and make a picture in a web; the characters fall from time to time into some attitude to each other, or to nature, which stamps the story home like an illustration'. This is 'the highest and hardest thing to do in words', 'to embody character, thought or emotion in some act or attitude that shall be remarkably striking to the mind's eye.'[28] English critics since Dr Johnson had explored the originality of the novel as a modern form; but Stevenson sees contemporary fiction resting on much older foundations, and echoes Aristotle's account of the literary artwork as the imitation of an action. When he writes about romance Stevenson is not offering an alternative to realism so much as reflecting on aspects of narrative art on which every story depends. But if the novel is defined primarily as 'realistic', meaning faithful to life as we experience it, the novelist must disavow those formal aspects of the art, such as pattern and plot, which may not strike us as particularly truthful but on which its success depends.

Stevenson's comments on detail in the same essay are also revealing. The presence of exact particulars – for example Defoe's catalogue of the materials Crusoe is able to rescue from the shipwreck, but we might also think of Stevenson's list of the contents of Billy Bones's chest in *Treasure Island* – is valuable not because it locates the action in a 'realistic' world but because it makes the reader's daydreams real. 'No art produces illusion' argues Stevenson: description, location and fidelity to the world are satisfying when they resonate in the mind of the reader. Rather than establishing a convincing and 'typical' background, these concrete particulars become striking incidents in themselves.[29] This suggests a further secret of Stevenson's style – its compression. Nothing is required in the story which does not contribute to the overall pattern. In turn, the idea of pattern tells us that Stevenson's use of romance draws to the surface the artistic elements of the novel, the conscious artifice and the deliberate organisation of words on the page. As a result the romance begins to look something like a novel which reflects particularly intensely on its own stylistic possibilities.

Strange Case of Dr Jekyll and Mr Hyde offers us a good example of how Stevenson's romances work in practice, structured as it is around a series of striking scenes and incidents, observed or described: a shady-looking doorway recalls the trampling of a young girl by a sinister figure; the revolting appearance of Hyde himself is impressed on all who see him; the brutal murder of Carew is watched from above; the discovery of the ransacked chamber and twitching body of Dr Jekyll. It is these 'epoch-making scenes' which have stuck in the minds of Stevenson's readers: 'we may forget the words, although they are beautiful; we may forget the author's comment, although perhaps it was ingenious and true.'[30] It is the actions that are significant not their subsequent interpretation as part of an explanatory narrative. As Vladimir Nabokov argues, 'Stevenson's story is – God bless his pure soul – lame as a detective story. Neither is it a parable or an allegory, for it would be tasteless as either. It has, however, its own special enchantment if we regard it as a phenomenon of style.'[31] His are not works that dwell on the subtleties or complexities of human character, except in so far as those are directly revealed through decisions and choices made in extraordinary circumstances. Nor is he especially concerned to reveal the material or social underpinnings of the society in which his characters live. His fiction offers us riddles, but like the series of documents and memoranda which promise explanations in *Dr Jekyll and Mr Hyde*, their dramatic resolution fails to cancel out the original impression of mystery on which the artistic success of the venture hangs.

This is reading as Stevenson describes it in his essay: '[T]he process should be absorbing and voluptuous; we should gloat over a book, be rapt clean out of ourselves, and rise from the perusal, our mind filled with the busiest, kaleidoscopic dance of images, incapable of sleep or continuous thought.'[32] But it is also the fate that befalls Mr Utterson, the apparently prosaic observer of Jekyll's downfall, whose imagination is not merely 'engaged' but 'enslaved' by his encounters with Hyde.[33] Indeed, the focal transformation in the novel is not that of Jekyll into Hyde, but of Utterson into 'Mr Seek'.[34] The psychology of both reading and writing are for Stevenson connected to the unconscious, and the power of romance stems in large part from its access to those sources that our everyday life must block out. Enflamed by the story he has been told by Enfield, Utterson's fancy summons the image of a sleeper awakened by 'a figure to whom power was given, and even at that dead hour he must rise and do its bidding.'[35]

The figure is of course Utterson's personification of Hyde's inexplicable power over Jekyll, but we can see that it is also an internal mental dissociation, figuring the power of the image over the dreamer himself, and the threat to Utterson of the fancy he has sought to suppress. His dream uncannily foreshadows Jekyll's own moment of horror in awakening, when he sees Hyde's hand upon the pillow, and realises that he has ceded power over himself to another. If the scene here recalls Victor Frankenstein awoken by his own monstrous creation, so Stevenson's account of the genesis of *Dr Jekyll and Mr Hyde* echoes Mary Shelley's, both authors putting down their demonic creations to the inspiration of the nightmare. As Nicholas Rankin has argued, Shelley was very likely in Stevenson's mind during the composition of this story during his residence in Bournemouth, owing to his proximity to her former home. Even without such contextual information, *Dr Jekyll and Mr Hyde*, like so many of Stevenson's stories, is clearly in large part a drama of reading and writing.

The ambiguity of the romance's appeal to the imagination serves to underline the extent to which Stevenson's powerful moral concerns, expressed at length in his published and manuscript essays, cannot be directly read off from his fictional creations. As he puts it in 'A Gossip on Romance', 'There is a vast deal in life and letters both which is not immoral, but simply a-moral.'[36] But this is itself a moral lesson of sorts, and in one of his early essays he specifically identifies successful romance writing with the establishment of moral significance: 'every situation is informed with moral significance and grandeur'. But this does not mean a moral lesson so much as an 'organising principle'; Stevenson is not interested in '"the novel with a purpose"', 'the model of incompetence' in which 'the moral [is] clumsily forced into every hole and corner of the story, or thrown externally over it like a carpet over a railing.'[37]

A good example here is *Treasure Island*, a work whose moral complexity stems directly from the effort to bypass the pointing of moral lessons. A highly compressed and stylised *bildungsroman*, the story depends upon Jim's ability to acquire a strategic and inventive capacity to outwit the pirates. His maturity – even his survival – depend upon Jim's ability to learn from Long John Silver, whose ability to flatter and deceive is matched by extreme violence when necessary. Silver outmanoeuvres both his pirate crew and the officers and gentlemen on board the *Hispaniola*, while the fixed hierarchies of maritime life and the English social order seem as degenerate as the rough and ready democracy of the pirate's forecastle council.

This strikes the note of what Stevenson felt as his own 'confusion': 'Ethics are my veiled mistress. I love them, but I know not what they are.'[38] It should also remind us that although he is ostensibly writing for children, Stevenson believes he can serve them better by stocking their imaginations than by working on their conscience or sense of duty. Indeed, part of Jim's lesson in *Treasure Island* is that 'duty' is never in itself a sufficient guide to action, as he survives only by disobeying the orders of his superiors and breaking the rules. There are hints in this of the radical individualism that Stevenson found in the writings of Walt Whitman and Henry Thoreau, of his imaginative passion for the dissenting Protestantism of the Scottish Covenanters, and of his formative experiences of artistic Bohemianism as an antidote to the stifling Calvinism of his Edinburgh childhood. We are a long way from the pious hymns to duty – to God, to King and country, and to Empire – which would be codified in more didactic tracts of the turn of the century such as Baden-Powell's *Scouting for Boys* (1908).

The French critic Jacques Rivière characterises this aspect of Stevenson's work persuasively when, punning on the French *aventure*, he associates it with an openness towards the future: 'the perfect realisation of a novel lies in its perfect activity. It becomes "act" when it comes to the point of being composed only of actions.'[39] The effect of storytelling is 'a novel that advances through constantly new events'.[40] There is no sense of a larger pattern, fate or providence, unfolding in *Treasure Island*, but only the concrete and accidental outcomes of more or less spontaneous actions. Actions rewrite that which has gone before: 'Never does the past explain the present. But the present explains the past. I do not simply mean that it clarifies the enigmas, but that what happens modifies unceasingly the intent and the scope of what has happened.'[41]

This notion of the future has a polemical significance, in that it points to a conception of man struggling to open a future in which morality is not necessarily repudiated, but would become a matter of autonomy – living by one's own laws – rather than conformity to custom. Indeed Stevenson self-consciously exploits those aspects of the romance tradition that force us to challenge and question narrative authority. Like Hugo, whose ambition 'to "denounce" the external fatality that hangs over men in the form of foolish and inflexible superstition' Stevenson cites, this has a covert ideological force.[42] By challenging us to question the workings of Providence, it exposes history not as a drama of national heroism but as a more chaotic and lawless field in which the victor gets to tell his story at the expense of the victims. It is sufficiently prevalent in Stevenson's work to challenge any attempts to tie his work to imperialism, and reminds us that plotting is often subject to political manipulation.

This is particularly clear in *Treasure Island*. Jim Hawkins recounts his own story, recognising his impulsive and unlawful behaviour as 'the mad notions that contributed so much to save our lives' but refusing Livesey's temptation to see this as providential: '[T]here's a kind of fate in this [. . .] every step it's you that saves our lives.'[43] Stevenson's treatment of Benn Gunn, who like Defoe's Crusoe sees his isolation on the island as God's will, suggests that Providence is not perhaps to be trusted, providing only a convenient way of accommodating oneself to a situation which is outwith one's control. Moreover, the pirates whistle 'Lillibullero', a popular anti-Catholic song which became virtually a Whig anthem around the time of the Glorious Revolution of 1688 and ridicules Irish faith in prophecy, not on the grounds that such belief is mere superstition, but on the grounds that the English Protestants' faith in their divinely-guided victory is in fact correct. Subtly, Stevenson reacts against the mainstream of English political and histori-cal discourse, which celebrated that Providence by which liberty had been constituted.

This offers us a critical way of reading even an essay such as 'The English Admirals', which exemplifies the challenges posed by Stevenson to his modern reader. At first sight it appears to be an exercise in national mytho-poeia, celebrating the heroic exploits of exemplary men: '[W]e do not all feel warmly towards Wesley and Laud, we cannot all take pleasure in *Paradise Lost*; but there are certain common sentiments and touches of nature by which the whole nation is made to feel kinship.'[44] Religion and literature may not be able to unify the English, but the consciousness of noble deeds on the part of their ancestors can. Our affinity for the sea is predicated on our sense that its bottom is littered with 'the bones of our seafaring fathers' – Stevenson draws closely here on his source, the historian and essayist Froude's celebra-tion of the 'paving' of the sea with 'bones' in his well-known essay 'England's

Forgotten Worthies' which also inspired Kingsley's *Westward Ho!* and Tennyson's 'Ballad of the Revenge'.[45]

Yet there are touches of the sceptical eye that would more strongly inflect his later writing even in this early essay, which begins with a very characteristic anecdote. Stevenson recalls the Roman general, fighting barbarian warriors in the German forests, who exploits the sudden appearance of seven eagles, hailing them as Roman birds, and therefore as an excellent omen for the forthcoming battle. Such an ability to profit on accidental circumstances stands a real chance, Stevenson suggests, of changing the course of events: 'for it gives to the one party a feeling that Right and the larger interests are with them.' Prefaced in this way, Stevenson's prose encomium stands on shifting foundations. It is not the inherited characteristics of the English, but those stories that they believe, which constitute that 'feeling [. . .] seated beyond the reach of argument.'[46] What Stevenson describes in his Dedication as 'bracing, manly virtues' derive here from actions undertaken without thought of consequences, and certainly without thought of posthumous fame. Even if a form of providence returns, it is one that has been severed from racial or national destiny: 'Our affections and beliefs are wiser than we; the best that is in us is better than we can understand; for it is grounded in experience, and guides us, blindfold but safe, from one age on to another.'[47]

It is this sense of the unconscious forces operating on man that Stevenson sees as beginning with the work of Walter Scott: '[W]e begin to have a sense of the subtle influences that moderate and qualify a man's personality; that personality is no longer thrown out in unnatural isolation, but is resumed into its place in the constitution of things.'[48] It hints too at the cultural resources offered by romance which Stevenson seeks to mobilise against the vogue for the realist novel. Whereas a realist novel takes for granted that the forces which govern man's social and existential predicament can to a large extent be analysed and assessed, the romance warns us against the typically modern hubris of assuming that as the maker of his own environment, the resolution of all man's problems lies within his grasp. This might be at least one dimension of that elusive 'importance' to which Eliot alludes, and allows for the possibility of a strong conclusion: if Stevenson does not seem to fit into our history of the novel in English, then we need to rethink that history. Stevenson was an important reference point not only for Nabokov, but for other central figures of twentieth-century literature such as Gide and Borges. Italo Calvino is another, and his account of literature in 'Cybernetics and Ghosts' – an essay which reads like a digest of Stevenson's own critical writing – connects the idea of art as significant play with form and the power of storytelling to tap into mythic structures: 'the more enlightened our houses are, the more their walls ooze ghosts. Dreams of progress and reason are haunted by nightmares.'[49] As fiction in English has begun to respond to such writers over the last thirty years, and as boundaries between popular and literary fiction have again come under pressure, Stevenson's writing may yet be exercising an obscure magnetism on contemporary writing.

Under the hulk of Edinburgh Castle, in a quiet corner of Princes Street Gardens, seven silver birches shelter a path of stone slabs laid in the grass, leading to an upright stone on which is carved: 'RLS – A Man of Letters, 1850–1894.' The modesty of Ian Hamilton Finlay's memorial for Stevenson seems a fitting response to the grotesque Gothicism of the Scott monument, which towers up in another part of the Gardens, beyond the galleries on the Mound. The elegant, spare style of the former contrasts favourably with the overwrought architecture of the latter. Even the choice of tree is morbidly appropriate: birches are slender and relatively short-lived. Although the forms derive from Finlay's own neo-classicist artistic programme, they chime with key aspects of their subject's own aesthetic ambitions and posthumous fate. That the stone should be a truncated column while the trees double as the pillars of a woodland temple suggests a fusion of the romantic and the classical which suits Stevenson's own style; that the grove itself be the memorial suggests the capacity of Stevenson's work to nourish and sustain countless admirers; the relative blankness of the stone directs the viewer away from the image of the man towards the works whose value alone might excuse the extent of his myth.

The pun (RLS – letters) reminds us of Stevenson's humanist conception of literature. It is his equation of literature with romance that singles out Stevenson from the defence of the novel current at the time that he was writing; it is his manipulation of romance as sceptical rather than a didactic form that saves his work from moralism; and it provides the key to a formalism that never becomes an aestheticism. The realist subordinates art to the mundane world; the aesthete substitutes art for life: Stevenson reminds us that art and world represent two realities which cannot – indeed must not – be confused. The two themes announced in the passage cited earlier from 'A Gossip on Romance', of man's combination with man in society and of man's relationship to nature, point the distance between Stevenson and the organicist philosophy of Herbert Spencer by which he had been consumed as a young man, in which the study of human nature becomes an aspect of biology, a branch of something like a social physics. Stevenson's great themes are not man as a natural being, but man in conflict with nature; not man as a social animal, but the tensions and sympathies between man and his fellows. There is a materialistic undercurrent in Stevenson which is not the celebration of scientific knowledge, but a sceptical rejoinder to religious or philosophical idealism. Literature, for Stevenson, participates in and reflects on this struggle over man's nature. As Chesterton put it: 'Other men have justified existence because it was a harmony. He justified it because it was a battle, because it was an inspiring and melodious discord.'[50]

Endnotes

Introduction – Fielding

1. For Stevenson and the 'bookmen' see Penny Fielding, *Writing and Orality: Nationality, Culture, and Nineteenth-Century Scottish Fiction* (Oxford: Clarendon Press, 1996), pp. 132–52. For literary culture in general in the period see John Gross, *The Rise and Fall of the English Man of Letters: Aspects of English Literary Life since 1800* (London: Weidenfeld and Nicholson, 1969) and Peter Keating, *The Haunted Study: A Social History of the English Novel 1875–1914* (London: Secker and Warburg, 1989).

2. Men of Letters and bookmen *were* men. (Stevenson's wife Fanny Osbourne – divorced, American and forthright in her views – was much disliked by his male admirers). Despite the increasing appearance of women as cultural commentators, among them Margaret Oliphant, the literary scene continued to be dominated by a masculine ethos. In addition to her many novels, Oliphant single-handedly wrote large swathes of *Blackwood's Edinburgh Magazine*, describing herself as *Blackwood's*'s 'general utility woman'. Even so, she felt obliged to adopt an identifiably masculine voice in her journalism.

3. Andrew Lang, *Adventures among Books* (London: Longman's, Green & Co., 1905), p. 51.

4. Glenda Norquay, *R. L. Stevenson on Fiction: An Anthology of Literary and Critical Essays* (Edinburgh: Edinburgh University Press, 1999), p. 160.

5. Paul Maixner, ed., *Robert Louis Stevenson: The Critical Heritage* (London: Routledge, 1981) pp. 96–7. Saintsbury is a good example of the 'bookman' who could move seamlessly, during his long literary career, between his posts as journalist on the *Saturday Review* and as Regius Professor of English Literature at the University of Edinburgh.

6. See Alan Sandison, 'Masters of the Hovering Life: Robert Musil and R. L. Stevenson', in Richard Dury and Richard Ambrosini (eds), *Robert Louis Stevenson: Writer of Boundaries* (Madison, WI: University of Wisconsin Press, 2006), p. 316.

7. Norquay, *R. L. Stevenson on Fiction*, p. 2.

8. Stevenson, *Familiar Studies of Men and Books*, Tusitala Edition (London: William Heinemann, 1923–4), p. 85.

9. Ibid., p. 86.

10. *The Letters of Robert Louis Stevenson*, ed. Bradford Booth and Ernest Mehew, 8 vols, New Haven, CT: Yale University Press (1994–5), vol. 5, p. 171.

11. See Glenda Norquay, *Robert Louis Stevenson and Theories of Reading: The Reader as Vagabond* (Manchester: Manchester University Press, 2007), pp. 56–62.

12. Kevin McLaughlin, 'The Financial Imp: Ethics and Finance in Nineteenth-Century Fiction', *Novel* 29 (1996): 165–83 (pp. 170–3).

13. Stevenson, *Familiar Studies*, p. 87.

14. Maixner, ed., *Critical Heritage*, p. 293.

15. Stevenson, *The Merry Men and Other Tales*, Tusitala Edition (London: William Heinemann, 1923–4), p. 5.

16. Ibid., p. 29.

17. Norquay, *R. L. Stevenson on Fiction*, p. 61.

18. Ibid., p. 21.

19. *Letters*, vol. 8, p. 159.

20. Stevenson and Fanny van der Grift Stevenson, *The Dynamiter*, Tusitala Edition (London: William Heinemann, 1923–4), p. 1.

21. Quoted in Gross, *Rise and Fall of the English Man of Letters*, p. 150.

Chapter 1 – Duncan

1. F. R. Leavis, *The Great Tradition* (New York: New York University Press, 1969), p. 5, n. 2.

2. For Stevenson's exclusion from anthologies and surveys see Richard Dury's valuable reception history at <http://dinamico2.unibg.it/rls/critrec.htm> (accessed 1 December 2008). On his posthumous reputation see Paul Maixner, ed., *Robert Louis Stevenson: The Critical Heritage* (London: Routledge and Kegan Paul, 1981), pp. 42–4, and Richard Ambrosini and Richard Dury, eds, *Robert Louis Stevenson. Writer of Boundaries* (Madison, WI: University of Wisconsin Press, 2006), pp. xiv-xviii. Symptomatically, Stevenson is scarcely mentioned even in Patrick Parrinder's recent, comprehensive historical survey of the British novel, *Nation & Novel: The English Novel from its Origins to the Present Day* (Oxford: Oxford University Press, 2006).

3. Maixner, ed., *Critical Heritage*, p. 515.

4. Ibid., pp. 509 and 510.

5. Ibid., p. 508.

6. See Simon Dentith, *Epic and Empire in Nineteenth-Century Britain* (Cambridge: Cambridge University Press, 2006), pp. 105–6.

7. Robert Kiely, *Robert Louis Stevenson and the Fiction of Adventure* (Cambridge, MA: Harvard University Press, 1964), p. 268.

8. Maixner, ed., *Critical Heritage*, pp. 341–2.

9. Ibid., p. 349.

10. Ibid., p. 474.

11. Glenda Norquay, ed., *R. L. Stevenson on Fiction: An Anthology of Literary and Critical Essays* (Edinburgh, Edinburgh University Press, 1999), p. 82.

12. Ibid.

13. See Roger G. Swearingen, *The Prose Writings of Robert Louis Stevenson: A Guide* (Hamden, CT/London: Shoe String (Archon)/Macmillan, 1980), pp. 86–7 and 98–9.

14. Philip Waller, *Writers, Readers and Reputations: Literary Life in Britain, 1870–1918* (Oxford: Oxford University Press, 2006), p. 3.

15. Maixner, ed., *Critical Heritage*, p. 358.

16. Ibid., pp. 476 and 477.

17. Norquay, *R. L. Stevenson on Fiction*, p. 122.

18. Maixner, ed., *Critical Heritage*, p. 475.

19. *The Letters of Robert Louis Stevenson*, ed. Bradford Booth and Ernest Mehew, 8 vols (New Haven, CT: Yale University Press, 1994–5), vol. 7, p. 461.

20. See Robert Irwin Hiller, *The South Seas Fiction of Robert Louis Stevenson* (New York: Peter Lang, 1989); Vanessa Smith, *Literary Culture and the Pacific: Nineteenth-Century Textual Encounters* (Cambridge: Cambridge University Press, 1998).

21. Francis Russell Hart, *The Scottish Novel: From Smollett to Spark* (Cambridge, MA: Harvard University Press, 1978), p. 146.

22. Walter Benjamin, 'The Storyteller', in *Illuminations*, trans. H. Zohn (New York: Harcourt, Brace, 1968), pp. 87–8. On Stevenson and Benjamin see also Matthew Wickman, 'Stevenson, Benjamin and the Decay of Experience', *International Journal of Scottish Literature* (<http://www.ijsl.stir.ac.uk/index.htm>), 2 (2007); accessed 1 December 2008.

23. Benjamin, 'The Storyteller', p. 91.

24. Stevenson, 'My First Book: *Treasure Island*', in *Treasure Island*, Tusitala Edition (London: William Heinemann, 1923–4), p. xxvi.

25. Norquay, *R. L. Stevenson on Fiction*, p. 61

26. Ibid., p. 54.

27. Ibid.

28. Lloyd Osbourne, *An Intimate Portrait of Robert Louis Stevenson* (1924), pp. 107–8; cited in Swearingen, *The Prose Writings of Robert Louis Stevenson*, p. 131.

29. See Barry Menikoff, '*New Arabian Nights*: Stevenson's Experiment in Fiction', *Nineteenth-Century Literature* 45: 3 (1990), pp. 339–62; Alan Sandison, *Robert Louis Stevenson and the Appearance of Modernism: A Future Feeling* (Basingstoke: Macmillan, 1996).

30. Stevenson, *The Dynamiter*, Tusitala Edition (London: William Heinemann, 1923–4) p. 1.

31. Ibid., p. 6.

32. Norquay, *R. L. Stevenson on Fiction*, p. 85.

33. Ibid., p. 63.

34. Stevenson, 'Victor Hugo's Romances', in *Familiar Studies of Men and Books*, Tusitala Edition (London: William Heinemann. 1923–4) p. 6.

35. *Letters*, vol. 7, p. 246; see also p. 253.

36. Norquay, *R. L. Stevenson on Fiction*, p. 64.

37. For arguments that take seriously the status of *Kidnapped* as historical novel and epic see (respectively) Barry Menikoff, *Narrating Scotland: The Imagination of Robert Louis Stevenson* (Columbia, SC: University of South Carolina Press, 2005) and Dentith, *Epic and Empire*, pp. 192–4.

38. Stevenson, *Weir of Hermiston & Some Unfinished Stories*, Tusitala Edition (London: William Heinemann, 1923–4) p. 59.

39. *Letters*, vol. 7, p. 465. In the same month as *Waverley* was published, August 1814, Scott was on a tour of inspection of the northern Scottish coasts accompanied by Stevenson's grandfather, Robert Stevenson, the celebrated lighthouse engineer. In 1891 Stevenson found his grandfather's reminiscences of the voyage among his papers, and extracted them for publication with a preface by himself ('Scott's Voyage in the Lighthouse Yacht') in *Scribner's Magazine* (October, 1893).

40. Stevenson, *St Ives*, Tusitala Edition (London: Heinemann, 1923–4), pp. 85–6.

41. For the formulation see Karl Miller, *Cockburn's Millennium* (Cambridge, MA: Harvard University Press, 1975), pp. 178–80.

42. Stevenson named *Guy Mannering*, *Rob Roy* and *Redgauntlet* as the Scott novels he reread most often: Norquay, *R. L. Stevenson on Fiction*, p. 119. In the 1887 essay 'Books Which Have Influenced Me', however, Scott is conspicuous by his absence.

43. Maixner, ed., *Critical Heritage*, p. 467.

44. This is also true of Stevenson's earlier set pieces of narrative in Scots, such as the ghost story 'Thrawn Janet' or the inset 'Tale of Tod Lapraik' in *Catriona*. A comparison with their models, 'Wandering Willie's Tale' in Scott's *Redgauntlet* or any of Hogg's tales, will betray the worked-up, eye-on-the-dictionary quality of Stevenson's pastiche. The extensive passages of Scots dialogue in *Kidnapped* and *Catriona*, however, match the unobtrusive skill of the earlier authors.

45. Stevenson, *Weir of Hermiston*, pp. 71, 72, 72 and 83.

46. See Eric Massie, 'Scottish Gothic: Robert Louis Stevenson, *The Master of Ballantrae*, and *The Private Memoirs and Confessions of a Justified Sinner*', in William B. Jones, Jr, ed., *Robert Louis Stevenson Reconsidered: New Critical Perspectives* (Jefferson, NC: McFarland and Co., 2003), pp. 163–73.

47. Stevenson himself acknowledged the provenance of the Chevalier Burke in Thackeray's *Barry Lyndon*: 'The Genesis of *The Master of Ballantrae*', in

The Master of Ballantrae, Tusitala Edition (London: William Heinemann: 1923–4) p. xxv.

48. Ibid., p. xxv.
49. Cited in Swearingen, *The Prose Writings of Robert Louis Stevenson*, p. 120.
50. Stevenson, 'Note to The Master of Ballantrae', in *The Master of Ballantrae*, p. 238.
51. Maixner, ed., *Critical Heritage*, p. 355.
52. Stevenson, *The Wrecker*, Tusitala Edition (London: William Heinemann, 1923–4) p. 289. Recent discussions alert to this aspect of the tale include Gordon Hirsch, 'The Commercial World of *The Wrecker*', *Journal of Stevenson Studies* 2 (2005): 70–98, and Roderick Watson, '"The Unrest and Movement of our Century": The Universe of *The Wrecker*', *Journal of Stevenson Studies* 4 (2007): 114–28.
53. Stevenson, *The Wrecker*, pp. 33–4.
54. Ibid., p. 36.
55. *Letters*, vol. 7, p. 180.
56. Stevenson, *The Wrecker*, p. 405.
57. Ibid., p. 404.

Chapter 2 – Irvine

1. See, for example, Patrick Brantlinger, *Rule of Darkness: British Literature and Imperialism, 1830–1914* (Ithaca: Cornell University Press, 1988) and Laura Chrisman, *Rereading the Imperial Romance: British Imperialism and South African Resistance in Haggard, Schreiner and Plaatje* (Oxford: Clarendon Press, 2000).
2. Glenda Norquay, ed., *R. L. Stevenson on Fiction: An Anthology of Literary and Critical Essays* (Edinburgh: Edinburgh University Press, 1999), p. 54.
3. Robert Louis Stevenson, *Treasure Island*, ed. Emma Letley (1883; Oxford: Oxford University Press, 1985), p. 117. Further page references are given in the text.
4. Norquay, *R. L. Stevenson on Fiction*, p. 61.
5. Christopher Harvey comments that the gentlemen of *Treasure Island* could be seen as 'an embattled microcosm of civil society [. . .] being menaced by the lower orders under brutal and materialistic leadership'. Christopher Harvey, 'The Politics of Stevenson', in J. Calder, ed., *Stevenson and Victorian Scotland* (Edinburgh: Edinburgh University Press, 1981), p. 120. David H. Jackson develops this idea in '*Treasure Island* as a Late-Victorian Adults' Novel', *The Victorian Newsletter* 72 (1987): 28–32.
6. Charles Kingsley, *Westward Ho!* (London: Dent, 1906), p. 65.
7. James Eli Adams notes that this mystification of gentlemanliness as 'an innate, physiological sensibility' is frequent among mid-Victorian commentators. *Dandies and Desert Saints: Styles of Victorian Manhood* (Ithaca: Cornell University Press, 1995), pp. 152–3 and 162–4.

8. Another useful contrast, from Stevenson's own generation, is Haggard's *King Solomon's Mines* (1885). In this boy's romance of adventure, written in answer to *Treasure Island*, the ideal gentleman, Sir Henry Curtis, is an aristocrat who can trace his family back to the Vikings, and a war in Africa allows him to demonstrate that he has inherited their skill in battle along with physical qualities such as his size and blond hair. Henry Rider Haggard, *King Solomon's Mines* (Oxford: Oxford University Press, 1989), pp. 11 and 226.

9. Stephen Arata, *Fictions of Loss at the Victorian Fin de Siècle* (Cambridge: Cambridge University Press, 1996), pp. 38–43.

10. Robbie B. H. Goh, 'Textual Hyde and Seek: "Gentility", Narrative Play and Proscription in Stevenson's *Dr Jekyll and Mr Hyde*', *JNT: Journal of Narrative Theory* 29 (1999): 158–183 (p. 176).

11. Norquay, *R. L. Stevenson on Fiction*, p. 61.

12. Stevenson, *New Arabian Nights*, Tusitala Edition (London: William Heinemann, 1923–4), p. 107. Further page references are given in the text.

13. Lisa Honaker, 'The Revisionary Role of Gender in R. L. Stevenson's *New Arabian Nights* and *Prince Otto*: Revolution in a "Poison Bad World"', *English Literature in Transition 1880–1920* 44 (2001): 297–319 (pp. 303 and 305).

14. The most sustained example is Alan Sandison, *Robert Louis Stevenson and the Appearance of Modernism* (Basingstoke: Macmillan, 1996).

15. Thomas Carlyle, *On Heroes, Hero-Worship and the Heroic in History*, in *The Works of Thomas Carlyle*, 30 vols (London: Chapman and Hall, 1897), vol. 5, p. 199.

16. Ibid., p. 196.

17. Ibid., p. 202.

18. Robin Gilmour, *The Idea of the Gentleman in the Victorian Novel* (London: George Allen and Unwin, 1981), p. 28.

19. Honaker, 'Revisionary Role', p. 304.

20. Stevenson, *Prince Otto*, Tusitala Edition (London: Heinemann, 1923–4), p. 63. Further page references are given in the text.

21. David Cannadine, *Ornamentalism: How the British Saw their Empire* (London: Penguin, 2001), p. 122.

22. Stevenson, 'The Ebb-Tide', in *South Sea Tales*, ed. Roslyn Jolly (Oxford: Oxford University Press, 1996), p. 125. Further page references are given in the text.

Chapter 3 – Reid

1. Edmund Gosse, *Critical Kit-Kats* (London: Heinemann, 1913), p. 279; Lloyd Osbourne, 'Prefatory Note' to 'Stevenson at Play: War Correspondence from Stevenson's Note-book', in Stevenson, *Further Memories* (London:

Heinemann et al., 1923), p. 191; Andrew O'Hagan, 'In His Hot Head', *London Review of Books* 27.4 (17 February 2005): 10–12 (p. 12); John Seelye, 'Introduction', in Stevenson, *Treasure Island* (London: Penguin, 1999), p. xi.

2. John Jay Chapman, 'Robert Louis Stevenson', in *Emerson and Other Essays* (London: David Nutt, 1898), p. 223.

3. Morag Styles, *From the Garden to the Street: An Introduction to 300 Years of Poetry for Children* (London: Cassell, 1998), p. 171; Ann C. Colley, '"Writing Towards Home": The Landscape of *A Child's Garden of Verses*', *Victorian Poetry* 35 (1997): 303–18 (p. 304).

4. Lloyd J. Borstelmann, 'Children before Psychology: Ideas about Children from Antiquity to the late 1800s', in Paul H. Mussen (ed.), *Handbook of Child Psychology*, 4th edn, vol. 1: *History, Theory and Methods*, ed. William Kessen (New York: John Wiley and Sons, 1983), pp. 18–26.

5. William Wordsworth, 'Ode: Intimations of Immortality from Recollections of Early Childhood', in Wordsworth and Samuel Taylor Coleridge, *Lyrical Ballads and Other Poems*, ed. Martin Scofield (Ware: Wordsworth Editions, 2003), p. 171.

6. Charles Darwin, 'A Biographical Sketch of an Infant', *Mind* 2.7 (July 1877): 285–94 (p. 288).

7. Robert B. Cairns, 'The Emergence of Developmental Psychology', in Mussen (ed.), *Handbook*, p. 63.

8. James Sully, *Studies of Childhood* (London: Longmans, Green and Co., 1896), pp. 4 and 8–9.

9. Stevenson, '"Rosa Quo Locorum"', in *Further Memories* (London: Heinemann et al., 1923), p. 1.

10. Sully, *Studies*, p. 27.

11. See Stevenson, 'Books Which Have Influenced Me', in *Essays Literary and Critical* (London: Heinemann et al., 1923), pp. 64–5; Herbert Spencer, *The Principles of Psychology* (1855), 2nd edn, 2 vols (London: Williams and Norgate, 1870–2), vol. 2, p. 627.

12. Stevenson, '"Rosa"', p. 1.

13. Sully, *Studies*, p. 229.

14. Styles, *From the Garden*, pp. 23 and 96; Humphrey Carpenter, *Secret Gardens: A Study of the Golden Age of Children's Literature* (London: Allen and Unwin, 1985), p. 3.

15. Carpenter, *Gardens*, p. 11.

16. Jeffrey Richards, 'Introduction', in Richards (ed.), *Imperialism and Juvenile Literature* (Manchester: Manchester University Press, 1989), pp. 4–5.

17. Stevenson, 'Popular Authors', in *Essays Literary and Critical* (London: Heinemann et al., 1923), pp. 31 and 21.

18. Roger Swearingen, *The Prose Writings of Robert Louis Stevenson: A Guide* (Hamden, CT: Archon Books, 1980), pp. 11 and 189.

19. Stevenson, 'Notes on the Movements of Young Children', in *Juvenilia and Other Papers*, *The Davos Press* (London: Chatto and Windus et al., 1912), p. 102.

20. Stevenson, 'Notes', pp. 98–100.

21. Sully, *My Life and Friends* (London: T. Fisher Unwin, 1918), p. 215.

22. Sully, 'Poetic Imagination and Primitive Conception', *Cornhill Magazine* 34 (1876): 294–306 (pp. 298–9).

23. Stevenson, 'Child's Play', *Cornhill Magazine* 38 (1878): 352–9 (p. 357).

24. Stevenson, 'Play', p. 357.

25. Sully, *Studies*, pp. 322, 323, 326 and 327.

26. Stevenson, 'Play', p. 355.

27. Sully, 'Poetic Imagination', pp. 295 and 298.

28. Stevenson, 'Play', p. 356.

29. Sigmund Freud, 'Creative Writers and Day-dreaming', in Peter Gay (ed.), *The Freud Reader* (London: Random House, 1995), p. 438.

30. Stevenson, 'The Lantern-Bearers', in *Further Memories* (London: Heinemann et al., 1923), p. 34.

31. Michael Rosen, 'Robert Louis Stevenson and Children's Play: The Contexts of *A Child's Garden of Verses*', *Children's Literature in Education* 26.1 (March 1995): 53–72 (p. 64).

32. Stevenson to Edmund Gosse, March 1885, in Bradford Booth and Ernest Mehew (eds), *The Letters of Robert Louis Stevenson*, 8 vols (New Haven, CT: Yale University Press, 1994–5), vol. 5, p. 85.

33. Stevenson to W. E. Henley, May 1883, in *Letters*, vol. 4, p. 113.

34. Stevenson, unspecified 'record, written probably about 1872', cited in Graham Balfour, *The Life of Robert Louis Stevenson*, 10th edn (London: Methuen, 1912), pp. 32 and 33.

35. Stevenson, 'Play', p. 358; Sully, *Studies*, p. 61.

36. Stevenson, 'Block City', in *A Child's Garden of Verses*, rpr. in *Collected Poems*, ed. Janet Adam Smith (London: Rupert Hart-Davis, 1950), pp. 393 and 364. Further page references are given in the text.

37. Sully, *Studies*, pp. 36 and 35.

38. Ibid., p. 95n.

39. See Stevenson, 'The Dumb Soldier' and 'The Kingdom', in *Garden*, pp. 402–3 and 390–1.

40. Stevenson, 'Play', p. 355.

41. Sully, *Studies*, p. 61.

42. H. C. Bunner, review, *Book Buyer* (May 1885), rpr. in Paul Maixner, ed., *Robert Louis Stevenson: The Critical Heritage* (London: Routledge and Kegan Paul, 1981), p. 158.

43. Jenny Bourne Taylor, 'Obscure Recesses: Locating the Victorian Unconscious', in J. B. Bullen (ed.), *Writing and Victorianism* (London: Longman, 1997), p. 141.

44. Sally Shuttleworth, 'The Psychology of Childhood in Victorian Literature and Medicine', in Helen Small and Trudi Tate (eds), *Literature, Science, Psychoanalysis, 1830–1970: Essays in Honour of Gillian Beer* (Cambridge: Cambridge University Press, 2003), p. 97.

45. [William Archer,] unsigned review, *Pall Mall Gazette* (24 March 1885), rpr. in Maixner, ed., *Critical Heritage*, p. 155.

46. Stevenson to William Archer, March 1885, in *Letters*, vol. 5, p. 97.

47. Hugh Cunningham, *The Children of the Poor: Representations of Childhood since the Seventeenth Century* (Oxford: Blackwell, 1991), p. 154.

48. Stevenson, 'System', in *Garden*, p. 372.

49. Stevenson, 'Memoirs of Himself', in *Memories and Portraits, Memoirs of Himself, Selections from his Notebook* (London: Heinemann, 1924), p. 149.

50. Stevenson, 'Memoirs', p. 156. Further page references are given in the text.

51. On 'night terrors', see Janet Oppenheim, *'Shattered Nerves': Doctors, Patients and Depression in Victorian England* (Oxford: Oxford University Press, 1991), p. 235.

52. Sully, *Studies*, p. 219.

53. Christina Hardyment, *Dream Babies: Child Care from Locke to Spock* (London: Jonathan Cape, 1983), p. 108.

54. Sully, *Studies*, p. 39.

55. Stevenson, 'Edifying Letters of the Rutherford Family', in Roger Swearingen (ed.), *An Old Song and Edifying Letters of the Rutherford Family* (Hamden, CT: Archon Books, 1982), p. 87; Stevenson, 'The Misadventures of John Nicholson', in Paul Binding (ed.), *Weir of Hermiston and Other Stories* (London: Penguin, 1979), p. 219.

56. Stevenson, 'Heathercat: A Fragment', in *The Ebb-Tide, Weir of Hermiston, Heathercat, The Young Chevalier* (London: Heinemann et al., 1922), pp. 444 and 457–8.

57. Sidney Colvin, 'Editorial Note', in Paul Binding (ed.), Stevenson, *Weir of Hermiston and Other Stories* (London: Penguin, 1979), p. 293.

58. Stevenson, *Weir of Hermiston*, in Paul Binding (ed.), *Weir of Hermiston and Other Stories* (London: Penguin, 1979), p. 61. Further page references are given in the text.

59. Stevenson, 'Memoirs', p. 157.

60. Shuttleworth, 'Psychology', p. 101.

61. James Stewart and James Stirling, *Naphtali, or the Wrestlings of the Church of Scotland for the Kingdom of Christ; a Deduction thereof from the Reformation until 1667. With the Last Speeches of Some Who Have Died for the Truth since 1660. Also a Relation of the Sufferings of Hew McKail* ([Edinburgh: n. p.,] 1667).

62. Stevenson, '"Rosa"', pp. 1–2.

63. Stevenson, 'The Pentland Rising', in *Essays Literary and Critical* (London: Heinemann et al., 1923), pp. 94 and 108.

64. Stevenson, 'Memoirs', p. 155.

65. Ibid., pp. 157–8 and 158.
66. Ibid., p. 155.
67. G. Stanley Hall, *Adolescence: Its Psychology and its Relations to Physiology, Anthropology, Sociology, Sex, Crime, Religion and Education*, 2 vols (London: Appleton, 1905), vol. 1, pp. xi and x.
68. See Penny Fielding, *Writing and Orality: Nationality, Culture and Nineteenth-Century Scottish Fiction* (Oxford: Clarendon Press, 1996), p. 180.
69. See Joseph Bristow, *Empire Boys: Adventures in a Man's World* (London: HarperCollins, 1991), pp. 122–3.
70. Fanny Stevenson, 'Prefatory Note', in Robert Louis Stevenson, *The Black Arrow: A Tale of the Two Roses* (London: Heinemann et al., 1923), p. x.
71. Stevenson, *Black Arrow*, p. 33.
72. See Fanny Stevenson, 'Prefatory Note', pp. vii-x.
73. Stevenson to Henley, August 1881, in *Letters*, vol. 3, p. 225; Stevenson to Henley, October 1883, in *Letters*, vol. 4, p. 188.
74. Stevenson, *Black Arrow*, p. 236.

Chapter 4 – Arata

1. 'A Chapter on Dreams', in Roger Luckhurst, ed., *Strange Case of Dr Jekyll and Mr Hyde and Other Tales* (Oxford: Oxford University Press, 2006), p. 154.
2. Ibid., p. 159.
3. Ibid., p. 154.
4. Frances Power Cobbe, 'Unconscious Cerebration: A Psychological Study', *Macmillan's Magazine* 23 (1870): 24–37 (p. 37).
5. Kelly Hurley, *The Gothic Body: Sexuality, Materialism and Degeneration at the Fin de Siècle* (Cambridge: Cambridge University Press, 1996), p. 1.
6. Stevenson, 'A Note on Realism', in Glenda Norquay, ed., *R. L. Stevenson on Fiction: An Anthology of Literary and Critical Essays* (Edinburgh: Edinburgh University Press, 1999), p. 69.
7. Stevenson, *Strange Case of Dr Jekyll and Mr Hyde*, ed. Richard Dury (Edinburgh: Edinburgh University Press, 2004), p. 47. Further page references are given in the text.
8. Sigmund Freud, 'The "Uncanny"', in James Strachey et al., eds, *The Standard Edition of the Complete Psychological Works of Sigmund Freud*, 24 vols (London: Hogarth Press, 1955), vol. 17, pp. 217–56 (p. 220).
9. Ibid., p. 240.
10. Ibid., p. 249.
11. Ibid., p. 250.
12. Richard Dury, 'Strange Language of *Dr Jekyll and Mr Hyde*', *Journal of Stevenson Studies* 2 (2005): 33–51 (pp. 45–6).
13. Stevenson, 'On Some Technical Elements of Style in Literature', in Norquay, ed., *R. L. Stevenson on Fiction*, p. 94.

14. Quoted in Dury, 'Strange Language', p. 39.

15. Ibid., p. 35.

16. Gerard Manley Hopkins, letter of 28 October 1886, in C. C. Abbott, ed., *The Letters of Gerard Manley Hopkins to Robert Bridges* (London: Oxford University Press, 1935), p. 239.

17. Jenni Calder, *Robert Louis Stevenson: A Life Study* (Oxford: Oxford University Press, 1980), p. 164.

18. Ian Duncan, 'Walter Scott, James Hogg and Scottish Gothic','in David Punter, ed., *A Companion to the Gothic* (Oxford: Blackwell, 2000), p. 70.

19. Paul Maixner, ed., *Robert Louis Stevenson: The Critical Heritage* (London: Routledge and Kegan Paul, 1981), p. 300.

20. Stevenson, 'Thrawn Janet', in *The Merry Men and Other Tales*, Tusitala Edition (London: William Heinemann, 1923–4), p. 110. Further page references are given in the text.

21. Stevenson, *The Wrong Box* and *The Body Snatcher*, Tusitala Edition (London: William Heinemann, 1923), p. 194. Further page references are given in the text.

22. 'The Merry Men', in *The Merry Men and Other Tales*. Further page references are given in the text.

23. *The Letters of Robert Louis Stevenson*, ed. Bradford Booth and Ernest Mehew, 8 vols (New Haven, CT: Yale University Press, 1994–5), vol. 5, p. 220.

24. Oscar Wilde, *The Picture of Dorian Gray*, ed. Michael Patrick Gillespie (New York: W. W. Norton, 2007), p. 367.

25. *Letters*, vol. 5, p. 211.

26. *Letters*, vol. 6, p. 56.

27. See William Veeder, 'Children of the Night: Stevenson and Patriarchy', in William Veeder and Gordon Hirsch (eds), *Dr Jekyll and Mr Hyde after One Hundred Years* (Chicago: University of Chicago Press, 1988), pp. 107–60; Cyndy Hendershot, *The Animal Within: Masculinity and the Gothic* (Ann Arbor, MI: University of Michigan Press, 1998); and Andrew Smith, *Victorian Demons: Medicine, Masculinity and the Gothic at the* Fin de Siècle (Manchester: Manchester University Press, 2004).

28. See Elaine Showalter, *Sexual Anarchy: Gender and Culture at the Fin de Siècle* (New York: Viking, 1990); and George E. Haggerty, *Queer Gothic* (Urbana, IL: University of Illinois Press, 2006).

29. See Linda Dryden, *The Modern Gothic and Literary Doubles: Stevenson, Wilde and Wells* (Basingstoke: Palgrave Macmillan, 2003); Robert Mighall, *A Geography of Victorian Gothic Fiction: Mapping History's Nightmares* (Oxford: Oxford University Press, 1999); and Stephen Arata, *Fictions of Loss in the Victorian Fin de Siècle* (Cambridge: Cambridge University Press, 1996).

30. See H. L. Malchow, *Gothic Images of Race in Nineteenth-Century Britain* (Stanford: Stanford University Press, 1996); Patrick Brantlinger and Richard

Boyle, 'The Education of Edward Hyde: Stevenson's "Gothic Gnome" and the Mass Readership of Late-Victorian England', in William Veeder and Gordon Hirsch (eds), *Dr Jekyll and Mr Hyde after One Hundred Years*, pp. 265–82; and Judith Halberstam, *Skin Shows: Gothic Horror and the Technology of Monstrosity* (Durham, NC: Duke University Press, 1995).

31. G. K. Chesterton, *Robert Louis Stevenson* (New York: Dodd, Mead and Co., 1927), p. 51.
32. *Letters*, vol. 5, p. 151.
33. 'Markheim', in *The Merry Men and Other Tales*, pp. 104 and 105. Further page references are given in the text.
34. *Letters*, vol. 6, p. 56.
35. Quoted in Katherine Linehan (ed.) *Strange Case of Dr Jekyll and Mr Hyde* (New York: W. W. Norton, 2003), p. 86.

Chapter 5 – Lumsden

1. Barry Menikoff, *Narrating Scotland: The Imagination of Robert Louis Stevenson* (Columbia, SC: University of South Carolina Press, 2005), p. 205.
2. Jenni Calder, 'Figures in a Landscape: Scott, Stevenson, and Routes to the Past', in *Robert Louis Stevenson: Writer of Boundaries*, ed. Richard Ambrosini and Richard Dury (University of Wisconsin Press, 2006), p. 127.
3. 'A Gossip on Romance', in Glenda Norquay, ed., *R. L. Stevenson on Fiction: An Anthology of Literary and Critical Essays* (Edinburgh: Edinburgh University Press, 1999), p. 55. Further page references are given in the text.
4. *The Letters of Robert Louis Stevenson*, ed. Bradford Booth and Ernest Mehew, 8 vols (New Haven, CT: Yale University Press, 1994–5), vol. 8, p. 67.
5. Walter Scott, anonymous review of *Tales of my Landlord*, *Quarterly Review*, January, 1817; reprinted in *The Prose Works of Sir Walter Scott, Bart.*, 28 vols (Edinburgh: Robert Cadell, 1834–6), vol. 19, pp. 55–6.
6. Julia Reid, *Robert Louis Stevenson, Science and the Fin de Siecle* (Palgrave Macmillan: Basingstoke, 2006), pp. 130–1.
7. Calder, 'Figures in a Landscape', pp. 127 and 129.
8. William Gray, *Robert Louis Stevenson: A Literary Life* (Palgrave Macmillan: Basingstoke, 2004), p. 54.
9. Stevenson, 'The Pentland Rising', in *Essays Literary and Critical*, Tusitala Edition (London: William Heinemann, 1924), p. 93.
10. *The Master of Ballantrae*, Tusitala Edition (London: William Heinemann, 1923–4), p. xxiii. Further page references are given in the text.
11. Stevenson, 'The Pentland Rising', p. 103.
12. Walter Scott, *The Lady of the Lake*, in *The Poetical Works of Sir Walter Scott, Bart.* (Edinburgh: Cadell, 1830), Canto 1, Stanza 5.
13. Stevenson, *Kidnapped*, Tusitala Edition (London: William Heinemann, 1923–4), p. 153. Further page references are given in the text.

14. Calder, 'Figures in a Landscape', p. 128.
15. Oliver S. Buckton, *Travel, Narrative and the Colonial Body* (Athens: Ohio University Press, 2007), pp. 136 and 146.
16. *Letters*, vol. 7, p. 12.
17. See for example Penny Fielding, *Writing and Orality: Nationality, Culture and Nineteenth-Century Scottish Fiction* (Oxford: Clarendon Press, 1996); Julian Meldon D'Arcy, *Subversive Scott: The Waverley Novels and Scottish Nationalism* (Reykjavik: University of Iceland Press, 2005); Ian Duncan, *Scott's Shadow: The Novel in Romantic Edinburgh* (Princeton: Princeton University Press, 2008) and Caroline McCracken-Flesher, *Possible Scotlands: Walter Scott and the Story of Tomorrow* (New York: Oxford University Press, 2005).
18. Walter Scott, *The Tale of Old Mortality*, ed. Douglas S. Mack (Edinburgh: Edinburgh University Press, 1993), p. 7.
19. Scott, *Old Mortality*, pp. 10 and 12.
20. Walter Scott, *Waverley*, ed. P. D. Garside (Edinburgh: Edinburgh University Press, 2007), p. 364.
21. Stevenson. 'The Pentland Rising', p. 93.
22. Ibid., p. 110.
23. Kerwin Lee Klein, 'On the Emergence of *Memory* in Historical Discourse', *Representations* 69 (2000): 127–150 (pp. 128 and 143).
24. Stevenson, 'Crabbed Age Youth', in *Virginibus Puerisque and Other Essays*, Tusitala Edition (London: William Heinemann, 1923–4), pp. 41–4.
25. Menikoff, *Narrating Scotland*, pp. 13 and 205–6.
26. Edward M. Eigner, *Robert Louis Stevenson and the Romantic Tradition* (Princeton: Princeton University Press, 1966), p. 142.
27. Buckton, *Travel, Narrative*, p. 133.
28. Stevenson, *Island Nights Entertainments* and 'The Misadventures of John Nicholson', Tusitala Edition (London: William Heinemann, 1923–4), p. 137. Further page references are given in the text.
29. Klein, 'On the Emergence of Memory', p. 145.

Chapter 6 – McCracken-Flesher

1. Bradford Booth and Ernest Mehew (eds), *The Letters of Robert Louis Stevenson*, 8 vols (New Haven, CT: Yale University Press, 1994–5), vol. 5, p. 230.
2. A quick review of available titles yields: J. A. Hammerton, *In the Track of R. L. Stevenson and Elsewhere in Old France* (Bristol: J. W. Arrowsmith, 1907); J. Patrick Findlay, *In the Footsteps of R. L. S.* (Edinburgh: W. P. Nimmo, Hay and Mitchell, 1911); Nicholas Rankin, *Dead Man's Chest: Travels after Robert Louis Stevenson* (London: Faber and Faber, 1987); Gavin Bell, *In Search of Tusitala: Travels in the Pacific after Robert Louis Stevenson* (New York: Picador, 1995); Hilary Macaskill, *Downhill all the Way: Walking with Donkeys on the Stevenson Trail* (London: Frances Lincoln, 2006); Alan Castle, *The Robert*

Louis Stevenson Trail: A Walking Tour in the Velay and Cevennes, Southern France (Milnthorpe: Cicerone, 1992).

3. James Buzard, *The Beaten Track: European Tourism, Literature and the Ways to Culture, 1800–1918* (Oxford: Clarendon Press, 1993), p. 1.

4. Judith Adler, 'Travel as Performed Art', *The American Journal of Sociology* 94.6 (1989): 1366–91 (p. 1368).

5. Nigel Leask, *Curiosity and the Aesthetics of Travel Writing, 1770–1840* (Oxford: Oxford University Press, 2002).

6. Mary Louise Pratt, *Imperial Eyes: Travel Writing and Transculturation* (London: Routledge, 1992).

7. Buzard, *Beaten Track*, p. 156.

8. John Prebble, *The King's Jaunt: George IV in Scotland, August 1822* (London: Collins, 1988); Caroline McCracken-Flesher, *Possible Scotlands: Walter Scott and the Story of Tomorrow* (Oxford, Oxford University Press, 2005), pp. 73–113.

9. Stevenson, *Edinburgh: Picturesque Notes*, ed. David Daiches (Edinburgh: Salamander Press, 1983), p. 14.

10. *Letters*, vol. 1, p. 141, and pp. 146–7.

11. Stevenson, *The Collected Poems of Robert Louis Stevenson*, ed. Roger C. Lewis (Edinburgh: Edinburgh University Press, 2003), p. 38.

12. Ibid., p. 74.

13. *Letters*, vol. 7, p. 79.

14. *Letters*, vol. 1, p. 142.

15. Ibid., pp. 168–9 and 178.

16. Stevenson, 'Ordered South', *Macmillan's Magazine* 30 (1874): 68–73. For the eighteenth-century comparison, see Henry Fielding's *Journal of a Voyage to Lisbon*, 1755, or Tobias Smollett's *Travels through France and Italy*, 1766.

17. Peter Radford's *The Celebrated Captain Barclay: Sport, Gambling and Adventure in Regency Times* (London: Headline, 2002), reviews Barclay's exploits. See William Wordsworth, *The Prelude*, for his walking in Europe, and Thomas Carlyle's letters, for the Scottish author's walking tours with Edward Irving and others.

18. Stevenson, 'Ordered South', p. 69.

19. Stevenson, 'Walking Tours', *Cornhill Magazine* 33 (1876): 685–90 (p. 685).

20. Stevenson, 'Ordered South', pp. 72 and 69.

21. Stevenson, 'Walking Tours', p. 685.

22. Some of the essays appeared first individually, under the title 'Notes on Edinburgh', *The Portfolio* 9 (June-December 1878). See Roger Swearingen, *The Prose Writings of Robert Louis Stevenson: A Guide* (Hamden, CT: Archon, 1980), p. 32.

23. Stevenson, *Edinburgh*, pp. 13, 9, 21–2 and 22.

24. Pratt, *Imperial Eyes*, p. 86. Pratt connects this tradition to earlier stories of 'shipwrecks, castaways, mutinies, abandonments and (the special inland version) captivities'.

25. Stevenson, *Edinburgh*, pp. 9–10.

26. Paul Maixner, ed., *Robert Louis Stevenson: The Critical Heritage* (London: Routledge and Kegan Paul, 1981), pp. 59–61.

27. Stevenson, *An Inland Voyage and Travels with a Donkey*, Tusitala Edition (London: Heinemann, 1924), p. xvii. Further page references are given in the text.

28. *Letters*, vol. 2, p. 189.

29. Buzard, *Beaten Track*, p. 2.

30. For *Travels with a Donkey*, see Stevenson, *An Inland Voyage and Travels with a Donkey*, Tusitala Edition (London: Heinemann, 1923–4), p. 129. Further page references are given in the text.

31. Stevenson, 'Fontainebleau: Village Communities of Painters', in two parts *Magazine of Art* 7 (1884): 265–72; 340–5 (pp. 265 and 343).

32. For Stevenson, *Across the Plains*, see *From Scotland to Silverado*, ed. James D. Hart (Cambridge, MA: Belknap, 1966). Further page references are given in the text. For the complex publishing history of these and other Stevenson essays, consult Swearingen, *The Prose Writings of Robert Louis Stevenson*.

33. Maixner, *Critical Heritage*, pp. 381, 387 and 381.

34. See *From Scotland to Silverado* for *The Silverado Squatters*, p. 203.

35. See *From Scotland to Silverado* for *The Amateur Emigrant*, which is used specifically for its return to Stevenson's unexpurgated manuscript for its text. Further page references are given in the text.

36. *Letters*, vol. 3, p. 5.

37. Cited by Hart, introduction to *From Scotland to Silverado*, p. xlii.

38. Hart explains the necessity to reassemble Stevenson's preferred text in the 'Introduction' to *From Scotland to Silverado*, pp. xiii-li.

39. Hart, *From Scotland to Silverado*, p. xxxix; Maixner, *Critical Heritage*, p. 381.

40. *Letters*, vol. 7, p. 79.

41. Stevenson, *In the South Seas* (London: Hogarth, 1987), p. 6. This edition includes 'The Marquesas', 'The Paumotus', 'The Eight Islands', 'The Gilberts', and 'The Gilberts – Apemama'. See Swearingen for the many iterations of this text. Further page references to *In the South Seas* are given in the text.

42. Fanny Van de Grift Stevenson, *The Cruise of the 'Janet Nichol' among the South Sea Islands: A Diary by Mrs Robert Louis Stevenson* (New York, Charles Scribner's Sons, 1914).

43. H. J. Moors, *With Stevenson in Samoa* (Boston: Small, Maynard and Company, 1910).

44. Nicholas Rankin, *Dead Man's Chest: Travels after Robert Louis Stevenson* (London: Faber, 1987).

45. Maixner, *Critical Heritage*, p. 398.

46. Maixner reviews *The Wrecker*'s publication and sales history in *Critical Heritage*, pp. 396–7.

47. Stevenson and Lloyd Osbourne, *The Wrecker* (London: Cassell, 1893), p. 232.

48. *Letters*, vol. 7, pp. 283 and 195.

49. Stevenson, *A Footnote to History: Eight Years of Trouble in Samoa* (New York: Charles Scribner's Sons, 1892), pp. 106, 61 and 105.

50. Stevenson, *In the South Seas*, intro. p. 2.

51. Stevenson, 'Walking Tours', p. 689.

52. Laurence Sterne, *The Life and Opinions of Tristram Shandy, Gentleman*, ed. Ian Campbell Ross (Oxford: Oxford University Press, 1983), pp. 385 and 386.

53. Laurence Sterne, *A Sentimental Journey and Other Writings*, ed. Ian Jack and Tim Parnell (Oxford: Oxford University Press, 2003), pp. 10 and 65. Here, Sterne follows Yorick in Europe. Yorick is central to *Tristram Shandy*, though dead at the time of its telling.

54. Maixner, *Critical Heritage*, p. 62.

55. *Letters*, vol. 7, pp. 29 and 101–2.

56. Stevenson, 'The Foreigner at Home', *Cornhill Magazine* 45 (1882): 534–41 (p. 536).

Chapter 7 – Fielding

1. Paul Maixner, ed., *Robert Louis Stevenson: the Critical Heritage* (London: Routledge, 1971), p. 259.

2. Stevenson, *Collected Poems*, ed. Roger C. Lewis (Edinburgh: Edinburgh University Press, 2003), p. 88. Further page references are given in the text..

3. A. E. Housman, *Collected Poems and Selected Prose*, ed. Christopher Ricks (Harmondsworth: Penguin, 1988), p. 222.

4. Matthew Arnold, *Culture and Anarchy*, ed. Stefan Collini (Cambridge, Cambridge University Press, 1993), p. 67.

5. For these and other poets of the 1880s and 1890s see Joseph Bristow, ed., *The Fin-de-Siècle Poem: English Literary Culture and the 1890s* (Athens: Ohio University Press, 2005).

6. T. S. Eliot, 'What is Minor Poetry?', in *On Poetry and Poets* (London: Faber and Faber, 1957), p. 47.

7. Holbrook Jackson, *The 1890s: A Review of Art and Ideas at the Close of the Nineteenth Century*, intro. Malcolm Bradbury (London, Cresset Library, 1988), p. 190.

8. Walter Pater, *The Renaissance: Studies in Art and Poetry*, ed. Adam Phillips (Oxford: Oxford University Press, 1998), pp. 151–2.

9. Arthur Symons, *Selected Writings*, ed. Roger Holdsworth (Manchester: Carcanet, 1974), p. 83.

10. Ibid., p. 27.

11. Maixner, ed., *Critical Heritage*, p. 395.

12. Glenda Norquay, *R. L. Stevenson on Fiction: An Anthology of Literary and Critical Essays* (Edinburgh, Edinburgh University Press. 1999), p. 104.

13. Pater, *The Renaissance*, p. 86.

14. Stevenson, *St Ives*, Tusitala Edition (London: William Heinemann, 1923–4), p. 224.

15. *The Letters of Robert Louis Stevenson*, ed. Bradford Booth and Ernest Mehew, 8 vols (New Haven, CT: Yale University Press. 1994–5), vol. 4, p. 206.

16. Maixner, ed., *Critical Heritage*, p. 268.

17. Linda C. Dowling, *Language and Decadence in the Victorian Fin de Siècle* (Princeton: Princeton University Press, 1986), p. 221.

18. Arthur Symons, 'Modernity in Verse', in *Studies in Two Literatures* (London: Leonard Smithers, 1897) p. 88. The 'revolutionary' modern poet here described is none other than Stevenson's friend W. E. Henley.

19. Dowling, *Language and Decadence*, p. 123.

20. Linda M. Austin, *Nostalgia in Transition: 1780–1917* (Charlottesville: University of Virginia Press, 2007), pp. 15–23; Cairns Craig, *Associationism and the Literary Imagination: From the Phantasmal Chaos* (Edinburgh: Edinburgh University Press, 2007), pp. 239–84.

21. John Hollander, *The Work of Poetry* (New York: Columbia University Press, 1997), p. 133.

22. Ibid., p. 134.

23. *Letters*, vol. 6, p. 337.

24. Ann C. Colley, *Nostalgia and Recollection in Victorian Culture* (Basingstoke: Macmillan, 1998), pp. 157–91.

25. Edward S. Casey, *Remembering: A Phenomenological Study* (Bloomington: Indiana University Press, 1987), p. 202.

26. Colley, *Nostalgia and Recollection*, p. 179.

27. In her groundbreaking first collected edition of the *Poems*, Janet Adam Smith thinks Stevenson originally wrote 'devoted' and this has been reprinted in some subsequent editions. The manuscript, however, does read 'denoted'.

28. Richard Le Gallienne, *Robert Louis Stevenson: An Elegy and Other Poems* (London: John Lane, 1895), p. 18.

29. Ibid., p. 13.

30. Although we should be cautious about spotting 'pre-echoes' of literary modernism in Stevenson, we might compare his poem of inaccessible vegetation myths, deathly clerks and senseless crowds moving over London Bridge with T. S. Eliot's *The Waste Land* (1922).

31. *Letters*, vol. 7, p. 26.

Chapter 8 – Jolly

1. Stevenson, *In the South Seas*, ed. Neil Rennie (London: Penguin, 1998), p. 6.

2. Stevenson, 'Walking Tours', in *Virginibus Puerisque and Across the Plains* (Oxford: Oxford University Press, 1926), p. 159; *The Letters of Robert Louis Stevenson*, ed. Bradford Booth and Ernest Mehew, 8 vols (New Haven, CT: Yale University Press, 1994–5), vol. 5, p. 81; Stevenson, *An Inland Voyage and Travels with a Donkey*, Tusitala Edition (London: Heinemann, 1923–4), p. 103.

3. Stevenson, *Inland Voyage*, p. 103; Stevenson, 'Walking Tours', p. 162.

4. Stevenson, *Inland Voyage*, pp. 207 and 208.

5. Stevenson, 'Across the Plains', in *Virginibus Puerisque and Across the Plains* (Oxford: Oxford University Press, 1926), p. 224.

6. Neil Rennie, *Far-Fetched Facts: The Literature of Travel and the Idea of the South Seas* (Oxford: Oxford University Press, 1995), pp. 83–140.

7. *Letters*, vol. 6, p. 420; vol. 7, p. 271; and vol. 7, p. 254.

8. Stevenson, *In the South Seas*, p. 6; Stevenson, *A Footnote to History: Eight Years of Trouble in Samoa* (London: Cassell, 1892), p. 1; Stevenson, *In the South Seas*, p. 9.

9. Stevenson and Lloyd Osbourne, *The Wrecker* (New York: Dover, 1982), p. 125. Further page references are given in the text.

10. Stevenson, *Footnote*, p. 1.

11. Stevenson, *In the South Seas*, pp. 14 and 13.

12. Roslyn Jolly, 'Robert Louis Stevenson, Henry Maine and the Anthropology of Comparative Law', *Journal of British Studies* 45 (2006): 556–80.

13. Stevenson, *In the South Seas*, p. 216.

14. *Letters*, vol. 6, p. 312.

15. Stevenson, *In the South Seas*, pp. 242–52.

16. Mary Louise Pratt, *Imperial Eyes: Travel Writing and Transculturation* (London: Routledge, 1992), p. 4; Paul Allatson, *Key Terms in Latino/a Cultural and Literary Studies* (Oxford: Blackwell, 2007), pp. 229–32.

17. Roslyn Jolly, 'Piracy, Slavery and the Imagination of Empire in Stevenson's Pacific Fiction', *Victorian Literature and Culture* 35 (2007): 157–60.

18. *Letters*, vol. 6, p. 206.

19. *Letters*, vol. 8, pp. 231–2 and n.

20. [Editorial], *The Times*, 4 June 1892, p. 13; and Arthur Johnstone, *Recollections of Robert Louis Stevenson in the Pacific* (London: Chatto and Windus, 1905), pp. 148–9.

21. Stevenson, *Footnote*, pp. 285–8; and *Letters*, vol. 7, pp. 320–2 and 338.

22. 'A New Stevenson', *Daily Chronicle*, 23 August 1892.

23. *Letters*, vol. 6, p. 276.

24. Stevenson, *Footnote*, p. 253.

25. *Letters*, vol. 6, p. 216.

26. Ibid., p. 276.

27. 'A Gossip on Romance', in Glenda Norquay, ed., *R. L. Stevenson on Fiction: An Anthology of Literary and Critical Essays* (Edinburgh: Edinburgh University Press, 1999), p. 53.

28. Stevenson, *South Sea Tales*, ed. Roslyn Jolly (Oxford: Oxford University Press, 1996), p. 184. This edition contains *The Ebb-Tide*, 'The Beach of Falesá' and 'The Isle of Voices' and page references are given in the text.

29. *Letters*, vol. 6, p. 274.

30. Stevenson, *In the South Seas*, p. 107.

31. Ibid., pp. 17, 19, 18.

32. Ibid., p. 108.

33. Ibid., p. 110.

34. Ibid., p. 116.

35. Ibid., p. 119.

36. Ibid., p. 120.

37. *Letters*, vol. 6, p. 332.

38. Stevenson, *In the South Seas*, p. 113.

39. Ibid., p. 43; Stevenson, *Footnote*, p. 23.

40. Stevenson, *In the South Seas*, p. 74.

41. Stevenson, *Footnote*, pp. 112, 138.

42. *Letters*, vol. 8, p. 269.

43. *Letters*, vol. 7, pp. 19–20.

44. Ibid., p. 27.

45. *Letters*, vol. 6, p. 60.

46. *Letters*, vol. 7, p. 93.

47. Ibid., p. 25.

48. Sidney Colvin, 'Editorial Note', *In the South Seas*, Tusitala Edition (London: Heinemann, 1923–4) p. vii.

49. Stevenson, *In the South Seas*, p. 50.

50. Fanny Van de Grift Stevenson, *The Cruise of the 'Janet Nichol' among the South Sea Islands: A Diary by Mrs Robert Louis Stevenson*, ed. Roslyn Jolly (Seattle: University of Washington Press, 2004), p. 91.

51. Ibid., pp. 102–3.

52. Stevenson, *In the South Seas*, p. 200.

53. Fanny Stevenson, *Cruise*, p. 120.

54. Ibid., pp. 158–61, 187, 202 and 160.

55. Roslyn Jolly, 'South Sea Gothic: Pierre Loti and Robert Louis Stevenson', *English Literature in Transition 1880–1920* 47 (2004): 38–42.

56. Francis Bacon, *The New Atlantis*, ed. G. C. Moore Smith (Cambridge: Cambridge University Press, 1900), p. 1; Rennie, *Far-Fetched Facts*, pp. 1–82.

57. Fanny Stevenson, *Cruise*, pp. 95–7.

58. Ibid., pp. 106–9.

59. Stevenson, *In the South Seas*, p. 230.

60. *Letters*, vol. 8, p. 68.

61. Stevenson, *In the South Seas*, p. 116.

62. *Letters*, vol. 6, p. 209.

Chapter 9 – Lyon

1. Henry James, *Letters*, ed. Leon Edel, 4 vols (Cambridge, MA: Belknap Press of Harvard University Press, 1974–84), vol. 4, p. 812. James's 'duties' also invokes a very important Stevensonian word and value.

2. See John Gross, *The Rise and Fall of the Man of Letters: English Literary Life since 1800* (Harmondsworth: Penguin, 1973); and Peter Keating, *The Haunted Study: A Social History of the English Novel, 1875–1914* (London: Faber and Faber, 1989).

3. James, *Letters*, vol. 2, p. 255.

4. *The Letters of Robert Louis Stevenson*, ed. Bradford Booth and Ernest Mehew, 8 vols (New Haven, CT: Yale University Press, 1994–5), vol. 3, p. 159.

5. Glenda Norquay, ed., *R. L. Stevenson on Fiction* (Edinburgh: Edinburgh University Press, 1999), p. 54.

6. *Letters*, vol. 3, p. 241.

7. Ibid., p. 245.

8. James, *Literary Criticism: Essays on Literature; American Writers; English Writers* (New York: Library of America, 1984), pp. 351–2.

9. *Letters*, vol. 3, p. 83.

10. James, *Literary Criticism: Essays on Literature*, p. 1242.

11. Stevenson, *Familiar Studies of Men and Books*, Tusitala Edition (London: William Heinemann, 1923–4), vol. 27, pp. 8–9.

12. Stevenson, *The Collected Poems*, ed. Roger C. Lewis (Edinburgh: Edinburgh University Press, 2003), p. 98; James, *Selected Tales*, ed. John Lyon (London: Penguin, 2001), p. 254.

13. Norquay, *R. L. Stevenson on Fiction*, p. 76. See Claire Harman, *Myself and the Other Fellow: A Life of Robert Louis Stevenson* (New York: HarperCollins, 2005).

14. William Ernest Henley, *The Letters to Robert Louis Stevenson*, ed. Damian Atkinson (High Wycombe: Rivendale, 2008), p. 362.

15. See Kenneth Graham, 'Stevenson and Henry James: A Crossing', in Andrew Noble (ed.), *Robert Louis Stevenson* (London: Vision Press, 1983), pp. 23–46; George Dekker, 'James and Stevenson: The Mixed Current of Realism and Romance', in Robert M. Polhemus and Roger B. Henkle (eds), *Critical Reconstructions: The Relationship of Fiction and Life* (Stanford: Stanford University Press, 1994), pp. 127–49; Hilary J. Beattie, '"The Interest of the Attraction exercised by the great RLS of those days": Robert Louis Stevenson, Henry James and the Influence of Friendship', in *Journal of Stevenson Studies* 4 (2007): 91–113; Anthony Neil Chilton, 'Doing His Best: "The Lesson of the Master"', in *Henry James: The Artist and 'Other People's Interest'* (Unpublished PhD thesis, University of Bristol, 2007), pp. 142–79.

16. Stevenson, *Virginibus Puerisque and Other Essays in Belles Lettres*, Tusitala Edition (London: William Heinemann, 1923–4), vol. 15, p. 16.

17. James, *Literary Criticism: Essays on Literature*, pp. 1233 and 1237.

18. James, *The Complete Notebooks*, ed. Leon Edel and Lyall H. Powers (New York: Oxford University Press, 1987), p. 43.
19. James, *Literary Criticism: Essays on Literature*, p. 1238.
20. Ibid., p. 1252.
21. James, *The Portrait of a Lady*, ed. Geoffrey Moore (Harmondsworth: Penguin, 1986), p. 622.
22. George Eliot, 'The Natural History of German Life', in Rosemary Ashton (ed.), *Selected Critical Writings* (Oxford: Oxford University Press, 1992), p. 263.
23. Eliot, *Adam Bede*, ed. Stephen Gill (London: Penguin, 1980), pp. 188 and 177.
24. Adrienne Rich, *Diving into the Wreck: Poems 1971–1972* (New York: Norton, 1973), p. 13.
25. Eliot, *Middlemarch*, ed. W. J. Harvey (Harmondsworth: Penguin, 1985), p. 226.
26. George Levine, *The Realistic Imagination: English Fiction from Frankenstein to Lady Chatterley* (Chicago: University of Chicago, 1981), pp. 18 and 22.
27. Keating, *The Haunted Study*, pp. 27–32 and generally.
28. James first published 'The Art of Fiction' in *Longman's Magazine* in September 1884. He subsequently revised the text for book publication and, as discussed here, some of these revisions seem a significant response to Stevenson's 'A Humble Remonstrance'. Two versions of 'The Art of Fiction' are cited here as appropriate. The first is the Writers of America volume of James's *Literary Criticism: Essays on Literature*, pp. 44–65, which prints the last version of the essay. The second is Janet Adam Smith's edition, which prints the original magazine version: *Henry James and Robert Louis Stevenson: A Record of Friendship and Criticism* (London: Rupert Hart-Davis, 1948), pp. 53–85.
29. James, *Literary Criticism: Essays on Literature*, p. 44 and Adam Smith, *Henry James and Robert Louis Stevenson*, pp. 53 and 55.
30. Adam Smith, *Henry James and Robert Louis Stevenson*, p. 56.
31. James, *Literary Criticism: Essays on Literature*, pp. 45 and 46. Some uses of the word 'compete' remain even in the revised essay. Roslyn Jolly has noted the ambiguity of the phrase 'compete with life': for Jolly the phrase aligns the novel 'with the representational discourse of history but also suggests (however undesignedly) its complicity with the oppositional discourses of jokes, lies and romance'. Jolly, *Henry James: History, Narrative, Fiction* (Oxford: Clarendon Press, 1993), p. 3.
32. James, *Literary Criticism: Essays on Literature*, p. 52 and Adam Smith, *Henry James and Robert Louis Stevenson*, p. 65.
33. James, *Literary Criticism: Essays on Literature*, pp. 52–3. The earlier version may be found at Adam Smith, *Henry James and Robert Louis Stevenson*, pp. 65–7.
34. James, *Literary Criticism: Essays on Literature*, p. 53 and Adam Smith, *Henry James and Robert Louis Stevenson*, p. 67.

35. James, *Literary Criticism: Essays on Literature*, p. 61 and Adam Smith, *Henry James and Robert Louis Stevenson*, p. 80.

36. Adam Smith, *Henry James and Robert Louis Stevenson*, pp. 80–1. James revised this to read, 'I have been a child in fact, but I have been on a quest for buried treasure only in supposition' (James, *Literary Criticism: Essays on Literature*, p. 62).

37. Adam Smith, *Henry James and Robert Louis Stevenson*, p. 94.

38. Ibid., p. 90.

39. Ibid., p. 92.

40. Ibid., pp. 91 and 100.

41. Peter Brooks, *Henry James Goes to Paris* (Princeton: Princeton University Press, 2007); Victoria Coulson, 'Sticky Realism: Armchair Hermeneutics in Late James', *The Henry James Review* 25 (2004): 115–26.

42. Adam Smith, *Henry James and Robert Louis Stevenson*, p. 89.

43. James, *Roderick Hudson*, ed. Geoffrey Moore (Harmondsworth: Penguin, 1986), p. 386.

44. James, *Letters*, vol. 3, p. 499.

45. Ibid., p. 58.

46. Norquay, *R. L. Stevenson on Fiction*, pp. 70 and 71.

47. Stevenson, *Familiar Studies*, pp. 7–8.

48. Norquay, *R. L. Stevenson on Fiction*, p. 56.

49. Brooks, *Henry James goes to Paris*, p. 4.

50. Ibid.

51. James, *Literary Criticism: French Writers; Other European Writers; The Prefaces to the New York Edition* (New York: Library of America, 1984), p. 1064.

52. Ibid., p. 1229.

53. James, *Literary Criticism: Essays on Literature*, p. 1249.

54. James, *Literary Criticism: French Writers*, p. 1230.

55. Adam Smith, *Henry James and Robert Louis Stevenson*, p. 52.

56. Leon Edel and Gordon N. Ray (eds), *Henry James and H. G. Wells: A Record of their Friendship, their Debate on the Art of Fiction, and their Quarrel* (London: Rupert Hart-Davis, 1958), p. 248; James, *Letters*, vol. 4, p. 770.

57. James, *Letters*, vol. 3, p. 406.

58. Ibid., p. 495; James, *Literary Criticism: Essays on Literature*, p. 1253.

59. Norquay, *R. L. Stevenson on Fiction*, p. 78.

Chapter 10 – Thomson

1. G. K. Chesterton, *Robert Louis Stevenson* (London: Hodder and Stoughton, 1927), p. 75.

2. Edwin Muir, 'Robert Louis Stevenson', in Andrew Noble, ed., *Edwin Muir: Uncollected Scottish Criticism* (London: Vision, 1982), p. 228.

3. Arthur Quiller-Couch, *Adventures in Criticism* (Cambridge: Cambridge University Press, 1923–4), p. 88.

4. Walter Raleigh, *Robert Louis Stevenson* (London: Edward Arnold, 1906), pp.13 and 46.

5. Ibid., p. 78.

6. Quiller-Couch, *Adventures*, p. 97.

7. Paul Maixner, ed., *Robert Louis Stevenson: The Critical Heritage* (London: Routledge, 1981), p. 497.

8. Ibid., p. 511.

9. Janet Adam Smith, *Henry James and Robert Louis Stevenson: A Record of Friendship and Criticism* (London: Hart-Davis, 1948), p. 46.

10. Richard Holmes, *Footsteps: Adventures of a Romantic Biographer* (London: Hodder and Stoughton, 1985). John Cairney, *The Quest for Robert Louis Stevenson* (Edinburgh: Luath, 2004), p. 187.

11. Nicholas Rankin, *Dead Man's Chest* (London: Faber, 1987).

12. Scott Nollen, *Robert Louis Stevenson: Life, Literature and the Silver Screen* (Jefferson, NC: McFarland, 1994), p. 165.

13. Peter Keating, *The Haunted Study: A Social History of the English Novel, 1876–1914* (London: Secker and Warburg, 1989).

14. Brian A. Rose, *Jekyll and Hyde Adapted: Dramatizations of Cultural Anxiety* (Westport, CT: Greenwood Press, 1996).

15. Muir, 'Stevenson', p. 228.

16. *The Letters of Robert Louis Stevenson*, ed. Bradford Booth and Ernest Mehew, 8 vols (New Haven, CT: Yale University Press. 1994–5), vol. 8, p. 372.

17. Stevenson 'The English Admirals', *Virginibus Puerisque and Familiar Studies of Men and Books* (London: J. M. Dent and Sons, 1925), p. 81.

18. Maixner, ed., *Critical Heritage*, p. 518.

19. Stephen Arata, 'The Sedulous Ape: Atavism, Professionalism and Stevenson's *Jekyll and Hyde*', *Criticism* 37.2 (1995): 233–58.

20. Quiller-Couch, *Adventures*, p. 88.

21. cited by Christopher Ricks, 'A Note on "The Hollow Men" and Stevenson's *The Ebb-Tide*', *Essays in Criticism* 51.1 (2001): 8–17 (p. 8).

22. Ibid., p. 9.

23. Jenni Calder, review of Maixner, ed., *Critical Heritage*, in *Modern Language Review* 77.1 (1982): 937–8 (p. 938)

24. Stevenson, *Treasure Island*, ed. John Seelye (Harmondsworth: Penguin, 1999), p. 3.

25. Stevenson, 'A Note on Realism', *Essays Literary and Critical*, Tusitala Edition (London: William Heinemann, 1924–5), p. 78.

26. Maixner, ed., *Critical Heritage*, p. 123.

27. Joseph Bristow, *Empire Boys: Adventures in a Man's World* (London: Routledge, 1991), p. 93.

28. Glenda Norquay, ed., *R. L. Stevenson on Fiction: An Anthology of Literary and Critical Essays* (Edinburgh: Edinburgh University Press, 1999), p. 56.

29. Ibid., p. 61.

30. Ibid., p. 56.

31. Vladimir Nabokov, *Lectures on Literature*, ed. Fredson Bowers (London: Weidenfeld and Nicolson, 1980), p. 180.

32. Norquay, *R. L. Stevenson on Fiction*, p. 11.

33. Stevenson, *Strange Case of Dr Jekyll and Mr Hyde*, ed. Richard Dury (Edinburgh: Edinburgh University Press, 2004), p. 15.

34. Ibid., p. 16.

35. Ibid., p. 15.

36. Norquay, *R. L. Stevenson on Fiction*, p. 54.

37. Stevenson, 'Victor Hugo's Romances', *Virginibus Puerisque*, p. 147.

38. *Letters*, vol. 5, p. 213.

39. Jacques Rivière, *The Ideal Reader*, trans. Blanche A. Price (London: Harvill, 1962), p. 63.

40. Ibid., p. 72.

41. Ibid., p. 73.

42. Stevenson, 'Victor Hugo's Romances', p. 138.

43. Stevenson, *Treasure Island*, p. 84 and p. 184.

44. Stevenson, 'English Admirals', p. 90.

45. Ibid., p. 87.

46. Ibid., p. 86.

47. Stevenson, *Virginibus Puerisque*, p. xi.

48. Stevenson, 'Victor Hugo's Romances', p. 135.

49. Italo Calvino, *The Literature Machine*, trans. Patrick Creagh (London: Vintage, 1997), p. 19.

50. Maixner, ed., *Critical Heritage*, p. 504.

Further Reading

Ambrosini, Richard and Richard Dury, eds, *Robert Louis Stevenson: Writer of Boundaries* (Madison: University of Wisconsin Press, 2006).

Arata, Stephen, *Fictions of Loss in the Victorian Fin de Siècle* (Cambridge: Cambridge University Press, 1996).

Buckton, Oliver S., *Cruising with Robert Louis Stevenson: Travel, Narrative and the Colonial Body* (Athens: Ohio University Press, 2007).

Calder, Jenni, *Robert Louis Stevenson: A Life Study* (London: Hamish Hamilton, 1980).

Calder, Jenni, ed., *Stevenson and Victorian Scotland* (Edinburgh: Edinburgh University Press, 1981).

Colley, Ann C., *Nostalgia and Recollection in Victorian Culture* (London: Macmillan, 1998).

Colley, Ann C., *Robert Louis Stevenson and the Colonial Imagination* (Aldershot: Ashgate, 2004).

Dryden, Linda, *Modern Gothic and Literary Doubles: Stevenson, Wilde and Wells* (Basingstoke: Palgrave Macmillan, 2003).

Dryden, Linda, Stephen Arata and Eric Massie, eds, *Stevenson and Conrad: Writers of Land and Sea* (Lubbock, TX: Texas Tech University Press, 2009).

Edmond, Rod, *Representing the South Pacific: Colonial Discourse from Cook to Gauguin* (Cambridge: Cambridge University Press, 1997).

Eigner, Edwin M., *Robert Louis Stevenson and Romantic Tradition* (Princeton, NJ: Princeton University Press, 1966).

Fielding, Penny, *Writing and Orality: Nationality, Culture and Nineteenth-Century Scottish Fiction* (Oxford: Clarendon Press, 1996).

Furnas, J. C., *Voyage to Windward: The Life of Robert Louis Stevenson* (New York: Sloane, 1951).

Jolly, Roslyn, *Robert Louis Stevenson in the Pacific: Travel, Empire and the Author's Profession* (Aldershot: Ashgate, 2009).

Harman, Claire, *Robert Louis Stevenson: A Biography* (London: HarperCollins, 2005).

Keily, Robert, *Robert Louis Stevenson and the Fiction of Adventure* (Cambridge, MA: Harvard University Press, 1964).

Kucich, John, *Imperial Masochism: British Fiction, Fantasy and Social Class* (Princeton: Princeton University Press, 2007).

Lascelles, Mary, *The Story-Teller Retrieves the Past: Historical Fiction and Fictitious History in the Art of Scott, Stevenson, Kipling and Some Others* (Oxford: Clarendon Press, 1980).

Maixner, Paul, ed., *Robert Louis Stevenson: The Critical Heritage* (London: Routledge, 1981).

Menikoff, Barry, *Narrating Scotland: The Imagination of Robert Louis Stevenson* (Columbia: University of South Carolina Press, 2005).

Mighall, Robert, *A Geography of Victorian Gothic: Mapping History's Nightmares* (Oxford: Oxford University Press, 1999).

Norquay, Glenda, *Robert Louis Stevenson and Theories of Reading: The Reader as Vagabond* (Manchester: Manchester University Press, 2007).

Reid, Julia, *Robert Louis Stevenson, Science and the Fin de Siècle* (Basingstoke: Palgrave Macmillan, 2006).

Sandison, Alan, *Robert Louis Stevenson and the Appearance of Modernism: A Future Feeling* (London: Macmillan, 1996).

Smith, Vanessa, *Literary Culture and the Pacific: Nineteenth-Century Textual Encounters* (Cambridge: Cambridge University Press, 1998).

Veeder, William and Gordon Hirsch, eds, *Dr Jekyll and Mr Hyde after One Hundred Years* (Chicago: University of Chicago Press, 1988).

Wickman, Matthew, *The Ruins of Experience: Scotland's 'Romantick' Highlands and the Birth of the Modern Witness* (Philadelphia: University of Pennsylvania Press, 2007).

Notes on Contributors

Stephen Arata is the Mayo NEH Distinguished Teaching Professor in the Department of English at the University of Virginia. He has published extensively on late nineteenth- and early twentieth-century British literature and culture, including *Fictions of Loss in the Victorian Fin de Siècle* (1996). He is a general editor of the *New Edinburgh Edition of the Collected Works of Robert Louis Stevenson*.

Ian Duncan is Professor of English at the University of California, Berkeley. His books include *Scott's Shadow: The Novel in Romantic Edinburgh* (2007), *Modern Romance and Transformations of the Novel: The Gothic, Scott, Dickens* (1992), a co-edited collection, *Scotland and the Borders of Romanticism* (2004), and editions of novels by Walter Scott and James Hogg.

Penny Fielding teaches English and Scottish Literature at the University of Edinburgh. Her books include *Scotland and the Fictions of Geography: North Britain 1760–1830* (2008) and *Writing and Orality: Nationality Culture and Nineteenth-Century Scottish Fiction* (1996). She is a general editor of the *New Edinburgh Edition of the Collected Works of Robert Louis Stevenson*.

Robert P. Irvine is Senior Lecturer in English and Scottish Literature at the University of Edinburgh. His books include *Enlightenment and Romance: Gender and Agency in Smollett and Scott* (1999) and *Jane Austen* (2005). He is editing *Prince Otto* for the *New Edinburgh Edition of the Collected Works of Robert Louis Stevenson*.

Roslyn Jolly teaches English at the University of New South Wales. She is the editor of Stevenson's *South Sea Tales* (1996) and the author of *Robert Louis Stevenson in the Pacific: Travel, Empire and the Author's Profession* (2009). Her current research is on the idea of the South in nineteenth-century travel writing.

John Lyon has taught Literature at the Universities of Cambridge and Bristol and at the College of Wooster, Ohio. He is director of the Penguin Archive Project, funded by the Arts and Humanities Research Council. He has published on literature from the sixteenth century to the present day, including numerous editions of nineteenth- and twentieth-century novels.

Alison Lumsden is a senior lecturer in Scottish and English Literature at the University of Aberdeen. She has published on Scott, Stevenson and a number of twentieth-century Scottish writers. She is a general editor of the *Edinburgh Edition of the Waverley Novels* and co-director of the Walter Scott Research Centre at the University of Aberdeen.

Caroline McCracken-Flesher is a professor of English at the University of Wyoming. Her publications include *Possible Scotlands: Walter Scott and the Story of Tomorrow* (2005) and the edited volume *Culture, Nation and the New Scottish Parliament* (2007). She is currently editing *Kidnapped* for the *New Edinburgh Edition of the Collected Works of Robert Louis Stevenson*.

Julia Reid is lecturer in Victorian Literature at the University of Leeds, UK. Her book, *Robert Louis Stevenson, Science and the Fin de Siècle* (2006), considered Stevenson's engagement with evolutionary science. She is currently working on gender in late-Victorian anthropology, fiction and feminist political thought.

Alex Thomson is Lecturer in Scottish Literature at the University of Edinburgh. He is the author of *Deconstruction and Democracy* (2005) and *Adorno: A Guide for the Perplexed* (2006) and is a co-editor of the Edinburgh University Press series Taking on the Political. He is editing a volume of Stevenson's essays for the *New Edinburgh Edition of the Collected Works of Robert Louis Stevenson*.

Index